YOUNTSVILLE

The Rise and Decline of an Indiana Mill Town

RONALD V. MORRIS

University of Notre Dame Press
Notre Dame, Indiana

University of Notre Dame Press
Notre Dame, Indiana 46556
undpress.nd.edu

Published in the United States of America

Library of Congress Cataloging-in-Publication Data

Names: Morris, Ronald V., author.
Title: Yountsville : the rise and decline of an Indiana mill town /
Ronald V. Morris.
Description: Notre Dame, Indiana : University of Notre Dame Press, [2019] |
Includes bibliographical references and index.
Identifiers: LCCN 2019047735 (print) | LCCN 2019047736 (ebook) |
ISBN 9780268106614 (hardback) | ISBN 9780268106638 (adobe pdf) |
ISBN 9780268106645 (epub)
Subjects: LCSH: Yountsville (Ind.)—History. | Yount family. |
Mills and mill-work—Indiana—Yountsville—History. |
Company towns—Indiana—Montgomery County—History.
Classification: LCC F534.Y68 M67 2019 (print) | LCC F534.Y68 (ebook) |
DDC 977.2/48—dc23
LC record available at https://lccn.loc.gov/2019047735
LC ebook record available at https://lccn.loc.gov/2019047736

YOUNTSVILLE

CONTENTS

FIGURES

TABLES AND GRAPHS

TABLES

GRAPHS

ACKNOWLEDGEMENTS

I am grateful to Provost Terry King for his support of this project through an Immersive Learning Grant, followed by Special Assigned Time. I thank Allan and Barbara White for making this project possible through the use of their guest house by the archaeology crew; this project could not have happened without their support. Thanks also to Martha Morris and J. B. Bilbrey for reading early drafts of the documents. I further thank Erni Shields for preparing images for production.

Thanks are also due to the Crawfordsville District Public Library for their support in opening their collections, for allowing us to use their photographs (with special acknowledgment to Dellie J. Craig for additional support), and for hosting the exhibits of the projects that the students created. Thanks as well to the Wabash College Archives, Rotary Jail Museum, and the Indiana Historical Society for sharing their collections. I thank the Montgomery County staff for helping us find records and maps and the staff at Lane Place for help with checking sources. I further thank Mr. and Mrs. Mel Kelly and Bob and Donna Mills for their identification of Yountsville blankets and for letting us include photographs of their early Indiana textiles.

Thanks to the students in the Ball State University Archaeology 2014 Summer Field School: Tyler Goodwin, Lindey Jessie, Stephen Lacey, Colin Macleod, Nick Paris, and Michelle Yockey, as well as the students in the Ball State University 2014 Archaeology Analysis Class: Tyler Goodwin, Lindey Jessie, Stephen Lacey, Colin Macleod, and Nick Paris. I would also like to thank Breanne Friskney, Maeve Marino, and Abigail Wachs.

In many of the original documents presented throughout the book, spellings of names, family names, places, and other words were not always consistent or grammatically correct. I have chosen to present and retain data and information as it appears in the original inventories, letters, and other materials. Due to variation in the primary sources, and to avoid inelegant repetition, I have used "Yount's Mill" and "Yount Mill" interchangeably throughout the text.

Introduction

The Yount brothers established their mill in Indiana during the pioneer period, when only primitive industry was emerging on the frontier. Daniel continued to operate the mill through the economic boom of the 1850s and 1860s through sectional crises. His strong hands were at the levers of the mill during the rest of the 1800s. Through these times of economic prosperity and depression, everyone in Daniel's family had a relationship with the mill across three generations. In every decade of the mill's history, circumstances changed and the family adapted to the new realities.[1]

At the same time, textile workers came to work for Daniel. These immigrants and local people looked for and found a better life for their families in a woolen mill on the banks of Sugar Creek. Their children learned a good craft, brought wages into their homes, worked in proximity to relatives, and had a complete day off for leisure every week. The children prepared for a career that would make them employable in their adopted country. These immigrants experienced decent jobs, a steady income, a dependable future, and hope for their children's success through the economic prosperity produced through industrial apprenticeship.

Just four miles away, Caleb Mills was the president of Wabash College; he spent his life working for change in education. He provided leadership in educational reform, lobbying the state legislature for public libraries, higher education, and the provision of a public-school education to every student. He had a different view of the future, believing that students would need an education and values to perpetuate a democratic society. Some young men would even attend the university to learn the skills necessary to steer communities through education, religion, commerce, and politics. This was a future based on knowledge, and everyone would need to participate through the common schools, public libraries, or universities.[2]

In a small company town, the Yount family's mill owners and workers labored in a woolen mill, while educator Caleb Mills, located in the county seat, helped the community change to an education-based economy. Both those associated with the mill and the professor thought they would give children the best chance for the future, but both Daniel Yount and Caleb Mills died before it came to pass. Today communities working with industrialization and deindustrialization still work with educational reform to improve the lives of their children. In the contrast between the apprentice system of learning and public education, the extant industrial site serves as a metaphor through which to provide critical commentary for educational policy in the twenty-first century. The Yount family, who built a successful business and failed to change in the next generation, illustrated the process of industrialization and deindustrialization, illuminating the importance and function of the mill in the lives of the owners and workers in the mill company town of Yountsville.

In the Midwest, there are multiple stories about German working immigrants in urban areas, but there are few stories of immigrants as capitalists in rural areas. The story of the Yount family is a familiar one of an immigrant family who with talent, labor, and advantage built an industry. Local newspapers and magazines have told this story many times, but they rarely stress the fact that the Younts were an immigrant family. Forgetting the advantages they had in knowledge, skills, talent, and capital tends to lump all immigrants together as poor laborers, which is not the story of the Yount family.

Moreover, local people rarely told the story of the immigrant families who came to work in the mill. The stories of these people are revealed through census data that documents each person's ethnicity, family labor, and gender, which offered important narratives to explore in Midwestern life as a contrast to the well-told stories of people working in eastern mill communities. In a small rural town there were stories of working men, women with children, working single women, families working together in the mill, and immigrants from England, Ireland, and Scotland. While it was difficult to track the families after the mill closed in 1921, one thing was certain: most of the families left the area to find mill work elsewhere. Deindustrialization, dislocation, adaptation, and reuse were familiar problems in the Midwest.

Caleb Mills spent his entire life teaching and in service to education across the Midwest. He was a tireless advocate for educational reform, and the reforms he promoted had a definite effect on the families at Yountsville. Child labor laws with teeth were not enforced until after Yount's Mill closed. The termination of child labor caused declining incomes for families working in the mills, and the eventual barring of the youth population from the mill caused the mill owners to pay more money to employ older workers.

Public funding for education remains controversial. The Midwest does not have a uniform story to tell on educational reform, with some areas making rapid strides and other areas tardy and poorly funded. Then and now, nothing starts a fight in the Midwest like talking about how to fund the public schools. The controversy over spending time and effort on vocational education versus strengthening college preparation skills and liberal arts education remains pertinent in the twenty-first century. In an age in which people can expect employment in seven different jobs in a career, preparing for a variety of careers rather than one job might be the most prudent course to take.

Educational reform was a symptom of the rapid changes occurring during industrialization. Caleb Mills led the forces of change and helped students who had a future adapting to new industry. He saw the establishment of libraries, public schools, and private universities as the tools to prepare for the future of the community. Citizens in the twenty-first century look to these same tools to adapt to change in their economic circumstances.

At the same time, Caleb Mills worked for change in education, rapid industrialization called for changes in business and industry. Nearly every American has had to deal with the wider historical processes that gave them the capacity to make a living. This preparation for life might be found in the home, in the school, or in the community, but every generation of young people found a way to educate themselves. Dan Yount addressed these opportunities to use the most up-to-date technology, the turbine, which led to having more power and produced a greater output for the mill. Positioning his mill to serve more clients meant that he could provide a variety of products and a full production line processing fiber to finished goods for his community. In addition to working with technology, Dan employed more workers in the form of immigrants.

As time progressed, the business folded and the deindustrialization of the site began. The diaspora of people came first, as they found new opportunities, careers, or locations when the mill closed. The adaptive reuse of the mill as a boarding house followed next, serving as a residence and a bed and breakfast. The deindustrialization continued as the ruin played a role in the constructed memory of the local community.[3]

LOOKING FORWARD

The first chapter of this book details the rise of the common schools in Indiana. An education in technical, vocational, industrial, or informational fields allowed the student to link their preparation to their occupations or enjoy the felicity of learning for community improvement. The rise of the common schools provided a way for many young people across the Midwest to acquire the tools they needed for work and for participation in the democratic life of the community.

The ideological and political notion of economics affects citizens today as it did in the time of Mills and Yount, and the second chapter examines that interaction. The transition from hydropower to steam and the application of that power to textile mills in Indiana to spin and weave cotton from the South and from domestically produced wool produced stories of small-farm cotton production, slave labor, cotton production, and the work of the region's women to bring home sheeps' wool to clothe their families. At the same time, a new state constitution drafted after a financially disastrous flirtation with publicly financed internal improvement attempted to create a more perfect union of prosperity for citizens and communities.

Chapter 3 documents the production history of the mill. The mill at Yountsville played a regional role in the economy across nearly one hundred years. The mill responded to national events and played a part in the booming economy of the 1850s and 1860s. It remained a significant employer in the area, and it manufactured items used by soldiers in both the Civil War and the Spanish-American War. It was also unique in that the structures from the original mill remained standing, and do to the present.

But despite protective tariffs on imported wool and wool products, the mill eventually was not sustainable.

Chapter 4 illustrates the life of the Yount family. The family, like the mill, is also unique, and as German immigrants they built a family business in a small company town in a rural area. Ultimately the family was not able to sustain the mill as conditions in manufacturing, marketing, and transportation changed around them. The youngest generations of the Yount family embraced the future through receiving college educations. The members of the family lived modest lives while being generous and supporting institutions and the community.

While the story of the Yount family has been told in the community, the lives of the workers have not been discussed, and chapter 5 documents their lives in the mill, their graffiti, and their family lives. The mill workers came from the British Isles, bringing their textile skills with them. Families worked together in the mill—fathers, mothers, sons, and daughters—to make a living turning wool into cloth. These families lived in Yountsville for generations while the mill was open. Single people lived in the boarding house or with a family. Families of workers lived in housing close to the mill, but as soon as the mill closed most of the workers left the area to seek textile work in other mill communities.

Chapter 6 documents both the changes to the site and the preservation efforts that stabilize the remaining buildings. As the decade progressed the Yount family changed the geography of the mill site; they added and subtracted structures and upgraded their source of power. As the site evolved over a century, they created a residential site on the hill and an industrial complex in the valley. The site continued to change after the Yount family left the area and landowners made modifications to the land to improve it for their uses. People almost immediately valued the location on the banks of Sugar Creek and the history of the site.

Chapter 7 illuminates how nineteenth-century rural Midwesterners imagined the future, primarily the ways they imagined the relationship between education and industry. To do this, a very detailed description of Yount's Mill and a general portrait of Caleb Mills's life is included. The story paints a fine-grained picture that provides a rich illustration of social life and materiality. The discovery of abandoned warehouses, buildings, foundations barely rising above the grass, or in this case mills and boarding houses, causes the visitor to wonder about the past. Hopefully, this narrative will encourage the reader or the visitor to the site to stop to think about the history those parts of the landscape embodies, as well as what they symbolize and mean for the present.

Examining the foundations of public education at a time when it was under attack shows the promise that public education holds and why people are willing to support it. At a time when immigrants are demonized, it is important to see how past immigrants worked to contribute to their communities and to build better lives for their children. When local rural communities are seen only as hotbeds of meth production, places full of opioid dens, or economic wastelands it is important to remember that these areas are important manufacturing centers and productive communities, and they hold the keys to a high quality of life where people engage with their communities in a democratic society. These communities were once wildernesses that flowered with economic change, and they hold the promise for the next flowering of economic opportunity based on fresh water, recreation, and clean power, which all contribute to a good quality of life.

A NOTE ON SOURCES

To ameliorate the problems created by the gaps in the written records and to compensate for the fact that neither the Younts nor the mill workers can speak for themselves, the investigation of the site required multiple sources of evidence to tell the story of the people. The features lay hidden underground awaiting interpretation, such as the homes of Daniel and his brother Alan Yount. The results of that investigation revealed a very simple and tidy lifestyle across multiple years. Archaeology confirmed the demise of Daniel Yount's house with a cluster of evidence from the 1940s backfilled over the site. Archaeology also explored the undocumented features of the site, such as the existence of a mill pond and the undocumented development of a sewer line for a proposed amusement park. Material culture and especially landscape played influential roles in the understanding of the site. People have continued to live at the site since the founding of the mill. While a bulldozer-loving owner changed some sections of the site, much of it remained untouched, providing an extant landscape of residences of owners, workers, and industrial buildings. The powerful layout of the land by Daniel Yount led to the interpretation of well-defined social and work spheres, and the combination of data from different sources created a case study that described an everyday rural life that revolved around the transformation of work and school during the nineteenth century.

The archaeological exploration of the evidence provided by primary documents gave good clues as to what life was like at the mill. However, many of the documents of the mill have been lost over time, so the inclusion of archaeological and architectural data augments incomplete records. Few first-hand accounts were left either by the Yount family or by the mill workers. The large number of primary sources included in the book reflect the reality that sources on the Younts were held in many collections. The sources were both difficult to access and in danger of disappearing as records passed from one generation to another. While all of the sources for the records were acknowledged at the time of publication in the next decade, there is a very real possibility they will be in different locations than those names. Other documents, such as census records, provide details about the lives of the workers. Census documents and the collections of Caleb Mills, which help to flesh out his life, were both readily available. The variety of historical records provided a context for understanding both the location and the time. Archaeological analysis considered information from interviews with past owners, visual observation of ruins and the surviving structures at the mill site, the relationship between the sites of the buildings, the graffiti left in the buildings, artifacts found through archaeological excavation, and artifacts located in the community. The structures that existed provided evidence of their original use and changes, including graffiti, and the ruins provided unmistakable evidence of their relationship to commerce and industry.

ONE

Education in Indiana

Four miles from the great mill at Yountsville, Caleb Mills looked out the six-over-six-pane windows of his house to see the young Wabash College. He could not see the town of Crawfordsville from his sylvan retreat, but it was a growing community of civic-minded men and women who called themselves the Athens of the West. He had come to Indiana from New England in 1833 with a family tradition of books, religion, and ideas, plus his diploma from Dartmouth.[1] He came to Crawfordsville with his bride-to-be as the first professor of Greek and Latin of Wabash College; three years later, his 1836 home was quite comfortable.

He walked across the carpeted oak random-width floorboards toward the paneled doors and glanced through the fan light over the door and flanking windows to see morning sunlight in the warp of the glass before turning the brass key, lock, and latch.[2] He needed to tend his strawberries before the sun got too hot; then he returned to the white clapboard house with the three bays and shutters on both floors, which was topped with a shake roof. He started a return letter to missionary S. B. Munger, who was attempting to set up a school in India to save souls. Next he would write more letters to New England soliciting support from individuals and in-tuitions. Wabash was in better shape than before he arrived, but it was still important to be vigilant in communicating how important the work at Wabash College was to his students. "Whether they will have the disposi-tion to meet their obligation and do their duty to the earthly world, will depend upon the character of the intellectual and moral training the rising generations receive," he wrote.[3]

Caleb Mills taught school for a while before rising to accept the role of president at Wabash College. He brought a penchant for work and success in identifying and tackling problems his neighbors either did not notice or were complacent about. His religious beliefs as a New Light Presbyterian supported an element in his character that was striving for social reform.

In the early days of Wabash, factions of Old Light and New Light Presbyterians sparred around the formation of the college. Many more students were in the preparatory academy than in the college program, which was grounded in liberal and classical studies. The school also experimented with a short-lived labor system whereby students learned agricultural skills they could use to feed themselves and also learned building trades that would help them pay their tuition bills. Mills's male students thrived, and in his leisure time Mills started calling for public support of education. As early as 1844 he addressed public meetings and the Indiana Legislature on his chosen topic of education. As a professor in a sectarian college, he had no trouble advocating for an education in common schools that would be Protestant if not Presbyterian in purpose.[4] Neither he nor noted Indianapolis diarist Calvin Fletcher would object if the state-sponsored Indiana Academy at Bloomington were to be disbanded and the funds given to the sectarian Indiana colleges.[5] Mills would revisit his education theme many times across his life.

As a citizen of a progressive Midwestern state, Mills knew that to give young men a bright future they needed an education and that Indiana needed those young men to be the leaders in government, commerce, philanthropy, and culture. Every man could have an opportunity to rise in Indiana by improving his fortunes through education. At Wabash College, in 1862 there were six faculty members, but by 1872 that number had doubled to twelve members of the faculty, with two hundred students and twenty-four students who had earned degrees.[6] Wabash had $9,000 that was just barely floating above a sea of red ink when in 1873 railroad investor Chauncey Rose gave a $50,000 gift to match the $134,000 endowment, which gave Caleb Mills a little bit more breathing room as he continued to raise funds for Wabash College.[7] This was the bastion of one particularly rigorous educational reformer.

EDUCATION FUNDING

Section sixteen of each Indiana township looked like just about every other mile-square section of 640 acres, but it was special. It was reserved by the federal government to be sold by the state.[8] The money raised from that sale would be used to fund public education in Indiana forever through the creation of an endowment fund. The Indiana Legislature passed a series of laws to establish schools and seminaries in pioneer Indiana, culminating in the 1824 law to establish district schools. The idyllic one-room Indiana school did not always exist, and public education came at the cost of heavy lobbying across multiple years.

By the 1830s, the pioneers had moved beyond the struggle for imme-diate survival and the economy was better, thus allowing people to afford more luxuries. The population had soared, which meant that there were lots of children who needed to be educated and more people in communities that could support a school. As people remembered the fifty-year anniver-sary of the revolution, their civic feelings extended to education for all sponsored by state and local funding. Forward-thinking Whig governor Noah Noble encouraged education in an 1831 speech; two years later, he advised the legislature on attracting and preparing quality teachers. At the educational conventions of the 1830s and 1840s, Caleb Mills made annual speeches in support of establishing common schools in Indiana.[9]

The rapid change of industrialization spurred educational reform, but the imperative was lost on a mostly agrarian population until indus-try started to develop. All factions joined together in Madison in the for-mation of the Association for the Improvement of the Common Schools, which paralleled Caleb Mills's ideas on public education.[10] The members of this group recommended institutions for teacher preparation, and the 1833–34 legislature chartered the Indiana Teacher Seminary at Madison and the Wabash Manual Labor College and Teacher Seminary to pre-pare teachers for the common schools.[11] Furthermore, religious reform movements, especially among Protestant sects, acted to improve society on issues such as temperance, education, prisons, mental health, emanci-pation, and eventually the role of women. Education conventions orga-nized in 1837 and 1839 supported education regardless of party or reli-gious denomination, and by 1840 the statewide bipartisan Presbyterian, Methodist, and Baptist coalition for common schools was eventually successful in creating the political will necessary for the Indiana Constitution of 1851.[12]

As of 1840, the school district was the key administrative organization. No taxation was provided for schools; if people desired to build a school, they provided in-kind contributions of labor or supplies. Most schools were not just "blab schools" (ones in which students recited their lessons out loud and at the same time). And it was a myth that teachers delivered excessive corrections for misbehavior of a trivial nature.[13] By 1843, even though there were over twenty pages in the Indiana statutes dedicated to improving education, there was still no common school system.[14] Schools were perceived by the taxpayers to be local problems. Free schools were equated with pauper schools, and paying taxes for the children of others seemed unjust in the popular sentiment.

Public Involvement

In 1844 Caleb Mills wrote a letter that was published and circulated in Massachusetts about the state of education in Indiana. One-seventh of the Hoosier population was illiterate compared to one-eighteenth of Ohio's. Although there was little precise data about education in Indiana, it was obvious that thousands more illiterate citizens would be recorded as illiterate in the next federal census. Mills placed the blame not on immigrants but on the native-born population and the fact that common schools, academies, and colleges were not adequate in either in numbers or quality.[15] He proposed establishing a property tax to support common schools. While fines had been used to support county seminaries and high schools, these institutions could not keep up with the number of students who needed to be educated. Trustees of the county seminaries were not competent in selecting quality teachers. Mills explained that denominational jealousies prevented religious sects from providing enough education for students. He explained that Indiana needed female teachers but had no means to train them.

The next year, Mills delivered a speech to the Council of Prayer for College, a group specifically gathered to encourage and support sectarian universities. He defined his views on the importance of a university education as being a combination of wisdom and moral culture.[16] The civilization he sought was making others happy in addition to himself through knowledge and benevolence. The function of education in the community was to elevate state and national leaders, legislators, and instruct citizens. Thus, didactic knowledge contributed to the commonwealth as a tangible benefit to the people. He also applied this underlying value structure to the importance of the common schools.

In 1846 Governor James Whitcomb called for public schools, but he did not suggest how to pay for them.[17] That was the problem, of course. The congressional township fund was held locally. It was not equitable, and it was guarded jealously. The major problem was the fact that the land was of differing qualities. The land varied, from rich to swampy, rocky, prairie, tree-covered, or covered with thin soil. When the land was sold, it raised different amounts of money; as a result, some townships were wealthy, others poor, and still others did not have a viable school fund. People were not willing to share their funds with other townships or counties.

Creating a common school fund required consensus on the need for common schools. This consensus required, in part, that citizens understand that all of society benefited from an educated citizenry, and this benefit to society needed to be paid for by all citizens, even if they did not have children in the schools. In addition, common schools could not be supported if public money was also used to support private or religious schools.[18]

At this time Royal Mayhew, the state treasurer and ex officio common school superintendent, presented the first report on the state of education in Indiana; it was not pretty. He blindly called for slight modifications to education while reporting that 64 percent of Indiana children were unschooled.[19]

Addressing the Legislature

In 1846 Caleb Mills addressed the Indiana Legislature and the people of Indiana through columns in the *Indiana State Journal* in which he addressed problems of the common schools, seminaries, and higher education. He contended that education was bipartisan, bidenominational, and bisectional because it benefits every group by improving the capital of citizens and improves every part of the state. The state eagerly took on debt for the construction of railroads and canals for improving the transportation advantages of the state. All children, regardless of rank or color, deserved the opportunity for an education, and now was the time for investment with a currency that would never depreciate: knowledge and virtue.

The state of Indiana education was grim. In Putnam County one in six people was illiterate. In both Montgomery County and Parke County, one in five people was illiterate. In Clay, Dubois, Jackson, and Martin counties one-half of the people were illiterate. Since only one-third of the children of school age were served by the common schools in Indiana, the illiteracy problem was only going to increase. The one bright spot in his report was that the 9,348-member population of Wayne County had only 42 people who were unable to read; that was one in 222. With an average of one-seventh of Indiana illiterate, Caleb Mills believed that this problem needed a solution.

The common schools should be as free as the air we breathe, Mills said, and they should be funded by a property tax. There were free public schools in Connecticut, Michigan, and Ohio, which should be models for Indiana. "We have *borrowed* millions for the physical improvement of our State, but we have not *raised* a dollar by ad valorem taxation to cultivate the minds of our children," he wrote.[20] Hoosiers had recently invested heavily in internal improvements, but why not schools? New England was moving en masse to solve their literacy problem through establishing schools and training teachers. The Midwest was taking steps toward educating their students, but there was little infrastructure with which to work.

Support for quality education was lacking. There was a need for competent teachers and suitable schoolbooks, but little enthusiasm in the community, a lack of adequate funds, and no means of procuring such funds. Furthermore, the burden of educating the rising generation rested very unequally upon the community; the poor were burdened and the rich exempted from contributing their share. "All [citizens] have an equal *personal* interest in the protection which the government extend to themselves and families, and this equality is expressed by the poll-tax that they pay," Mills wrote.[21] He continued by illustrating the burden on families to educate their children: "I once found in a log-cabin a family of ten children, not one of whom could read, and upon inquiry, if they were sent to school, was told by the mother that they were not able to pay the tuition, and that if they sent their children at all, they must pay their portion of the whole expense of the quarter."[22] Caleb Mills did not believe the wealthy members of the community would object to paying property taxes for public education: "Certainly not, if he [the taxpayer] reflects that this property is not only affected in its value, by the character of the immediate community in which it is located, but also by the legislation of the State where it is vested."[23] The legislature was competent and understood that honesty and patriotism could be best ensured if there was a thinking electorate. There might be opposition, but if the legislators waited for complete harmony of sentiment from their constituents, they would never accomplish anything.

Caleb Mills was not pleased with the stewardship of the federal school lands fund. The US government intended that all students should benefit from the sale of public lands, but each county or township held its own funds and spent them in their own county. Some land was worth more than other land when sold, creating inequities, and some funds were wasted by not renting or improving the land prior to sale. New counties needed the money, but three new counties were excluded from the funds because they were created out of previously existing counties. Mills contended that all funds should be held in common and paid on a per-child bases.

Mills also suggested that a county superintendent count the number of students, divide tax money, select teachers, visit schools, establish the conditions of schools, and report to the state superintendent. County seminaries were supposed to generate teachers for the common schools, but the standards were so low that people were often not qualified to be teachers. Mills wished to improve the seminaries by sending all fines to pay for the academies, make the power of compounding interest work in favor of the sum collected from both fines and forfeitures, send tax money to only one academy per county, sell all extra seminary buildings and return the money to donors, and return state money to state coffers to provide aid to the county seminaries. Mills further suggested that free tuition be given to people who pledged to be teachers, but they must teach for the same number of quarters that they received public funds.

Mills believed that as soon as counties were formed they needed access to the funds necessary to create an academy. Many of the academies were poorly built and not designed for instruction, and there should be oversight of educational construction. Of course Mills thought that higher education in Indiana should be left alone, but that the schools should report information about their progress, character, and courses of study. However, state money for higher education required more reporting by the schools about their effectiveness, the state of their finances, the number of teachers produced, the curriculum, and faculty salaries. Mills believed that the state should pay for all students, but if the state did not have enough money for that, the state should pay only for the impoverished students.

Mills had a plan for regents to examine all colleges and receive reports on the state of the higher education they offered. Regents would not be connected to the five Indiana colleges, but each college president would be an honorary member to provide experience to the group. To be members of this group, colleges would pledge to educate two men from each county by providing them with lectures on education, and professors would spend three months traveling for the regents giving lectures on education. Each university that participated would receive $1,000. Mills also desired schools for both law and medicine, to be located in the capital. In the last paragraphs of his letter, Mills put forward a plan to dissolve the state college at Bloomington and transfer the value of the funds back to the state. He supposed that the state college would be purchased by the Methodists and operated by them as one of their institutions.

WAYNE COUNTY QUAKERS

Quakers confounded the romanticized view of the illiterate Hoosier living in a log cabin. In contrast with the illiteracy, ignorance, and lack of public education on the other side of the state, by 1840 the Society of Friends quietly made Wayne County, Indiana, an island of education. By educating boys and girls they had the lowest rate of illiteracy in the state, with only one in 222 people unable to read. Quakers opened schools in their meetinghouses and operated monthly meeting schools and Friends subscription schools. They improved their meetinghouses and schools from log to frame, then from frame to brick or stone. The school equipment, maintenance, and fuel were financed by each meeting. The meeting also paid for those families who could not afford to send their children to school.

Initial Quaker opposition to public schools was not opposition to education. Quakers were concerned that public schools were being funded in part by the militia fines for exemptions leveled against Friends so that they would not violate their peace testimony. If the public saw militia fines as a way to raise public-school funds, the fear of the Friends was that these fees would be increased to a point at which it would become a great hardship on their community to pay these fines. Because they expected to pay for children from their meeting to go to school, the idea of paying taxes for other community children to attend school did not irritate them. Quakers were also afraid that the state would not provide quality character education, but as early as 1834 Quaker schools started receiving state tax money. Quakers came to believe that good state-funded schools were advantageous to small parochial schools, and Friends became strong supporters of maintaining high standards in local schools.

Education of the body was learned through farm labor, training of the intellect was done in the schoolroom, and inspiration of the heart was conducted in the meetinghouse. Instruction was not just a function of the schools; rather, the entire community had a role to play in the education of its youth. Quakers believed in teaching children, not subjects, and in order to accomplish this they emphasized the building of character as well as intelligence.[24] Education was part of Quaker religious training, with an emphasis on being able to read the Bible as well as character and science. Little geography was taught in early Quaker schools since the Bible stated that the Earth was flat. Prior to the Civil War, the curriculum for most Quaker schools included spelling, arithmetic, handwriting, drawing, oral reading skills, and comprehension, with students reciting as well as demonstrating that they understood what they read. Values such as manners, simplicity, and sincerity were also included as part of the curriculum. At the higher levels, students received instruction in Latin, natural philosophy, and geometry. By 1859, orthography, reading, writing, geography, arithmetic, and English grammar were expected to be taught in Quaker schools. By 1869, spelling, writing, arithmetic, geography, grammar, physical geography, the history of the United States, algebra, geometry, German, and scripture were all required.[25] Geography lessons were frequently sung. Many Friends schools had a one-hour midweek meeting with elders that would start in silence. As would be expected of a Friends school, moral suasion or expulsion rather than corporal punishment was part of learning responsibility, discipline, and working with the community.

Assessment of the schools was done during frequent visitations by committees of weighty Friends from either the monthly or quarterly meeting, and they carefully selected the texts to be used by the students. Weighty Friend Elijah Coffin wrote in his diary in 1850, "First-month 22—Acting committee, boarding-school. Several interesting matters were acted upon. The scholars appear to be doing well. The superintendents are agreeable and the teacher very satisfactory."[26]

Coffin took his oversight responsibilities gravely, and also made sure students had appropriate books to develop their moral health. In the fifth month of 1850 he wrote that he went

Table 1.1. Categories of Information Found in Reports of Quaker Students,
1829–1849

Item Number	Category
1	Number of Friends of a suitable age to go to school.
2	Number of Friends educated exclusively in Monthly Meeting schools.
3	Number of Friends taught by Friends but not under the care of a Monthly Meeting.
4	Number of Friends taught in school not set up by a Monthly Meeting or taught by Friends.
5	Number of children of a suitable age to go to school but receive no instruction.
6	Number of school pupils in schools maintained and controlled by the Monthly Meeting and for what portion of the year.
7	Number of meetings with no Monthly Meeting school in their area.

Source: Data compiled and transcribed based on Jay, *Indiana Yearly Meeting Minutes.*

to the boarding-school after meeting. I distributed, in the girls' department, about twenty-three copies of Guney's Hymns, which had been sent to me by a Friend in Philadelphia for distribution.

12th – Distributed about thirty-five copies of Gurney's Hymns, in the boys' department, at the boarding-school after Scripture reading this afternoon.[27]

In proper Quaker fashion, reports on progress were given on each school visited. Table 1.1 shows some of the categories of information found in the reports. Quakers kept records and reports to provide transparency on Quaker education and to ensure assessments that demonstrated that their youth received a rigorous education. The reports made a case for additional funds for education in selected areas. After 1840, more questions were asked about education in scripture [Sunday] school. Quaker schools employed more female teachers than other schools in Indiana. and by 1884 there were 91 men and 106 women teaching in Quaker schools.[28] Regardless of the gender, there were the daily tasks of splitting enough wood to heat the schoolroom for the day, hauling the wood into the school, building fires, and removing ash, which compounded the work of preparing lessons and correcting assignments. The Quakers demonstrated the possibility of education reform in their communities, which led to their rapid adaption to new situations.

THE TURNING OF THE TIDE

The 1847 legislature organized a state common-school convention in Indianapolis and urged preparations to pass common-school legislation in the next session.[29] However, the colleges at Bloomington, Crawfordsville, and Greencastle were all afraid of the power of their rivals. They were particularly afraid that state funding would go to one college over their institution, and each religious sect was afraid the legislature would show a preference for another church school.

The Committee of Seven, a group of educational reformers, determined that the common schools should be free to all, that schools should be supported by taxation, that compensation should be elevated for teachers, and that there should be a vigorous superintendent to oversee the common schools.[30] In the thinking of the time, illiteracy was linked to crime, mobs, poverty, and repudiating debts. It was estimated that the cost of private schools was five times the price of common schools and that all the children of Indiana could be educated in the common schools for what was being spent on private education.[31]

The legislature put the idea of common schools to a vote by the people in 1848, and the northern Indiana counties carried the vote in favor of the referendum. The next year a state property tax of .10 per $100 dollars and .25 per poll tax raised revenue for the common schools and shared it on a per-child basis. It was ironic that the poll tax, now permanently stained with segregation and excluding voters from the ballot box, was viewed as a way to improve the community by funding common-school education. The local congressional township funds were absorbed by the state and equalized statewide. A local tax could be levied to extend the school year, furnish or supply the school with at least three months of school, and provide for qualified teachers. Local taxes could be in-kind contributions. Three township trustees would supervise the one district trustee. Private schools could be incorporated into the common schools. An unusual feature of this legislation was that each county had to vote for the law to be put in place in their county; sixty-one counties immediately accepted it, and twenty-nine rejected the common schools. The vote would be taken every year until a county accepted the common schools. In 1850, when Indiana opened its first publicly funded high school in Evansville, the Quakers had a dozen such institutions in operation.[32]

THE COMMON SCHOOL LAW, 1848–1849

In an address concerning the 1848–49 school law, Mills said in a series of five articles that a spineless legislature had passed a law that required the voters to determine by referendum whether or not it would be enacted.[33] Mills did not approve of the fence-sitting of the legislature when the Indiana Constitution clearly said that Indiana should provide free common schools for its children, but he did want people to vote for it. The big problem with the bill in Mills's view was that it put the responsibility on the local community rather than the state, and he knew this meant there would be inequities in funding the common schools. Mills also knew that unequal funding of education was undemocratic; people living next to each other in the same township would have different amounts of money spent on their children.

In his next article Mills suggested that, in order to fix the problems of the 1848–49 Common School Law, a general education fund should be created, and he promised local control of taxes except to pay for poor counties.[34] He approved of the mandated statistics gathered by the State Treasurer in order to inform the legislature as to the state of education each year, including attendance, population, tax money expenditures, school land available for sale, gender of the teachers, disciplines taught, and books used. Mills also approved of combining the township land money into a common fund and dividing the money per pupil.

Mills's third article about the Common School Law examined the financial implications of the law, and he pointed out that the law did not provide enough money to fund the public schools from property and poll taxes.[35] He reminded the voters that this was merely a place to start; he hoped to see education fully funded in the future and hoped to make this a demonstration program. He also observed that people were changing their minds about free public education as the common schools demonstrated their effectiveness. Mills believed that people did not go to community school meetings because they saw no direct interest in it, but they would become interested once they were taxed. They would want the best improvements for their money on the building, teachers, books, and equipment. Mills cited the example of New York, a state that, through public education, brought the cost of education for all down to $1.73 per student. Mills believed that democracy was demonstrated when all classes of students came together in public schools and students learned to be citizens of a republican government. By waking the intellect of its youth, Indiana improved the undeveloped resources it possessed. Mills further observed that inventors who improved society did not come from the unschooled.

Again, Mills addressed the populace through the newspapers by providing reasons why they should vote for the Common School Law of 1848–49.[36] He articulated that it was the best legislation possible, and experience would provide corrections over time. People would be interested in the common schools because they were being taxed, and the schools would benefit all. It was a constitutional duty to educate the youth of the commonwealth. The tax was so small that it was not a burden to the citizen, and free schools provided common ground where all friends of education met and operated.

In his final newspaper appeal, Mills provided analysis of why the voters disliked the law presented to them even though they wanted public education.[37] He observed that the statistics that appeared in the law would help the legislature make good decisions. He objected to the county control idea, but the consolidation of the congressional land sale proceeds into a state fund apportioned per pupil was a good idea. In a five-county change from the previous year, sixty-one counties to twenty-nine favored the new school law. The legislature wisely prepared for rapid changes of the 1850s' bullish economy and rapid industrialization by starting the process of providing public education in the Hoosier state.

The interaction of a charged economy and a workforce prepared to perform the required tasks in a factory operation meant that communities with schools were ready for industry to enter either the rural or the urban community. Both rural and urban locations had students provided with a common-school education, and both would continue to prepare future workers. More educational reform was still needed, but rural sites with natural advantages could capitalize on them as soon as the right entrepreneurs came on the scene.

TWO

The Growth of Industry in the United States

In the eastern United States, the Industrial Revolution ignited the textile industry, first at Slater Mill in Rhode Island. That was quickly followed by the development of the Merrimack River at Lowell, Massachusetts, and the rivers of Connecticut. Wool production—and, after the invention of the cotton gin, cotton production—quickly became staples of the New England economy.[1] Women left the farms to move into mill towns to make textiles and created a new type of work force—the factory working women. Entrepreneurs harnessed the power of falling water through large-scale engineering projects that would reshape the course of rivers. Fortunes were made by individuals, partnerships, and corporations because industrialization had come to the United States. This rapid change caused by the Industrial Revolution required an educated workforce.

INDUSTRY

Industry depended on power. People needed industrial power to make machines do their will and the repetitive, exhausting work of the mills. In Roman times, engineers put the weight or the flow of water to work in mills

This chapter was written with the assistance of J. B. Bilbrey.

for grinding grain and also harnessed the power of the wind and of animals to power mills for grinding grain, sawing lumber, or producing textiles. When the Industrial Revolution came to the United States, people quickly engineered old sources of power to accommodate new manufacturing processes. By the mid-nineteenth century, the federal census reported that there were tens of thousands of mills across the country.[2] By the early 1800s, the most substantial mills in the United States were run by hydropower, and in the middle of the century many of them transitioned to steam.

The factory system was invented in Britain in the late 1760s when Richard Arkwright created the water frame and the carding machine and converted a house into a workshop.[3] The factory system evolved and spread quickly throughout Britain and was brought to America by Samuel Slater in 1790. As it developed, the factory system in America took on a different shape than the original in Britain. The English factories generally relied on steam, with large concentrations of child labor in large cities. American factories mostly relied on water power and female (in the Lowell system) or family labor (in the Slater system) in small mill towns throughout the countryside.[4] Additionally, British factories were built of stone or brick with cast-iron columns. The early Slater factories were two-story wooden constructions that relied on the heavy timber available in America.[5] The construction of mills and the organization of factory towns in America would change after the 1830s as the Slater system of small family labor gave way to the sprawling industry of the Lowell system.[6]

Outside of the construction and operation of the factory itself, American and British industries shared a common reliance on the Sunday School as a means of discipline. First created in Britain in 1781, the Sunday School was adopted by manufacturers to teach discipline and values that would benefit the factory, such as punctuality and obedience.[7] Samuel Slater was trained in the industry under Jedediah Strutt, one of the early manufacturers to adopt the Sunday School, and Slater brought that to America when he began establishing his own factories in the 1830s and 1840s. The Sunday School was combined with the community church, Methodist for both British industrialists and Slater, to create a disciplined and reliable workforce.[8]

In Massachusetts Horace Mann looked at the rapid rise of industrial and textile enterprises and the needs of the citizens to have more knowledge to succeed in a swiftly changing manufacturing world. He, like Massachusetts and the rest of New England, championed state support for public education to ensure that the commonwealth and all its citizens would profit from public education.[9] He lobbied heavily for the abolition of ignorance by using public expenditures for common schools controlled by the state as a civic necessity. Children, regardless of their background, would be welcome in the school, which would be sustained by an interested and nonsectarian public. Schools would reflect the philosophy, methods, and responsibilities of citizens in a democracy. Professional teachers would be properly trained, and Horace Mann labored to spread his vision of common schools across the nation.

As Horace Mann advocated for this cause, Caleb Mills from New Hampshire moved to Indiana, bringing these ideals with him. Mills worked for common schools paid for by public tax funds. The common schools taught punctuality, responding to the schoolhouse bell as to the mill bell, and following directions. The schoolteachers also taught basic communication skills that would assist their pupils in factory operation by doing sums, writing, and reading directions.

Hydropower

With technology borrowed from Great Britain, the flow of water, the fall of water, and the torque of water allowed the American textile industry to start a manufacturing revolution in America. At the beginning, hydropower required a significant fall from the water source to allow for an overshot water wheel to fill each of the buckets and the weight of the water to pull the mill wheel down to a point at which the water dumped from the bucket and the empty bucket would travel to the top to be filled repeatedly. Breast water wheels would work where there was less of a fall. Undershot wheels worked well on rivers, and some wheels were towed from place to place on the Ohio River.[10] Tub wheels required less depth but would not work unless the water could be rapidly moved away from the exit of the mill. After 1800 but prior to the introduction and widespread use of the hydraulic turbine, large industry generally relied on breast wheels, and smaller industry relied on overshot wheels.[11] Hydropower was inexpensive and dependable, but it required significant engineering skills and cooperative geography.

While drought and freezing weather remained obstacles for the miller, the inability to get flowing water through the mill stopped production. The invention of the turbine radically changed the possible locations of mills; now a three-foot drop was all that was required to install a mill. The turbines came as standardized pieces, so there was a greater chance of high efficiency, and cast-iron equipment could handle increased torque, higher speeds, and greater weights. All these improvements in technology contributed to the spread of mills from site-specific locations to population-specific locations. Contrary to the myth of the rural miller mindlessly grinding corn into meal, the grist mills were early mechanized agrobusiness industries served by mechanical engineers. Milling also became less of a part-time sideline of farmers who were handy tinkers and became a full-time occupation for millers with specialized knowledge. With burr stones and sifters set for corn and wheat, mills took on special functions. Acme Evans sifters, grain transportation by belts, and gravity feed all improved the movement of grain in the mills.

As the mills grew, the process of providing power to the numerous machines used grew increasingly complex. By the 1830s, many medium-scale mills would occupy four or five floors of the mill buildings, with the hydropower coming from the basement. Iron shafting, combined with pulleys and couplings, would be distributed several floors up and across each floor to provide power for each machine. The equipment required to maintain this large-scale industry could weigh twenty or more tons.[12] Rather than being designed for this dispersal of power, many mills grew over time, introducing equipment and technology gradually as the industry grew. In the second half of the nineteenth century, the large-scale factories would leave hydropower behind and transition to the superior steam engine.

Steam Power

Steam power was produced by burning wood to boil water and create high-pressure steam, and the wood eventually transitioned into bituminous coal. Steam power brought the additional benefit of hot water and steam heat for buildings that had depended on fires that produced soot that would mar factory products. Steam power was reliable without the vagaries of drought or flood. Constant attention was needed to maintain proper water and fire levels or steam pressure and to prevent explosions and scalding. New equipment was expensive and required the remodeling of existing structures. But when implemented the steam engine was able to provide consistent power to a factory (and much more power than a water turbine) and produce superior goods (particularly in textile industries), and it could be established in any location.[13]

For growing cities that did not have access to rivers or other water sources for hydropower, the adoption of steam power was the only path to industrialization. While steam power might have been more of a cost initially (when compared to hydropower), being able to choose the ideal location for trade and a workforce was a promising benefit to factory owners and investors. The transition of factories into major cities, powered by steam, began in the 1840s and became common in the 1850s and 1860s.[14] The rising use of the steam engine coincided with the use of railroads as the primary means of shipping and transportation across the country in the 1860s.[15] The access to railroads, along with the growing urbanization of the nation, made the cities ideal locations for the large-scale factories that would utilize the steam engine.[16]

INDUSTRY IN INDIANA

While most of the mills in Indiana are gone now, the early industry of the state provided jobs for many workers. By the 1840s and 1850s, gristmills were ubiquitously spread across every county and in many communities of the Hoosier state.[17] Though many mills, like Keller's (Jennings County), Snoddy's (Fountain County), Snyder's (Montgomery County), Valley Mill (Montgomery County), and Thompson's (Edinburg) were removed, Jasper erected a replica to honor its milling heritage.[18] Other Indiana mills still stand in honor of their service, such as Red (Bardstown), while others, like Stockdale (Wabash County), Adams (Carrol County), Bonneyville (Elkhart County), Mansfield (Parke County), and Bridgeton (Parke County), continued to grind and sift flours as they had for over 150 years. Grinding grain was important to every community because, without modern preservatives or freezing, the natural oil in flour would become rancid in under a month. In addition to offering food production, mills performed a social function by providing places where people could meet and exchange news or stories.

Hydropowered sawmills once stood at Markle Mill in Vigo County and at Miami Indian Mill in Wabash County, but in the twenty-first century the mill works of Hamers gristmill at Spring Mill State Park greatly

Table 2.1. Numbers of Indiana Mills Producing Different Products, 1880

Type of Industry	Number of Establishments	Capital Invested	Number of Employees
Flour–Gristmill	996	$9,484,023	3,159
Lumber (sawed)	2,022	$7,048,088	10,339
Woolen Goods	81	$2,273,705	1,741

Source: Data compiled based on Thornbrough (1965) and US Bureau of the Census, *Compendium of the Census* (1880), 965–966.

overshadowed them.[19] Produced using a simple water wheel, the hydro-power operated a vertical sawblade, hoisting it up and forcing it down again and again. It simultaneously moved the log carriage forward at measured intervals to provide boards of uniform width. Anyone who had ever working on a saw pit to cut boards from timber would really appreciate the efficiency of the sawmill. Cut timber allowed people to side their cabins, build frame additions to their houses, or create frame houses. Mills were the hydropowered factories of the settlement period. The surprising number of mills (Table 2.1) employed a large number of people. The mills produced products of incredible value for that time.

Because of the limestone building-stone present in southern Indiana, hydropowered rock-cutting mills once stood at Muscatatuck (in Jennings County). Larger mills replaced the smaller mills that were not commercially viable, but these smaller mills allowed builders to get the products that they needed. At the same time, they supplemented the incomes of workers in the local economy, creating mixed agricultural and industrial jobs in the community. Small mills cut rock for foundations, steps, cabin supports, chimneys, thresholds, and lintels. Waste rock became quicklime for mortar, buffering for farm fields, whitewash, or plaster; it could also be used for chinking or gravel.

In addition to its gristmill, sawmill, and stone-cutting operation, Tunnel Mill, in Jennings County used hydropower to create explosives in their powder mill.[20] The explosive growth of the DuPont black powder works in Delaware was directly tied to the needs of farmers opening the forest land west of the Appalachian Mountains. The highly dangerous work was also highly profitable because every farmer wanted black powder to blow the stumps from their newly cleared fields. Compared to pulling stumps with teams of oxen or horses, prying them out of the ground with a lever, slowly burning them, or plowing around the stumps, blowing stumps out of the ground was a fast and easy way to clear a field. Of course black powder was also used in the ubiquitous hunting activities of the frontier. Independence Day was not complete without turning an anvil upside down, packing the hollow with gun powder, inserting a fuse, setting the hollow of another anvil on top of it, lighting the fuse, and running. Blowing an anvil was guaranteed to lend excitement to a Fourth of July.

The mill at Metamora (in Franklin County) processed feed, flour, and cotton on a small scale. The once massive, steam-powered cotton mills still stand at Cannelton, Evansville, and Madison.[21] The one at Madison stands vacant; that at Cannelton has been adapted and reused as senior citizen housing, and the structure in Evansville has been adapted to making infant food. These Ohio River mills took raw cotton and spun it into cotton thread on bobbins, and the bobbins were taken to power looms for weaving into bolts of cloth. The millers dyed the cotton cloth or printed the resulting fabric with a pattern. The inexpensive transportation of raw cotton via Ohio River shipping and the river or railroad shipping of finished cotton goods made the river banks great locations for textile distribution. These local producers would obviously have lower transportation costs than those shipping cotton from the Mississippi valley to the east coast and then by rail back to the Midwest.

While Bartholomew County, Lowell, Mishawaka, New Harmony, and Tell City once had wool mills, Beck's Mill (in Washington County) was the only place that wool-processing equipment was on display in Indiana in its original building, but those operations were for carding.[22] Yountsville offered the largest collection of the remaining mill-related structures dedicated to wool production and weaving at one site. The town's industrial history, the story of its labor, women's history, use of child labor, manufacturing, and economics during the 1800s presented a great example of what a Midwestern woolen textile production center was like. Other examples of East Coast mills exist, but the companion Midwestern stories were missing.[23] The archaeological exploration of Yount's Mill provided a reason to reexamine a site that was recognized at the time of the sesquicentennial of the Civil War as one of the most historic sites in the Hoosier state.

The land had multiple streams and springs, deep rocky canyons, and a natural fall to Sugar Creek; that body of water itself possessed a rapid fall that was perfect for mill dams. Millers searched the land for these types of geographic advantages, and they found them in Ripley Township of Montgomery County. The land held the promise of economic opportunity. The ability of skilled craftsmen and mechanics to read the land and turn that picturesque countryside into a sustainable form of power and harness that power to create a sustainable way of life for both mill owners and mill workers meant that this valley held potential different from that of the flat tableland just a few yards away. There were many mills in Montgomery County, primarily for grain and the production of lumber, but the county also had wool mills and wood products. Many of the mills were close to Yountsville. Many of them lasted just a few years, and the ones that had staying power had multiple owners.[24] The astonishing number of mills in Montgomery County (Table 2.2) shows a dense concentration of industry. The industry was aided by the changes in elevation, water, and people with mechanical skills.

Cotton Mills

Between three and four hundred people and their machinery came from Massachusetts to the Indiana Cotton Mills at Cannelton and used local coal and building stone. Capital from Louisville and Southern cotton allowed the mill to produce cloth on 372 looms.[25] Other Ohio River cotton mills at Evansville and Madison also produced textiles. The geography of the Cumberland and Tennessee Rivers made the Ohio River a natural center for producing and processing cotton for Midwestern markets with low transportation costs. Farmers could float their cotton downstream across Tennessee and Kentucky, then use steam power to move it upriver to factories. The introduction of the railroads perpetuated the existing growth, trade, processing, and marketing pattern. Finished cotton cloth could be distributed throughout the Ohio River valley and, if the market would bear it, continue following the Mississippi and Missouri rivers or be transported by railroad to the East Coast.

Indiana Wool

In the 1850s the price of a pound of wool was approximately 28 cents, and the 1850 US Census showed a million sheep, with the Indiana herd

Table 2.2. A Sample of Montgomery County, Indiana, Mills and Dates Established, 1800–1977

Name	Started	Ended	Product	Location	Builder
Yount's Woolen	c. 1843	1907c	Wool	Yountsville	Daniel Yount
Snyder	1830	c. 1941	Grain	Yountsville	Abijah Oneal
Sperry	1838				Maj. Isaac C. Elston
Deer	1829	1887	Grain	Waveland	Joel C. Deer
			Lumber		
			Wool		
			Wool	Ladoga	
Stitt			Lumber	Crawfordsville	John Stitt
Hill			Grain	Crawfordsville	
Franklin	1847		Flour	Darlington	Silas Kenworthy
			Flaxseed		
			Carding		
Pine Hills	1849	1887	Wool		William J. Canine
Pine Hills	1868	1876	Wool		Zenith Hallet
			Lumber		
Metropolitan			Grain		J. M. Troutman
Meyers	1831		Grain	Ladoga	John Meyers Jr.
Bateman					
Britts					
Honey Creek	1892		Grain	Darlington	John Cox
Griffin					
Hall					
Harlan					
Troutman	1836			Darlington	John and William Cox
Mankers					
Wood					
Mote					
Clouser	1820s	1886	Grain	Darlington	John Clouser
John's	1832			Thorntown	Hiram Lafollette
Mote					
Stovers	1830			Crawfordsville	
Elston					
Potts	1854	1901		Back Creek	John Potts
Craig	1856	1886	Grain		Robert Craig
Troutman					
Guntle	1828	1878		Yountsville	Dr. Winton
Spring		1900			
Gilkey	1843			Yountsville	
Hibernian					
Clark	1840			Alamo	Elijah Clark

Table 2.2. A Sample of Montgomery County, Indiana, Mills and Dates Established, 1800–1977 (*cont.*)

Name	Started	Ended	Product	Location	Builder
Grimes and Hybarger	1856			Alamo	
Deere and Canine	1831			Pine Hills	Joel Deer
Flashour	1848			Pine Hills	White and Hybarger
Chamber	1868			Happy Hollow	William Chambers
	1833		Flaxseed Fulling	Darlington	Benjamin Cox
	1860		Wool	Darlington	William Cox
Finkle	1865			Darlington	
	1838	1977	Lumber	Darlington	J. A. Marshall
Boldt	1873		Grain	Waynetown	Gray Brothers and William Ryder
Meyers	1832		Lumber Grain	Ladoga	
Anderson	1862		Grain	Ladoga	C. H. R. Anderson
Morris			Carding	Ladoga	Peter Morris
Ladoga Woolen Mills	1863	1880	Wool	Ladoga	Daniel C. Stover
Anderson Sorghum Mills		1895	Sorghum	Ladoga	M. B. Anderson
Epperson Heading Mill			Staves	Ladoga	
Hoosier Veneer Mill		1912	Veneer	Ladoga	
Ashby			Grain	Ashby	
Blackbear Hotel	1886	1914	Grain	New Richmond	
Ladoga Water Mill				Ladoga	
Champion Planing Mill			Planing	Crawfordsville	J. H. Markley and Co.
Mote	c. 1850		Lumber	Garfield	Jerry and Washington Mote
Gunkle	1852	1862	Grain	Union Twp.	Michael and Samuel Gunkle

Source: Data compiled from *Montgomery Magazine*, Montgomery, IN.

Table 2.3. Indiana Wool Production, 1850–1880

Year	Pounds of Finished Wool
1850	2,610,287
1860	2,552,318
1870	5,029,023
1880	6,167,498

Source: Data compiled from Thornbrough and US Bureau of the Census, *Compendium of the Tenth Census*, 1888.

declining prior to 1860 (Table 2.3). With the arrival of the Civil War, states sent purchasing agents across the nation and to Europe to purchase wool cloth to equip soldiers for national service. Wool was required for socks, pants, vests, jackets, coats, hats, blankets, and canteen covers, and a bidding war commenced. The spike in wool prices, up to 96 cents a pound, led to larger herds of three million sheep in the war years, according to the Department of Agriculture, and Indiana had the fifth-largest sheep herd in the nation.[26] After the war, wool prices tumbled, and the herd turned into a food supply. The volume of wool produced after the Civil War confounds present understanding of Indiana as a corn and hog state. It flies in the face of conceptions of what farmers produced.

Across the couple of decades after the Civil War, the Indiana sheep herd diminished, but wool production continued to increase at the same time due to the importation of improved breeds of sheep. The new breeds grew more wool by volume and had a better-quality wool. The new wool also helped Indiana weavers improve the variety of their goods. Farmers hesitated to purchase expensive thoroughbred breeds because roving packs of dogs killed unguarded sheep. As of 1861, dogs were licensed and then taxed by township trustees to compensate farmers for sheep lost to dog attacks. Cotswold and Southdown sheep were imported in the 1870s, and the Indiana Wool Growers Association formed in 1876 to help their members to improve the breeding of sheep and the production of wool.[27]

While there were many small woolen mills in Indiana, the 1870 Indianapolis Woolen Exposition presented cloth from Columbus, Indianapolis, Lawrenceburg, Peru, Richmond, and Terre Haute. This state trade exhibition promoted domestic wool and presented the variety of manufactured yarn. Exhibitors displayed machinery and sample cloth. Some of the cloth was coarse for blankets or jeans, but some of it rivaled that produced by more established and larger eastern mills.[28] The quality of the manufactured goods inspired local farmers and manufactures as well as creating new local, regional, and national markets. All of this interest in farm-to-factory manufacturing supported the existing Indiana wool industry. And all of this industry required a well-educated workforce.

CONSIDERING CONSTITUTIONAL CHANGES

At the time the Indiana Legislature was considering creating a new state constitution, Caleb Mills gave a fifth address describing what they might do to improve the state of education in Indiana.[29] The popular tide had turned in support of public education. For the past two years, the majority of the state population had voted in favor of common schools, and Caleb Mills declared that the most important issue was education and that the voters would both favor it and value it in the future. Indiana as a commonwealth, along with the citizens of Indiana, had changed since the first constitution was approved. In the thirty-four years since the 1816 constitution, in which Indiana had promised to provide universal free education, the state had made large strides in developing as a commonwealth. Indiana could now afford the promise of free schools because of the changes that had occurred in the state. From 1816, tax revenue rose from $6,000 from 9,000 voters; in 1848, tax revenue was $508,000 from 153,000 voters.[30] Mills believed that both Massachusetts and Connecticut illustrated the need for taxes that provided a foundation for the support of common schools. Both of those systems flourished because they could depend on consistent funding for their schools based on taxation. Farmers might consider tax levies as falling primarily on them, not on mechanical ventures, even though the measures to both needed an educated workforce. Industry also paid taxes on their improved land, but not in the proportion to farmers who were large landowners.

Even though Congress granted Indiana 650,317 acres of land, Mills contended that poor management limited the value of that gift to provide a base for school funding.[31] Other instances of poor management resulted when Hendricks County sold land for $1,000, but after improvements and a couple of years had passed, the land sold again for $5,000.[32] While Tippecanoe County sold its land for more than $10,000 and Vigo County sold its land for $18,000, other counties raised far less, resulting in unequal funding that perpetuated itself over multiple years.[33] Mills argued that if any advantage should be given, it should be given to those who were disadvantaged in soil and their situations in order to help most those who had the least and aid those who required the most assistance. Mills further argued that if Michigan was right in her use of the grant, then Indiana was wrong, because Michigan helped all receive an education and Indiana was helping only those communities that already had established schools. Mills maintained that the US Congress expected the grant to be used to help all, regardless of township lines, intelligence, or wealth. Congress never expected that one township would get more funds or that the funds would be used to help the rich at the expense of the poor. Mills maintained that it was slander to attribute to the legislators unstatesmanlike and anti-democratic motivations, and he believed that spreading the congressional land to increase its value rather than giving it in one large tract attracted community attention and created improvements in the surrounding land. Thus, placing school land as close to the center of the township as possible helped draw attention to it and get the highest price to support common schools. Michigan even went so far as to survey school land as town lots when practical. If the operation of the fund aided the rich and disfavored the poor, then the town could honor both the original legislators and the next generation by doing the right thing and fixing the system. Providing for all children was in the best interests of the state because people moved frequently and would not stay in their townships forever. When revising the Constitution, Mills said, the people should fix the common fund for school land and create a property tax for education; furthermore, funding streams should come from five accounts for common schools plus one for academies and one for universities. Those five funds included those for congressional lands, the State Bank of Indiana tax, a saline fund, and funds for forfeitures of recognizance and county fines. As a side note, Mills believed that the governor should not have the power to pardon criminals since that reduced the amount of money available to the fund.

Mills next addressed the problem of county seminaries, which he believed were important and should not be discontinued but were mismanaged and did not produce the desired results. His conclusion was that all institutions above the grade of the common school should not be operated by the state because he believed that voluntary associations and private enterprise did a better job of supervision. He contended that banking, like education, was a matter of internal improvement; therefore, friends of education established academies only when and where they thought they would be successful. In addition, the state paid for a portion of the work done for the public by these seminaries. For example, New York gave money for the number of students studying academic subjects.

Next Mills suggested creating three education funds: for the common school, university, and library. The common school fund included the bank fund that, without bonds or mortgages and with a tax of $.002 on each dollar of property, created enough capital to fund the schools and provided relief to those paying for the education of their children. Under his plan he believed that two-thirds of the taxpayers would pay no more than they paid for one admission to see a circus or menagerie. At about 25 cents, a poll tax would not be burdensome either. The largest tracts of land were owned by nonresidents who paid the most taxes to support the public schools. It was reasonable to Mills to tax property to pay for the protection and enhancement of that land through the educational advancement of its citizens. Making taxes statewide would allow for a fair tax on property, as would the poll tax that should be created to a poor man who improved his land that was next to land owned by a wealthy man of another state, who paid nothing for the education of the children of the region.

The legislature established the literary fund to create libraries in the common schools and seminaries. To help the literary fund, the present academies' fund should be given to the local school fund, and future funds from the saline fund, fines, forfeitures, and bank tax should also go to libraries and seminaries. Mills encouraged patrons to read for leisure books on history, biography, travel, the arts, science, and literature. He excluded all works of fiction and romance, which he found to be worthless. He also excluded religious books from the book list because there were plenty of these in Sunday schools and private libraries, and he desired to prevent denominational bickering and suspicion. By following the lead of Massachusetts and New York in purchasing low-cost American-manufactured books, local libraries raised money to match state funds each year for five years. After five years, the money could be split between academies and common schools for apparatus and libraries.

Caleb Mills also wished to develop competent teachers, and he used this analogy: just as the justice system needed higher courts, education needed higher education. Furthermore, Indiana must have a source of competent teachers, and they must come from higher education. A few teachers came from other states, but Indiana educators must produce the majority of their future teachers. Both Massachusetts and New York had established state-funded normal schools, which provided free tuition and travel expenses to and from school. Massachusetts had three normal schools and multiple teacher institutes, by county or smaller, across the state, with each lasting two to three weeks. In the teacher institutes common-school teachers learned teaching methods, content, and something about government before they returned to improve their schools.

Mills took the role of West Point in providing scientific and accomplished officers for the Army as similar to the role of normal schools in creating leaders for education. Mills believed there was economy in grafting normal schools to existing institutions, but he did not want to try to use the existing county seminaries. After all, New York had tried the idea and failed, and while academies were valuable, they did not replace the need for normal schools. Academies had limited means and were unstable; furthermore, they did not possess adequate teachers, apparatus, or library resources. Finally, academies could not compete with universities. The Indiana colleges did not have the same problem as academies in supporting normal schools. Mills suggested that each college establish a full-time and experienced teacher preparation professor to provide mentorship and create a peer group of future teachers.

College funds given by Congress and the Indiana Constitution did not impinge on state funding or collage operation. Mills believed that it was time for Indiana to create a group of university regents. Their duties would be to distribute the literary and college appropriations of the legislature, oversee the colleges by visiting them annually, and attend and participate in the final examinations of the colleges. They would also receive the annual reports of the Indiana colleges from their respective boards of trustees and compile a report to the legislature on the state of the Indiana colleges. A dozen regents would be selected with enough background in literature and science that they could examine the course of study at each college, and no more than two would be from any one religious sect.

Mills put forward a plan for creating an Indiana university, not to be confused with the existing state college at Bloomington, that would consist of every college that adopted a course of study that satisfied the regents. To remain in good standing, each college would furnish an annual report of its income and expenditures; would provide an enumeration of faculty and students; would report the course of study required for admission and graduation, plus the accomplishments of each class; would disclose the library holdings, laboratory equipment, and instructional materials; and would create a professorship of normal teaching. To prove they were a university, they would need to have cash and property, have a normal professor give a course of common-school teaching lecturers during the year, help with the teacher institutes, and address the community members to persuade them of the value of well-prepared instructors. Furthermore, they would admit one student from each county to receive free tuition in exchange for teaching the same number of quarters as it took to educate him. The student would give a bond for the full amount, which would be cancelled by certificates issued from the trustees under whom he had taught. The refunded tuition would be added to the college funds budget. The regents would divide university funds equally between the colleges, and the only compensation the regents would receive would be per diem and travel costs.

Mills again proposed the idea that the Bloomington campus should be sold to a sect and the money added to the university fund for training fifty common-school teachers every two years. He believed that only the privatized Bloomington college and the law college would join the existing colleges, but in the future other colleges would be welcomed to join the university. Colleges remained at liberty to control their affairs and would not exclude future colleges, and Mills believed that he would recruit private institutions to accomplish state goals. Moreover, no private property would be involved in the change, nor had it been united with the state, so it steered clear of constitutional objections. Once again Mills questioned the money spent on the Bloomington university versus the number of common-school teachers produced or the principals of county seminaries created.

THE NEW CONSTITUTION OF 1851

In the context of a state embracing the industrial age, a significant amount of the new constitution was devoted to the issue of education and reform. It charged the legislature to create legislation "to prove, by law, for a general and unified system of Common schools, wherein tuition shall be without charge, and equally open to all."[34] Mills addressed the community in support of the changes to the constitution, which he explained were not a partisan issue.[35] The constitution must be changed to make sure that Indiana had the power to protect state school funds from politicians who would seize the state funds and return them only to their locality. Students who should have been in school seven months a year had been turned out of their schools for three-fourths of a year. The state should provide money for six months of school for all, and the locality should provide money for additional periods of school. Mills observed that there were two ways to amend the constitution, and the legislature selected the quickest way. He felt that this was good, because it provided the most expedient way to change the constitution, thus providing education for more students faster as opposed to waiting multiple years to change the constitution and missing multiple students in the process. Moreover, Mills explained that the constitution started by guaranteeing the rights, privileges, and protections of adults but left minors to the whims of the legislature. He called both for a statement of the right to a public-school education and for a guarantee of seven months of school.

Mills was pleased with the Constitution of 1851 because he saw the education of youth as important to the commonwealth, but he wanted it to go further.[36] He believed that vice and crime were restrained and virtue and enterprise stimulated by the common schools. He saw ignorance, both individual and national, as diminishing effort while it disrupted indolence, poverty, and ruin. The creation of intelligence, however, was the mark of progress, invention, discovery, science, art, and virtue. Grounded in his sect, he equated education with cultivating a moral acquiescence in the controlling arrangements of a Higher Power, but he also saw the mental and moral culture developed by education as systematic of a government that ameliorated the social and political condition of society. He contended that to awaken the mind and reject indolence was to claim liberty for both the self and others and that education fostered individual and national energy by creating civic, social, and political institutions.

Moreover, Mills explained that the framers of the Indiana Constitution wanted to eliminate the inequity of burden and the inequity of privilege in their support of the common schools. The state both provided and supervised education through the creation of the position of the Superintendent of Public Instruction, and by combing all of the permanent funds for a revenue stream. The constitution required the legislature to provide free common schools to all students with no partnership with local units until the baseline obligation of creating and funding public schools was fulfilled. The legislature included many of the people who drafted the constitution and was in sympathy with what it should do for education, as demonstrated by their 1852 Common School Act, where they placed a tax of $.001 on one dollar of property and established a 50-cent poll tax to fund public education. He reminded voters that neither of the past two legislatures had increased the school tax or restored the library tax. And he declared that the framers had rejected the three-month school, to be supplemented by the wealth or poverty of the community, in favor of a six-month school, which he thought was as much as a rural population needed.

Mills concluded that the state had the power to correct and punish through state-funded reformatories and prisons, and therefore Indiana also had the power to prevent vice through the construction of state-funded free schools. He called for amendments to the constitution to add six months of school, with the locality to add more time to the term. Mills also called for an amendment that specifically regulated the amount of tax money raised in order to be fair to all students in all communities and to make sure that the legislature did not raid the education funds for other purposes. Finally, Mills suggested that the term of the Superintendent of Public Instruction be lengthened from two years to four years. Unfortunately for Mills, no amendments were added to the Indiana Constitution. While he was ready to go even further to promote education, the Hoosier voters had bitten off enough reformed education and needed to chew and digest it before they would be ready to take another bite of reform.

The development of industry in Indiana using hydropower and later steam power for wool and cotton mills paralleled the production history of Yount's Mill. The mill provided an important service when it started, and it played an important role in the regional market. At a time when Indiana was making important constitutional changes that would be used to support education, the burgeoning economy propelled the mill to prosperity.

THREE

The Production History of Yount Mill

In the last Ice Age, the great ice sheet melted over what would become Montgomery County, Indiana. The water pouring out of the glacial ice found soft glacial till to move around as aggregate that drilled through soft Mansfield sandstone or hit more determined shale. The variation of the bedrock and the effervescent cascading melt water carrying aggregate carved a path for Sugar Creek, a steep-sided valley rising to the surrounding tablelands. While Sugar Creek is not very long, it has one of the fastest falls in Indiana. As side streams carved their way down to reach Sugar Creek, they also left steep-sided rock-bottomed creeks with waterfalls and springs. The glaciers were good for the millers who were to come later.

STARTING THE MILL

In 1840 Allen and Daniel Yount came to Montgomery County intent on the manufacture of woolen goods, and with them they brought a piece of the Industrial Revolution.[1] The brothers had one burning question on their minds: Could they make a life for themselves and their families at the confluence of Mill [now Spring] Creek and Sugar Creek by operating a mill? Later they looked for employees who could help them. The Yount brothers knew the dangers of milling only too well; they had survived floods while operating their mill in Tippecanoe County. Hydropowered mills were prone to flooding, and neighbors were prone to ask for credit if times were hard, stressing a business until it folded. The Younts had knowledge of hydrology, engineering, building skills, and manufacturing. They also knew how to work hard and accomplish tasks in order to create and run a successful business.

Daniel and Allen selected a location, and in 1840 they attempted to purchase the water rights from Silas Wright, who was leasing the rights to the power for a small carding mill near the mouth of Spring Creek. Daniel and Allen realized that they would bind their capital to the water rights and not be able to build what they really wanted.[2] They each had a thousand dollars from their father, and in addition they had access to even more capital because they had both sold their farms. They were looking for an investment and a future. In the meantime they took possession of and ran Snyder Grist Mill on Mill Creek, three-fourths of a mile from its entrance to Sugar Creek. Just before the water-rights lease expired in 1843, Daniel and Allen bought the land from Abijah O'Neal, making the water rights a moot point.[3] Wright moved the machinery, dismantled his mill, and hauled the building to another location.

When the water was low, the Yount brothers constructed a brush dam across Spring Creek and dug a millrace to provide power for their first carding mill. They hewed and mortised the timbers for the frame building.[4] At this mill they would scour wool, a washing process sometimes called finishing, which sometimes also included dyeing. They provided combed wool to housewives, who would spin their own wool thread into yarn. The women could knit or weave this yarn into fabric for their families or combine it with linen to create linsey-woolsey, a durable fabric with a linen warp and a woolen weft.[5] In retrospect, Daniel described how the mill was established: "We did not want to go into manufacturing, but after a time they [the women in the community] got tired of doing the work themselves, and wanted to exchange their wool for cloth, so we had to make it."[6] While the memory was condescending toward the women, it reflected how Daniel viewed the beginnings of the mill. The Younts engaged in trade, taking a percentage of the finished wool in exchange for processing the wool for the farm wives since currency was in short supply; they also judiciously extended credit only to the most established neighbors. The women eagerly exchanged a portion of their wool, since it cut many hard hours of labor from their lives as they constructed clothing for their growing families.

In 1849 Daniel and Allen extended their mill race one hundred fifty yards down the creek to their new frame mill.[7] To power this mill they built a thirty foot overshot wheel, and they took their profits and plowed them into new spinning and weaving equipment. Now the Yount brothers could control the entire process of wool production from raw wool to finished product. Again, the women of the community were thrilled with this luxury of trading raw wool for woven cloth or yarn, which they could use to clothe their families.

THE NEW ECONOMY

On the top of the hill near the road, Allen and Daniel built their homes and a guesthouse for their customers. When they realized that they were becoming successful, they overhauled the mill in 1849 with new equipment to allow them to spin and weave.[8] The business was known as Yount's Woolen Exchange Mill, as farmers from many miles around brought wool to be weighed in the mill store by the Younts. Dan remarked, "Our customers were from all the country around here within a radius of 100 miles. They came from Illinois, and a few who moved to Kentucky still send their wool to us."[9] The farmers then would receive credit in the store to purchase from the variety of woolen products sold in the store. A farmer typically took a bolt of wool fabric home to make into garments. Some farmers would need to spend the night at the Younts' prior to returning home the next day.

In 1857, before Allen and his family moved West looking for new opportunities, he sold his $8,000 half of the property, equipment, and business to Arthur Russel.[10] Russell had worked in mills for most of his life, at Burnettsville, Monticello, and on the Wea River in Indiana, as well as a mill in Norway. With more than just a passing interest in milling, Arthur had the good sense to marry Rhoda Yount, the daughter of Daniel and Sarah Yount. He brought capital into the firm from the sale of his last mill at Monticello, Indiana. On January 1, 1858, the day he was to take possession of his half of the partnership, unfortunately he died of typhoid fever.[11] At the public estate sale, Daniel Yount, as the highest bidder, purchased the other half of his own mill from the court estate administrator. In agreements with the court on March 28 and June 10, 1863, Daniel provided a trust for his grandchildren, Byrun R. Russell and Lydia L. Russell, to be aided by their guardians Arthur McConaha, Achsa McConaha (perhaps relatives of Sarah), John Townsely, Daniel's new son-in-law, and Daniel's daughter and the mother of the children, Rhoda Townsely.[12] Now the sole proprietor, Daniel ran the mill by himself.

Daniel and Allen had prospered during the booming industrial economy of the 1850s, but as good as those years had been, nothing could have prepared Daniel for the economy of the 1860s. In the war years industry exploded, and the business economy of the United States erupted in profits. It was good for Daniel, too. Daniel produced $170,000 worth of goods during the Civil War at the height of his production, compared to his usual production of about $70,000 per year.[13] This also made him a major employer and taxpayer in the region.

At low water in 1864, Daniel built a seven-and-a-half-foot-tall notched wooden crib dam filled with rock and locked together with iron pins across Sugar Creek just before the Spring Creek joins it. He harnessed the swift and powerful flow of Sugar Creek and created a pond that would provide him with a stable power system nearly year -round. Only a hard freeze or a parching drought could stop production, and his mill stood strong on the bank so that floods could not confound the operation of the mill. The power for the entire mill complex was produced by his turbine wheel, located in the frame shed next to the river, and he connected the turbine to his two-story, fifty-by-seventy-five-foot brick mill.

By 1864, eleven buildings stood at the mill site. Daniel continued building in 1867 by adding a second brick mill, a structure measuring fifty by eighty-four feet that he connected to the same power source.[14] He produced products valued at $75,000 per year, rarely lost a customer, and did not need to advertise at this time.[15] In addition, an old naïve painting shows the smokestack south of the dye house.[16] The main road metaphorically came down the hill from the west of the boarding house and ended at the front doors of the mills, seemingly at the gate of prosperity.[17]

Unfortunately, Daniel had a problem: he did not have clear title to the water rights for Sugar Creek. As usual, there was no litigation. On August 16, 1866, Joseph M. Hopping sold his water rights to Daniel Yount.[18] On February 12, 1867, Daniel purchased half of Sugar Creek from Sylvester and Susan Hopping.[19] Daniel followed this purchase with one on August 31, 1867, from Abijah and Ellin O'Neal, when they sold an acre of land, giving him control of the water on Sugar Creek where he had built his new mill.[20] On October 8, 1867, Jacob M. and Mary Troutman sold their water rights to their father-in-law and father, Daniel Yount.[21] Daniel now had an uncontestable claim to the power source for his mill.

In order to feed his family and the occupants of the boarding house, in 1870 Daniel Yount purchased graham flour, cornmeal, and wheat flour for baking. He also purchased bran, screenings, and chaff for livestock feed and nails for $38.32 from Spring Mill, the grist mill near Yountsville.[22] Daniel's account at the same mill in 1874 shows that he owed $248.08 for shorts for grits, flour, butter, hauling, and wool.[23] Always looking for an income stream, on December 28, 1875, Daniel sold forty oak trees as timber on the mill side of the creek for $150.[24]

In 1875 Daniel brought his sons, Andrew and John, and his son-in-law, Wycliff C. Whitehead, into the partnership, now known as Daniel Yount and Sons, Woolen Manufacturers and Merchants Proprietors of Exchange Woolen Mills.[25] John died in 1876 in a Crawfordsville railroad accident, leaving his widow with four sons from ages twelve to two months. When John died, Wycliff C. and Anna Whitehead sold part of the Yount Woolen Mill to Daniel on April 29, 1876, and on the same day Andrew Yount sold part of the company to Daniel in order to reorganize the company.[26] This left Daniel the senior partner of the company, with 14.05 shares, while Andrew had 5.30 shares and W. C. Whitehead 8.30 shares of their partnership, which included the nine structures and undivided acreage. For some reason, Daniel wanted Whitehead to have more shares than his son Andrew until Whitehead left the partnership.[27]

On January 19, 1880, a letter came to Daniel Yount from his son-in-law, Wycliff Whitehead, in Pataskala, Ohio, who had previously been in partnership with the firm. The letter is addressed "Dear Father" and refers to the author's wife as Daniel's daughter.[28] There is a reasoned plea for the satisfaction of some settlement of the Whiteheads' long-term efforts for the mill. Whitehead was heavily in debt and was counting on being paid for his efforts. The cause for the separation was described as illness from miasma of both husband and wife from working at the mill; however, the separation was obviously not amicable. This might have been the root of the story of the attempt to sell the mill, which resulted in the burning of the contract with Whitehead, who, seeing the rise of larger mills in the East, favored the sale, while Daniel was firmly against it. Daniel had been involved in several past dissolved partnerships; he might have separated from his father, John, or Allen in a similar manner.

Andrew Yount took the teaching exam and received a twelve-month teaching license in 1884, but, in ill health, Daniel Yount sold the mill to Andrew Yount on February 23, 1887. Daniel continued to give advice and direction as he was able.[29] Daniel observed, "We employ thirty hands now."[30] Daniel and Andrew were in partnership as Daniel Yount and Son to provide wool, woolens, and cotton staple goods.[31] Their colors ran from black, grey, brown, indigo, or red to white. They did a vigorous business in multiple types of finished woolen goods and added cotton products to their retail business. They had accounts with merchants who purchased goods for their stores. The addition of cotton yard goods gave their customers more of a selection of fabrics. Customers purchased flannel, gingham, shirting, and yarn.[32] The father and son continued to provide services, including selling patterns, while maintaining their wool exchange business. Even though they claimed that they bartered their woolen goods exclusively for wool, everything on the invoices (Figure 3.1) was sold for cash. People traveled to the mill to trade their wool for goods, but the railroads also carried parcels through the postal service from farmhouses to the factory and back in a cash business. Merchants purchased woolen stock from Daniel and Andrew, and orders came in from Missouri, Illinois, and Indiana.

In 1890, Andrew traded with the major cities of Chicago and Detroit as well as the local town of Crawfordsville (Table 3.1). Andrew turned to Chicago for fabric dye and to Detroit for the soap he needed. Andrew was able to get machine parts locally, including two spur wheels and a crankshaft for the mill. The business was not self-sufficient; it traded widely for goods ranging from machine parts to baby chairs. It also had expensive bills for important items to run the business.

It was profitable when Daniel did his own distribution and consignment. People like George A. Gilbert wrote to Daniel in 1890 saying, "I am in business here and if I could make anything in handling your good[s I] would like to do so."[33] Daniel seemed to be eager to consign goods to multiple stores; sometimes, though, they were perhaps too close to one another. That same year M. Herzog wrote in complaint, "I do not think you ou[gh]t to sell your goods to anyone else in this town as the trade is too small to pay a profit for two."[34] Obviously Daniel was supposed to stop selling his goods to Mr. Herzog's competitor. Daniel traded in Indiana, Illinois, Missouri, and Kentucky, four states, with thirty-three small vendors, mostly

D. Yount & Son
Manufacturers of
All Kinds of Staple
Woolen Goods
Exclusively in
Exchange for Wool
105
17

Statement
Yountsville, Ind., *6/13/1889*
C Schrnek
Parwifa
In Acc't with D. Yount & Son,
Manufacturers of and Dealers in
Wool, Woolen
and
Staple Cotton Goods

[On lined paper]

2	Sks Yarn	33⅓	.66
5	Cuts @ Brown	15	.75
3½	Flannel	35	1.22
5	Table Linen	55	2.75
3 Piece 14	Gingham	9	1.26
6	Muslins	9	.54
10	Muslins	8	.80
8	Muslins	6	.48
23	Shirting	10	2.30
8	Pattern	12½	1.00
3	@	15	.60
			$12.36

Figure 3.1. Invoice for Various Goods, 1889. Transcribed from the papers of Allan and Barbara White.

Table 3.1. Yount Mill Correspondence for Purchases, 1890

State	Town	Party	Description
IN	Crawfordsville	Lyle and Smith Founder and forging Machinists	cast 2 spur wheels (turned machine steel) changed crank shaft, Casting
MI	Detroit	James Hartness Soap Company Fulling and Scouring Soap for Woolen and Hosiery Mills	purchase soap
IN	Crawfordsville	Zach Mahorney & Sons	4 screen windows 4 yards rope 6 yds netting Tacks screen door hinges Tea kettle – Albert 1 granite kettle 4 pot lids 1 chair bottom 1 china plate 1 child's high chair
IL	Chicago	N. Spencer Thomas Peerless Dyes	dye

Source: Data compiled and transcribed from the Yount Woolen Mill Papers of the Rotary Jail Museum and Tannenbaum Cultural Center, Crawfordsville, IN.

dealing in two-ply wool yarn, blankets, and cloth. A more typical local order from The New York Cash Store in Ladoga, Indiana, requested six blankets in three colors and fifteen bundles of two-ply wool yarn in two colors, to be shipped immediately (Figure 3.2). Finished colored blankets continued to play a role in the business. The mill sold raw yarn for housewives who wanted to create their own clothing.

Daniel explained his assessment of the wool business resulting from the disruptions of the Civil War. In his opinion, the lack of cotton forced cotton manufactures to switch to wool production, which proved unsustainable.

The war stimulated the market unnaturally. Immense supplies of blankets and cloth were manufactured for the army. Cotton could not be had, and some of the cotton mills in the East were turned into woolen mills. In

W. R. Hostetter   C. Ashby   W. M. Mills
The New York Cash Store
Hostetter, Ashby & Mills,
Proprietors,
Ladoga, Indiana, Sep 22 1890

Andrew Yount
    Yountsville
        Please ship us at once
2 pr. Red Blankets
2 pr Gray Blankets
2 pr White Blankets
10 bundles sheeps gray yarn 2/ply
5 bundles steel mix yarn 2 / ply

Yours very truly
Hostetter Ashby & Mills

Figure 3.2. Local Order, 1890. Transcribed from the papers of Allen and Barbara Brooke White at Yountsville Mill, Yountsville, Indiana.

the readjustment that followed this great demand, there was a necessary falling off when the war ended. Then the West was overrun with peddlers who sold shoddy, an inferior type of blanket that was turned out by the Eastern mills, or cloth they had in stock, and Daniel admitted that his mill could not compete with them. Prices of goods were never as high as they were after the war. At the end of the war, unwashed wool was worth 25 cents, and washed wool was one-third higher. The average price had been about that since then. There was not nearly as much wool made in the section around the mill as there had been. A lessening of the tariff in 1883 reduced the supply to about 15,000,000 pounds.[35]

Daniel also blamed the "peddlers," which in some regions was a code word used by those with anti-Semitic attitudes. Additionally, prior to the Civil War, shoddy was a type of wool blanket, but during and after the war it took on the present meaning of inferior quality. Daniel concluded that a protective tariff was needed.

In 1888 Daniel remarked about the fluctuation in wool prices over time, "For the last ten years, while war prices have not been reached and never will be again, they were 25 or 30 per cent higher than they were prior to 1860. I used to buy unwashed wool for 16 cents, but even now we cannot get it for that."[36] The deflation in the market had been devastating, wiping out half a dozen local wool mills and shuttering mills in the East. "The price has been gradually declining," Yount said. "War prices we could not expect to maintain as there is no longer that unusual demand; but still with the proper protection it would be a good business, and people could make a good living at it."[37] Daniel had confidence that protectionist tariffs would allow wool manufactures to remain competitive.

Daniel was particularly hopeful with the prospect of Benjamin Harrison entering the White House. He believed that the rise in the wool market was tied with "the almost absolute certainty of General Harrison's election and the attendant defeat of the Mills bill in Congress. The market is extremely sensitive to all such influence, and our correspondents plainly attribute it to this—not because they are biased politically but because it is a commercial fact. If there were an equal prospect of Mr. Cleveland's election there would be an immediate decline. The tariff agitation of the past few years, the Democratic intention to reduce the tariff has unsettled the market."[38]

Wool cloth that was brushed or combed, like flannels, were called worsteds. Daniel felt this was an area that was particularly vulnerable to imported wool products from Europe. He blamed Democrats for a betrayal of campaign promises that led to the demise of the American wool industry: "The discrimination made in favor of worsteds, which have the lowest tariff when it ought to be the highest, has also had a disastrous effect. The Democrats promised that the old tariff should be restored, but they have not kept their word. The manufactures wanted the President [Grover Cleveland] to interfere, but he has excused himself on the ground that, as we are likely to have free wool, it wouldn't be worthwhile. We believe that wool is not and will not be properly protected so long as there is this unjust discrimination against worsteds."[39]

Daniel heard the calls for free trade in the press and by politicians and roundly rejected them. He did not believe there were any wool producers or manufacturers East or West who wanted free-trade wool or wool products.[40] He wrote: "How can anyone suppose that the uncertain supply from a foreign market, subject to loss and interruption by foreign wars and international disputes, could be as reliable and certain as a home market within our own boundaries and at our own doors. There would be a diminution in the supply at inconvenient times; an over supply at others; with corresponding fluctuation of the market that would be injurious if not fatal to many manufacturers. There is nothing like a steady home market, and it should be fostered and encouraged."[41]Daniel's communitarian spirit saw the advantages of being independent from foreign entanglements and rejecting free-trade overtures. His views on business were consistently protectionist. He responded to falling local production and prices, and he desperately wanted to save his mill and protect his family.

THE END OF THE MILL

The mill traded with thirty-three stores and towns in Indiana, Illinois, and Kentucky, selling mostly blankets by the pair, wool by the skein, and flannel and jeans by the piece (Table 3.2). A variety of colors were represented. Large orders traveled from the mill to these stores, located across the region. The mill provided an important service to the small-town stores it worked with.

In a photo Daniel Yount wears a dark coat with cloth buttons and no lapels, a white shirt, and a white tie. While his attire was simple, it all came from his mill and store. He has no hair on the top of his head, crow's feet gather at the corners of his eyes, and he wears an expression of concern on his countenance.[42] Daniel Yount, aged eighty-three, died at 3:00, on Sunday morning, September 31, 1890, at his home, crippling the company.[43] His obituary (Figure 3.3) reflects the respect for him in the community, referencing a nickname for him. The members of the community had depended on him for benevolence, and he had honored them with his philanthropy.

The newspapers decried Daniel's passing, and vendors sent condolences.[44] After Daniel's death, people reminisced, "Was there anywhere in the county any set of men of greater strength of character than Daniel Yount"?[45] It was a completely different world in Yountsville after Daniel's death.

At the time of Yount's death, he had a prosperous business. Daniel had 63,260 pounds of wool on hand, scoured, combed, and ready to weave—about $15,500 worth of inventory (Table 3.3). He also had 2,033 yards of wool in the looms worth about $605 (Table 3.4); these included twilled gray, white, and brown flannels, cashmeres, doeskin, and two dozen blankets. It seems surprising that a relatively small mill could be in the process of producing so

Table 3.2. Yount Mill Trade Correspondence, 1890

State	Town	Purchaser	Amount	Color	Product	Description
IL	Edgar	C. W. Lelark	2	White	Blankets	Pair
			1	Red	Blankets	Pair
				Sheeps–Grey	Flannel	
				Red		
	White Lick	Faught & Surber				
IN	Dudley	Geo. A. Gilbert	1 lbs.	Black	Yarn	2 ply
			1 lbs.	Indigo	Yarn	2 ply
				Blue		
IN	Russellville	Grimes, Ross & Co.				
IN	Wilkinson	Morrison Brothers		Black	Yarn	2 ply
				Navy blue	Yarn	2 ply
IN	Waynetown	M. Herzog	40 skeins	Grey	Yarn	2 ply
			20 skeins	Grey	Yarn	2 ply
			20 Skeins	Black	Yarn	2 ply
			40 Skeins	Red	Yarn	2 ply
			20 Skeins	Brown	Yarn	2 ply
			1 pr.	White	Blankets	
IN	Conroe			Sheep Grey & blue mix		2 ply
IL	Champaign	G. C. Willis			Fancy and Staple Dry Goods, Cloaks, Curtains and Draperies	

Table 3.2. Yount Mill Trade Correspondence, 1890 (cont.)

State	Town	Purchaser	Amount	Color	Product	Description
IL	Indianola		5 skeins	White		
			7 skeins	Sheeps Grey		
IN	Newtown	R. Campbell & Son Dealers in General Merchandise				
MO	St. Louis	Reade Manufacturing, Co.	2 skeins	Grey		
			1 skein	Black		
IN	Lebanon	John H. Perkins & Co.				
IN	Wilkinson	Morrison Bros.				
IN	Russiaville	C. S. Wadman	2 pair	White	Blankets	
			2 pair	Scarlet	Blankets	
			1 pair	Any other	Blankets	
			1 pair	Scarlet	Blankets	
			Flannel			
			10 lbs.	Navy		2 ply Heavy Twilled/ napped back
KY	Winchester	W.H. Forman				
IL	Claytonville		2 skeins	Black	Yarn	

Table 3.2. Yount Mill Trade Correspondence, 1890 (*cont.*)

State	Town	Purchaser	Amount	Color	Product	Description
IN	Ladoga	The New York Cash Store	1 piece	Steel gray	Jeans	
			1 piece	Sheeps gray	Jeans	
		Hostetter, Ashby & Mills	1 piece	Steel grey	Flannel	
			1 piece	Red	Flannel	
			1 piece	Indigo blue	Flannel	
			1 piece	Opera Suite	Flannel	
			2 pair	Red	Blanket	
			2 pair	Grey	Blanket	
			2 pair	White	Blanket	
			10 bundles	Sheeps gray	Yarn	
			5 bundles	Steel mix	Yarn	
IN	Colfax	E. H. Johnson				
IN	Bainbridge	Putnam County Agricultural Association				
IN	Ladoga	Kyle, McGinnis & Mayhall	6 pair	White	Blankets	
			4 pair	Red	Blankets	
			1 pair	Steel mix	Jeans	
IN	Lebanon	John H. Perkins and Co.	4 skein	Sheep grey	Yarn	2 ply
			4 skein	Black	Yarn	2 ply
			4 skein	Red	Yarn	2 ply
			4 skein	Navy blue	Yarn	2 ply

Table 3.2. Yount Mill Trade Correspondence, 1890 (*cont.*)

State	Town	Purchaser	Amount	Color	Product	Description
IL	Chery Point					
IN	Kentland			White	Yarn	
IN	Sheridan					
KY	North Middletown					
IN	Lebanon	John H. Perkins and Co.	4 skein	Indigo	Yarn	2 ply
			8 skeins	White	Yarn	2 ply
			4 skeins	Gray mixed	Yarn	2 ply
				Black		
IN	Veederburg	Osborn Bros.				
IN	Hazelrigg	S. Klepfer				
IN	Sheridan	Stanley and Weaver	100 skeins	Black	Yarn	2 ply
			10 skeins	Brown	Yarn	2 ply
			20 skeins	Grey	Yarn	2 ply
			20 skeins	Grey	Yarn	3 ply
IN	Crawfordsville		1 yd		Flannel	
IL	Claytonville		7 skeins	Sheeps grey		2 ply
			2 cuts	Grey		3 ply
IN	Roachdale	Dodd & Edwards	40 cuts	Black steel	Flannel	
			40 skeins	Mixed		2 ply
IN	Darlington					

Source: Data compiled and transcribed from the Yount Mill Collection, Marian Morrison Local History Collection at the Crawfordsville District Public Library, Crawfordsville, IN.

Daniel Yount, the veteran woolen manufacturer, died at his home in Yountsville, at 3 o'clock Sunday morning aged 83 years. The funeral services were held on Tuesday at 10 o'clock at the Methodist Church in Yountsville. Daniel Yount was the son of Andrew and Eve Yount, and was born in Warren County, Ohio, November 3, 1807, his ancestry coming from Germany about the year 1740 and settling in North Carolina. At the age of eleven years he began work in a woolen mill, then owned by his father near Dayton, Ohio. In 1827 he came to Tippecanoe County, settling about five miles south of Lafayette on the Wea. In 1835 he removed to Attica, where in company with an elder brother he established a woolen factory remaining there until 1839, when he purchased a farm on which he lived about one year. Early 1840 he removed to what is now Yountsville, erecting in company with his brother Allen a small carding mill, which has since grown to its present proportions. April 30, 1830, Mr. Yount was married to Sarah Price, who was born in Maryland in 1811. She died greatly respected June 19, 1878 they had five children, Rhoda, now Mrs. Townsley, Mary, now Mrs. Troutman, Andrew, John M., deceased, and Annie, now Mrs. Whitehead. "Uncle Daniel" as he was familiarly known was brought up in the faith of Friends but in 1842 there being no such organization at Younstville he united with Methodist Episcopal Church, a pillar of which he has since been. He led a busy and useful life, having been a class leader and trustee of his church since his connection with it. It was always his custom at the close of the conference year to ascertain the collections made from the congregation and give his check for whatever deficiency existed. His charity was instantaneous and only bounded by the opportunity for giving presented to him. He never in a single instance refused a request for assistance. While as a business man he was very successful, leaving quite a large estate, yet his generosity has disposed of an amount equal perhaps to all he has left. For many years as winter approached it has been his custom to say to one of his clerks, "James, if you know of any poor families in the neighborhood needing clothing or blankets send them enough to supply their wants." During his last illness which was long and painful he directed one of his employees to collect the remnants of cloth and flannel in the store and send them to the Orphans' Home, and when informed that his son, Andrew had already done this he answered, "very well" as through satisfied that a duty had been performed. The incident simply illustrates a life-long custom. A column has fallen not easily replaced, his employees will morn in him a lost friend. The neighborhood will no longer have the benefit of his wise and devoted counsel. His fireside is deprived of his care and protection. They can rest alone in the remembrance of his deeds.

Figure 3.3. Daniel Yount Obituary, 1890. From the *Crawfordsville Journal*, September 6.

Table 3.3. Copartnership of Daniel Yount and Andrew Yount, Raw
Materials at Woolen Mill, 1891

Weight	Description	Count	Appraisement
5000 Lbs.	Brand & Common Wool	@ 20	1000.00
5000 Lbs.	Weaving Wool	@ 21	1050.00
10000 Lbs.	Combing Wool	@ 24	2400.00
40000 Lbs.	Medium Wool	@ 24	9,600.00
3260 Lbs.	Scoured Wool	@ 45	1,467.00
			$15,517.00

Source: Data compiled from the Montgomery County Clerk's Office Probate Files.

Table 3.4. Copartnership of Daniel Yount and Andrew Yount, Goods in
Process of Manufacture, 1891

Amount	Description	Appraisement
50 yds.	Twilled flannel	20.00
205 yds.	Gray flannel	8.00
25 yds.	White flannel	7.00
150 yds.	White flannel	33.00
25 yds.	Cassimere	12.00
128 yds.	Flannel in brown	25.75
575 yds.	Flannel in brown	115.75
175 yds.	Flannel in brown	35.75
175 yds.	Flannel in brown	70.50
25 yds.	Flannel in brown	10.00
175 yds.	Doeskin	84.00
100 yds.	Flannel	28.00
225 yds.	Cashmeres	90.00
3 Prs.	Blankets	12.00
3 Prs.	Blankets	11.00
4 Prs.	Blankets	36.00
2 Prs.	Blankets	7.00
		$605.25

Source: Data compiled from the Montgomery County Clerk's Office Probate Files.

many different products. At the time of Daniel's death he had a good supply of raw materials on hand for continued production. In his last days, the mill business was still optimistic about its future prosperity.

Daniel and Andrew had a store filled with $12,442.53 worth of inventory in textiles (Table 3.5). At a time when a working man might make a dollar a day, this was a fortune on the shelves of their store. These were mostly their own products, including yard goods of flannel, worsted, doeskin, cashmere, bed padding, twill, tweeds, blankets, and yarns. They had cotton yard goods including toweling, table linen, medical napkins, ticking, muslin, bunting, gingham, sheeting, drill (a strong cotton fabric with a diagonal weave or bias), denim, calico, dress lining, and canvas. They carried such specialty items as linen, sateen, silecio (a trade name for a silk fabric), and rubber tissue along with notions such as braid, bias, silk thread, cotton thread, pins, buttons, and needles. They had ready-made clothing, pants for men and boys, vests, suspenders, shirts, cuffs, handkerchiefs, waists, mittens, and socks. They also had ready-made quilts and napkins for the home. A cadre of young men educated in public schools operated the store and the records of transaction necessary for a retail establishment on an industrial site. The variety of products in the store indicated that the mill was also a major textile distribution and retail center. The value of the products described shows that there was a fortune of fabric in the mill store.

In June of 1891, Andrew Yount served as the executor of the estate of Daniel Yount.[46] On July 7, 1891, Andrew and Achsa M. Yount sold half of the mill to the wool company.[47] On February 24, 1891, the mill was incorporated.[48]

The industrial changes brought educational progress, and by the 1890s it was easy to select from many young men who could keep the records of the mill with their public-school education. Starting in 1892 and continuing until 1907, the mill clerk kept a record (Table 3.6) of significant correspondence, including correspondence regarding loan payments, offers to purchase the mill, possible employees, letters to attorneys, annual reports, and samples. It is a curious record made primarily to keep in mind the most important documents of business so that the details did not get lost in the shuffle of the day-to-day business correspondence. Strangely, it was not kept in chronological order and seems to be entered as a stream of consciousness. This gives us an interesting sense of the methodical books kept by Daniel compared to those kept by Andrew. It also shows that the company was in a constant scramble to stay afloat. In addition to the day-to-day transactions, the mill had more interactions with banks and with

Table 3.5. Copartnership of Daniel Yount and Andrew Yount, Merchandise in Store, 1891

Count	Description	Merchandise in Store Cash
19	Handkerchiefs	$2.46
1	Handkerchiefs	$.32
6	Handkerchiefs	$1.06
14	Handkerchiefs	$2.00
2	Handkerchiefs	$.40
5	Handkerchiefs	$.80
16	Handkerchiefs	$1.00
50	Handkerchiefs	$1.20
17	Handkerchiefs	$.95
13	Handkerchiefs	$.42
1	Handkerchiefs	$.25
12	Handkerchiefs	$.95
1	Handkerchiefs	$.13
1	Handkerchiefs	$.09
28	Braide	$9.50
80	8 oz. spool cotton	$27.35
16¾	8 oz. silk thread	$19.92
	Lot pins, buttons, needles	$16.13
10 yds.	Chls Chldle	$28
28 yds.	Worsted	$79.40
14½ yds.	Worsted	$13.50
1¾ yds.	Worsted	$4.05
5⅓ yds.	Worsted	$4.43
3⅓ yds.	Worsted	$4.58
4¼ yds.	Worsted	$9.52
6¼ yds.	Worsted	$12.50
5 yds.	Worsted	$14.45
10½ yds.	Worsted	$21.52
5⅛ yds.	Worsted	$12.45
7⅛12 yds.	Plain gingham	$39.84
48 yds.	Plaid gingham	$4.04
289 yds.	Plaid gingham	$19.60
367 yds.	Plaid gingham	$23.36
42 yds.	Plaid gingham	$3.30
164 yds.	Couting[a] cloth	$16.106
5 yds.	Couting cloth	$5.05
75 yds.	Couting cloth	$4.80
122 yds.	Couting cloth	$8.78
83 yds.	Chambray givey[a]	$7.95
3 yds.	Chambray givey	$6.55
52 yds.	Chambray givey	$5.50

Table 3.5. Copartnership of Daniel Yount and Andrew Yount, Merchandise in Store, 1891 (*cont.*)

Count	Description	Merchandise in Store Cash
41 yds.	Chambray givey	$3.30
7 per	Bias	$.28
250 per	Bias	$16
33 per	Bias	$2.65
11 per	Bias	$1.10
35 per	Bias	$1.80
42 per	Bias	$2.34
35 per	Bias	$7
123 per	Bias	$6.20
136 per	Bias	$20.44
31 per	Bias	$4.20
4 per	Bias	$.68
8 per	Bias	$1.76
13 per	Bias	$4.00
171	Linen collars	$13.60
7 pairs	Cuffs	$1.20
19 pairs	Suspenders	$2.60
3 pairs	Suspenders	$.70
5 pairs	Suspenders	$1.30
5 pairs	Suspenders	$.70
9 pairs	Suspenders	$.50
3 pairs	Suspenders	$.30
66	Unlaundered shirts	$20
4	Laundered shirts	$2.40
55	Gauze Vests	$16.70
8	Gauze Vests	$1.20
9	Gauze Vests	$.90
19	Gauze Vests	$1.13
20	Gauze Vests	$5.40
24	Gauze Vests	$6.40
5	Gauze Vests	$1.30
1	Gauze Vests	$.15
8	Gauze Vests	$3.20
141 yds.	Cashmeres	$56
10 yds.	Cashmeres	$3.20
11 yds.	Cashmeres	$5
133 yds.	Cashmeres	$58.50
27 yds.	Cashmeres	$13
53 yds.	Cashmeres	$31.75
27 yds.	Cashmeres	$14
30 yds.	Dress goods	$6

Table 3.5. Copartnership of Daniel Yount and Andrew Yount, Merchandise in Store, 1891 (*cont.*)

Count	Description	Merchandise in Store Cash
22 yds.	Bulk brilliantine	$6.71
19 yds.	Serviette cloth (napkins)	$12.65
36 yds.	Plaid dress goods	$10.10
33 yds.	Brown dress goods	$4.48
89 yds.	Zurnner and Sons goods	$14.30
43 yds.	Plaids	$3.50
5	Fine white blanket	$36
64	Common white blanket	$294.52
10 ½	Plaid blanket	$52.92
15	Red blanket	$72
?	Fine blanket	$12.80
?	Wool sock	$24
37	Mittens	$11.90
827 yds.	Jeans	$330.80
851 yds.	Satwett[a]	$374.44
69 yds.	Black trical[a]	$40.20
36 yds.	Twilled flannel	$17.30
144 yds.	Blue cassimere	$26.72
130 yds.	Black doeskin	$26.72
82 yds.	Black cassimere	$30.36
224 yds.	Black cassimere	$135.44
133 yds.	Brown cassimere	$69.15
524 yds.	Grey cassimere	$272.48
350 yds.	Brown mix cassimere	$252
186 yds.	Stripe and mix cassimere	$111.60
1208 yds.	Old stripe and mix cassimere	$628.16
295 yds.	Old tweeds	$94.40
259 yds.	Old tweeds	$113.96
114 yds.	Grey doeskin	$72.96
280 yds.	Cassimere	$179.20
287 yds.	Cassimere and tweeds	$157.64
55 yds.	Grey cassimere	$33
9	Course white blanket	$42.10
3 yds.	Ticking	$1.75
98 yds.	Ticking	$13.13
25 yds.	Ticking	$2
6 yds.	Ticking	$.60
7 yds.	Ticking	$.55
120 yds.	Med. Table liner	$33.20
41 yds.	White table liner	$13.40

Count	Description	Merchandise in Store Cash
28 yds.	Checked table liner	$16.80
13 yds.	Checked table liner	$5.20
13 yds.	A.1. table liner	$3.53
30 yds.	Table liner	$9.60
17 yds.	Table liner	$6.15
21 yds.	Table liner	$15.10
1	Table cloth and napkins	$4.80
2 dozen	Napkins	$1.05
2 dozen	Napkins	$1.55
5 dozen	Napkins	$10
2 dozen	Med. Napkins	$.65
84 dozen	Denim	$6.70
10 dozen	Denim	$65
117 dozen	Cottonade	$14.05
2 dozen	Mens' cold pants	$9.60
2 dozen	Mens' mixed pants	$8.00
5½ dozen	Boys' pants	$9.60
9	Mens' waists	$3.25
2½ dozen	Mens' shirts	$6.00
128 yds.	Pocket drilling	$8.24
200 yds.	Pants lining	$6.40
303 yds.	Cotton flannel	$19.50
191 yds.	40 inch sheeting	$10.70
111 yds.	40 inch sheeting	$5.36
55 yds.	Bunting	$1.52
1010 yds.	Bunting	$40.55
14 yds.	Bunting	$2.30
9 yds.	Bunting	$1.38
23 yds.	Bunting	$3.70
65 yds.	Bunting	$11.50
5 yds.	Casing	$.40
284 yds.	Bleached muslin	
111 yds.	Mason co. muslin	
89 yds.	Forwell muslin	
58 yds.	New Castle muslin	
59 yds.	Luesel muslin	$20.36
22 yds.	Sofine muslin	$1.39
65 yds.	Muslin	$4.20
	Shirting muslin	$1.10
14 yds.	Shirting muslin	$15.20
220 yds.	Awaheay muslin	$15.20

Table 3.5. Copartnership of Daniel Yount and Andrew Yount, Merchandise in Store, 1891 (*cont.*)

Count	Description	Merchandise in Store Cash
60 yds.	Muslin	$3.60
144 yds.	Muslin	$9.22
318 yds.	Muslin	$6.67
53 yds.	Coal lining	$21.20
29 yds.	Coal lining	$11.60
42 yds.	Coal lining	$19.70
11 yds.	Coal lining	$2.25
125 yds.	Bed padding	$9
	Canvas	$4.50
449 yds.	Silecio[a]	$45
25 yds.	Silecio	$4
24 dozen	Wadding	$6.80
340 yds.	Dress lining	$10.90
96 yds.	Drill	$3.80
360 yds.	Crash[b]	$23
133 yds.	Crash	$4.32
9 yds.	Crash	$.50
4 yds.	Towels	$1.60
4 yds.	Towels	$.80
336 yds.	Blue calico	$13.45
562 yds.	Blue calico	$20.80
54 yds.	Blue calico	$.90
3½ yds.	Rubber tissue	$4.25
21 yds.	Quilts	$17.60
7 yds.	Quilts	$4.65
7 yds.	Quilts	$4.75
349 yds.	Satine	$33.68
752 yds.	Flannel	$142.40
127 yds.	Flannel	$34.50
57 yds.	Flannel skirting	$18.40
151 yds.	Flannel	$36.30
195 yds.	Flannel	$52.00
193 yds.	Flannel	$42
252 yds.	Flannel	$68
394 yds.	Flannel remnants	$69
42 yds.	Flannel	$13.60
873 yds.	Flannel	$208
583 yds.	Flannel	$140.53
233 yds.	Flannel	$65
233 yds.	Flannel	$62.66
137 yds.	Flannel	$33

Table 3.5. Copartnership of Daniel Yount and Andrew Yount, Merchandise in Store, 1891 (*cont.*)

Count	Description	Merchandise in Store Cash
29 yds.	Flannel	$8
217 yds.	Flannel	$52.10
119 yds.	Flannel	$28.70
107 yds.	Flannel	$26
165 yds.	Flannel	$33.25
232 yds.	Flannel	$46
31 yds.	Flannel	$11.15
708 yds.	Flannel	$200
73 yds.	Flannel	$38
99 yds.	Flannel	$59.25
266 yds.	Flannel skirt	$181
22¼ yds.	Flannel	$76.60
676 yds.	Flannel	$149.52
149 Skein	Yarn	$30
295 Cut	Yarn	$30
532 Cut	Yarn	$30
159 Cut	Yarn	$20
	Old lat. Yarn	$2.40
15 Bundles	Yarn	$60
5 Bundles	Yarn	$24
6 Bundles	Yarn	$24
11 Bundles	Yarn	$44
46 Bundles	Yarn	$184
73 Bundles	Yarn	$292
7 Bundles	Yarn	$31
14 Bundles	Yarn	$67
311 yds.	Flannel	$75.30
240 yds.	Flannel	$64
118 yds.	Flannel	$34
66 yds.	Flannel	$19.50
123 yds.	Flannel	$39.20
116 yds.	Flannel	$33.30
55 Bundles	Yarn	$241.50
27½ Bundles	Yarn	$120.25
21 Bundles	Yarn	$120
24½ Bundles	Yarn	<u>$100</u>
		$49,201.11

Source: Montgomery County Clerk's Office Probate Files.
[a] not used as a fabric descriptor today
[b] a rugged fabric, usually linen with an irregular fiber weave

Table 3.6. Yount Mill Account Records, 1893–1908

Date (y/m/d)	Party	Record
1907	Yount Mill	Elston Nat'l Bank account
1900, Jan. 25	Wilkinson bros.	Request wool on account
1897, July 13	—	Credit note, payable Ind. Nat'l Bank
1901, Aug. 26	—	Letter from mill to party interested in the property + basin
1906?	—	Notes on "Bills Receivable" envelope about account w/Bank of Sinden?
1899, Jan. 10	Treasurer's report	Annual report of "Resources and Liabilities"
1898, April 30	—	Notes to Andrew Yount, principal $6600.00 @ 7%
1893, Oct. 31	—	Hamilton Autograph Co. memorandum of sacks Y' Mills
1897, March 4	Clerk's office	James M. Duncan vs. Y' Woolen Mills Co.
1907	" "	13 checks
1907, Jan.	—	Bank statements for Yount Mills
1907	Yount mills	Elston Nat'l Bank account
1907	S. B. Morris co.	Bill of sale
1907, Sep. 12	O. A. Shepard	Clothing, shoes, men's . . . bill of sale
1907	Yount mill	Elston Nat'l Bank × 2
1897	Treasurer's report	"Resources + Liabilities" × 2
1907	Younts Mill	Elston Nat'L Bank, checks × 6
1906	Lewis Black → Crawfordsville Envelope	Envelop=s>
1906	Robert P. Grant → Bishop	Letter – about Yount property + business
1900, Dec. 7	Yount Mills letter → D. C.	Concerning unpaid (?) account
1890	—	Elston bank account
1894	Treasurer's report	Resources + Liabilities × 2
1900	Lumber company	Letter from lumber company – Yount owed debt to

Table 3.6. Yount Mill Account Records, 1893–1908 (*cont.*)

Date (y/m/d)	Party	Record
1900	—	Letters
1897	James M. Duncan	Bill of sales
1892	—	Treasurer's statement
1905	—	Mont. Co. Treas. Tax receipts
1900	W. Greenwood to Yount	Asking about prop., etc.
1897	Yount Mills	Personal tax assessment
1907	Account w/L. Bishop	(the big store) stamped × 4
1905	—	Merchant acts
1907	Elston Nat'l Bank	Lots of checks
1906	—	Promissory note to Bishop
1906, Jan. 17	Freeman + Fox mfg. Co.	Request quotes + samples
1906	Yount's	Purchase statements (× 4) w/Building "E," eastern goods (checks returned)
1907	Yount + Elston Nat'l bk.	
—	Elston & co.	Promissory note of $5,000 to Elston & co.
1901, March 8	First Nat'l Bank of C'ville	Promissory note of $7,500 to First Nat'l Bank of C'ville
1907, Jan. 2	Elston Nat'l Bank	Account w/ Elston Nat'l Bank
1905, April 8	R.L. Whitney/Falls City Woolen Mills	Letter to Falls City Woolen Mills from R. L. Whitney
1906, May 8	Yount/James Shaw	Letter to Yount from James Shaw (he is in previous letter)
1896, Oct. 22	—	Renewal contract for mercantile agency
1894, Dec. 13	—	Renewal contract for mercantile agency × 4
1904, Dec. 13	Cunningham Bros./Yount	Cunningham Bros. Woolen Co. w/yount account
1904, Dec. 14	Cunningham Bros.	Cunningham rejects goods
—	Cunningham/creditors	Cunningham request agreement for creditors (?)
1904, Dec. 1	Cunningham/Yount	Letter to Yount from Cunningham/Yount debt

Table 3.6. Yount Mill Account Records, 1893–1908 (cont.)

Date (y/m/d)	Party	Record
1905	Yount	Yount agrees to bargain w/ previous letter
1908, Jan. 15	Elston Nat'l Bank	$262 paid to Elston Nat'l Bank
—	—	Letter assessing Clements + Evans acct. w/ Yount
1900	—	Renewal w/ mercantile agency promissory notes
1905, Dec. 5	Peter Hammels (Kansas) → Andrew Yount	Letter to Andrew Yount from Peter Hammels (Kansas)
1901, June 14	Robert Grant → Andrew Yount	Letter to Andrew Yount from Robert Grant
—	? → Robert Grant	Letter to Grant, from ?
1905, Nov. 27	—	Letter to Yount from Hammelheim (Topeka, KS)
1907	M. J. Voris	Letter from M. J. Voris about purchase
1905	Younts → Hanover Woolen Mills	Letter from Younts to Hanover Woolen Mills
—		about employee
1905	Younts → Topeka, Kansas	Younts writes Topeka, Kansas recommending same employee
1898	George Merrit & Co.	Phone message from George Merrit & Co. Wool
1906	—	Elston Bank statements × 2
1906	Freeman + Fox Co.	Letter from Freeman + Fox Co. decided on some samples/requested more
1907	New trade palace	Letter from new trade palace/enclosed payment
1906	Freeman + Fox Co.	Decided on samples
1908	Lindley, Penwell attorneys	Collected $7.11 from Jacob Peters
1907	Lindley, Penwell attornerys	J. C. Peters bankruptcy matter (letters)
1899	George Merritt + co.	Account statement
1903–5	—	Insurance statement on all buildings
1893	L. D. Kirkpatrick	Attorney Letter

Table 3.6. Yount Mill Account Records, 1893–1908 (*cont.*)

Date (y/m/d)	Party	Record
1894	L. D. Kirkpatrick	L. D. Kirkpatrick on settlement case
1898	George Merritt + Co.	Letter from George Merritt + Co. on settlement case
1907	C. S. Wadman	Letter from C. S. Wadman/enclosed payment
1896	Bank of Waveland	Bank statement (× 2), Bank of Waveland
1901, July 10	Rob . . . (?)	Letter from Rob . . . (?) Seeking employment
—	Freeman + Fox Co.	Freeman + Fox Co. Order Book
1907	Elston Nat'l Bank	Elston Nat'l Bank statements
1907	Clements + Evans Insurance	Clements + Evans Insurance acct. statement
1907	Elston or First Nat'l	Checks to either Elston or First Nat'l
1894	Farmers Bank	Farmers Bank letter about Kirkpatrick
—	—	Envelope full of checks
—	—	German American insurance Co. (Clements + Evans)
—	—	Dwelling policies
—	—	A lot of checks!

Source: Transcribed from Yount Mill papers, 76.21/76.28, Rotary Jail Museum and Tannenbaum Cultural Center, Crawfordsville, IN.
Note: — indicates that the mill has borrowed money from the Indiana National Bank.

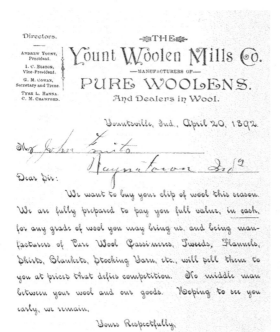

Figure 3.4. Form Letter, Yount Woolen Mills to John Fruits, 1894. From Noah Fruits, election material, 1892–1902, S492, Indiana State Library.

those from whom it was trying to recover debts. The entries also reflect searches for competent employees and proposals to part with the mill.

In 1892 Andrew Yount ended the days of not advertising when he offered to purchase wool through a direct-mail campaign. He talked about the wide variety of products the mill created, and C. Elston was listed as a vice president of the corporation for the first time. The company still championed its exchange of wool for goods. The advantage of direct transactions cut middleman out of the process and the overhead they charged (Figure 3.4). In 1893 Andrew offered to sell yarn to the Milton Hosier Company.[49]

Even though accounts were kept in dollars and cents on the store books, it is easy to see that labor was credited in a company-store arrangement of swapping clothes for lumber with a percentage of the commission allowed for debt collection (Figure 3.5). Some people in the community were working for bare necessities to keep themselves covered from the elements so they could continue to work outside during winter weather. Andrew sold lumber from his land as another way to create income from the property. The wood provided the power for the steam plant.

Jan th 22 1894 Mr Andrew Yount
Dear sir will you please let Mr. Al Kelsey have goods to the amount of
five dollars $5.00 and charge the same to me. and the lumber that I am
hauling in for you. I have hauled two loads of lumber for you since I was
over to surgeon. Mr. Kelsey has been helping me cut logs & he is in need
of some clothes and there will be more lumber than what I will want
more than what we agreed you will not command any one I can collect
the note on Harvey Llewellyn for you if you will treat me right about it.
I will not ask you to pay for more than one third the amount of the lumber taken in until what we owe you is settled in full. We have taken in for
you about 3 or 4 thousand feet.
Your Candy Llewellyn

Jan 29/94
Let Mr. Kelsey have Five Dollars in goods on this order by Andrew
Yount Pres.

Jan 30th 1894
Candy Llellen
Per Order To Kelsy
1 pr wool mittens 40
1 spool 5
2 pr. cotton socks 25
1 run outing 35
Cloth & lining pants 2.50
$3.55
1 shirt .50
$4.05

Figure 3.5. "He Is in Need of Some Clothes," 1894. Transcribed from Yount Woolen
Mill Papers, Rotary Jail Museum and Tannenbaum Cultural Center, Crawfordsville,
Indiana.

Representatives for the company attempted to collect outstanding
out-of-state debts, to no avail (Figure 3.6). Considering the number of
people that the company corresponded with for business, it is surprising
there are not more letters like this one. Downturns in the economy com-
promised small businesses that, with embarrassing finances, could not pay
the mill.

> Keithsburg Ill 6/23 1894
> The Yount Woolen Mills Co
> Yountsville Ind
> Gentlemen
> In answer to your inquiry regarding claim v. Bever Magel & Co will say
> that the prospect for collection same is not any better . . .

Figure 3.6. Attempt to Collect Debt, 1894. Transcribed from Yount Mill papers, Rotary Jail Museum and Tannenbaum Cultural Center, Crawfordsville, Indiana.

Yount Mill acted as a subcontractor creating Spanish-American War uniforms for the federal government. Geo. Merritt & Co., Woolen Manufactures and Wool Dealers of Indianapolis, put forward a contract for 20,000 yards of navy blue wool cloth, and the Yount Mill submitted a bill for 1,000 pairs of dark blue blouses (Figure 3.7). Not only did the Yount Mill make wool cloth for the military, but it also created readymade clothing for the war effort. Yount had expenses for shipping and for dye but also made a greatly needed profit on this contract. Since Geo. Merritt & Co. was established in 1856, this may have been the same contractor Daniel Yount used if he got a Civil War contract with Indiana or the federal government for uniforms and blankets, but no record of that partnership exists. Yet this may be the root of the often-told story of the mill's making Civil War uniforms and blankets. The other root of that story may be the often-discussed quiet benevolence of Daniel Yount when responding to calls from Governor Oliver P. Morton for blankets for Indiana troops. There is a good chance that Yount blankets were just donated at no cost and with no paperwork.

A photo from 1901 showed the connection between the brick mill buildings on the third floor for a belt to pass through to provide power. The rock wall behind the turbine shed was backfilled with dirt before the annex, and the dam seemed to be all wood.[50] Without Daniel there was more work than the family could perform. Andrew had many tasks; he could not run the office and the mill floor at the same time, so he conducted a national search for engineering talent. Potential applicant W. H. Greenwood asked about how the mill would be managed, what type of equipment was in the mill, and how large the town was (Figure 3.8), but he did not go to the mill.

In the series of letters that followed (Figure 3.9), the mill representative wrote to applicant Robert Grant saying that the next mill operator

George Merritt, Pres. Established 1856   Worth Merritt, Sec'y and Treas.
Geo. Merritt & Co.,
Woolen Manufacturers and Wool Dealers
Flannel Skirts, Flannel, Blankets, Yarns
No. 811 West Washington St.
Local and Long Distance Telephone telephone 607
Indianapolis, Oct. 6., 1898

Concerning Bid for making 20000 Yds. Of D. B. Blouse Flannels for Government Eid. First Ten Thousand at 89-4/10 Cts. Per Yd. Sedon Ten Thousand at 93-4/10 Cts. Per Yd.

It is agreed if both bids be accepted the price be equalize and made 91-4/10 Cts. Per Yd., for Ten Thousand Yds. Made by the Yount Woolen Mills Co., and the same price for Ten Thousand Yds. Made by Geo. Merritt & Co.

It is agreed that should only the Bid for Ten Thousand Yds. At 89-4/10 Cts. Per Yd. be accepted, that at the option of the Yount Woolen Mills CO., the said Geo. Merritt & Co., agrees to make and furnish 5000 Yds. At that price. The Yount Woolen Mills Co. the other 5000 Yds., and Geo. Merritt & CO. also have the option of claiming 5000 Yds., and Geo. Merritt & Co. also have the option of claiming 5000 Yds. To make at the last named price if they desire.

Each Party to this agreement is to be responsible to the government for the quality of the good he shall make and for all expenses of transportation or otherwise connected therewith.

In consideration of the fact that Geo. Merritt & Co. have been at all the expense of the initial proceedings and will make the Bid, furnish the Bonds, and all expenses connected therewith, it is agreed that Geo. Merritt & Co., shall collect the money from the Government in the usual manner and when so collected pay over to the Yount Woolen Mills Co., that portion for which the said Yount Woolen Mills Co. has furnish the goods, less five per cent of said sum which is to be retained by Geo. Merritt & Co., as a commission for affecting the sale.
Geo. Merritt & Co.

George Merritt, Pres. Established 1856   Worth Merritt, Sec'y and Treas.
Geo. Merritt & Co.,
Woolen Manufacturers and Wool Dealers
Flannel Skirts, Flannel, Blankets, Yarns
No. 811 West Washington St.
Indianapolis, Aug. 8th, 1899

The Yount Woolen Mill Co.
        Yountsville, IN
                Gentlemen –
                        We send your statement & offer a check for $4690.66 As yet—we have not received anything …
        Kindly acknowledge accepting of check.
                Yours truly
                        Geo Merritt and Co.

```
Monthly Statement
Indianapolis In Aug 8 1899
The Yount Woolen Mills Co
Yountsville Ind
In Account with Geo. Merritt & Co.
411 West Washington St.
                    Per
Dec.     7      By dye                          10.04
                By 1000 pair D. B. Blouse       9140.00      9150.04
Nov      7      To dye stuff                    23.24
         7      To dye stuff                    72.76
         14     To dye stuff                    182.56
         21     & flannel C Kacteer             10.00
         21     Dyeramo                         50.00
Dec      10     to dye stuff                    76.94
         20     dye stuff                       77.60
1899
Jan      2      To liar loo                     6.83
         14     To cludyo                       78.23
Feb      21     To 2shipping gi & c             2.80
Mar      28     To drayage                      .50
April    26     to carage Phila                 1.60
May      24     To check                        2000.00
June     2      To Loop yarn                    21. 42
July     29     To cartage Phila                8.40
Aug      8      To commission 10000 yds         457.00
Aug      8      to 1500 yar Come ho ho chin     1387.50
Aug      8      To cestage grig & altiery up    2.00
Aug      8      to check                        4690.66      $9150.04
```

Figure 3.7. Spanish-American War Documents, 1898 and 1899. Transcribed from Yount Woolen Mill Papers, Rotary Jail Museum and Tannenbaum Cultural Center, Crawfordsville, Indiana.

April 15, 1901

Gents

Please send me the particular in regard to your woolen mill advertised. Will you run it? If not what are your best terms? What is the power water or steam, pleas describe each machine how large is the town? and at once Your trc.

WH Greenwood

Figure 3.8. Request to Run Mill, 1901. Transcribed from Yount Mill papers, Rotary Jail Museum and Tannenbaum Cultural Center, Crawfordsville, Indiana.

June 01
Robt. P. Grant
East Brookfield. Mass.
Dear Sir
Your of the 7th . . . asking if we were in need of a man to superintend our Mill.
Just received we have a superintendent of our mill a man of good ability as a designer and manipulator of stock but is not satisfactory on account of his intem-
perate habits. And the probabilities are that we may have to discharge him and in
such event we shall require a man of unquestionable temperate habits good
ability as a designer and manufacturer industrious of good temper in one management of help should pleased to hear from you in answer to the following
question

What is your age? Are you in good health and able to do the work that is
necessary and required of a man in small mill . . . to design and give your best attention and time to all the detail of manufacturing from the raw stock to the finished fabric

Our mills Is only a 3 set 40 cards 10 broad looms drying and finish machinery All in fairly good condition located in a country village 4½ miles west of
Crawfordsville Ind the county seat

East Brookfield Mass June 14/1901
Yount woolen mills Co
Yountville INd
Gentleman
Your of the 10" came to hand yesterday P.M. & in reply say . . . reply to your questions. I am 58 years & 5 months old. I am in the very best of health & except for
having the Gripp last winter & that only for 3 or 4 days I have been in perfect
health for a great many years. I am thoroughly Able both Mentally and Physi-
cally to do all that is required of any person in a small mill including designing &
the direction of the work in every department of the Mill. My Experience has
been thorough & practical in all its details. I have grown up in the mill as Boy &
man. My father up to the time of his death (when I was 15 year old) was superintendent & designer of Jas R. Olive Mills at West Troy N. Y I am strongly temperate have never taken a glass of liquor or Beer in my life. As to salary I want
what the Mill is warranted in paying no more I know a 3 set mill is Small to you
cannot afford to pay as much as a 6 or 8 set mill can & I suggest that it would be
a good plan for me to go to you or pay 6 mo trial as the same salary as you are
now paying & at the end of that time of my services are not entirely satisfactory
to you I shall leave your employ but if they are satisfactory then the salary question to be fixed as we can agree, we will both be more inlightened & know each
other better then. I will say in advance you will find of me a reasonable man to
deal with & as to managing help I know human Nature pretty well & have never
had any trouble with help & I know what is required of Supt to get the best result
both from the help & machinery without any friction. I am sure I can meet all
your requirement satisfactorily. I could go to your with a notice of 3 or 4 days at
any time but I beg to say I am a correspondence with another Mill . I cannot say

& whither it will amount to anything or not, but I would prefer your position. I Enclose these recommends and can send more if you wish but I select these from firms that of James Frazer (you will notice he is Pres. of the Bank) was my first position as Sup. this was a 4 set mill & I was promoted form Boy Weaver to Designer to Supt & designer the next is about 4½ year later from Wendell Fabales who were selling agents for the Boston Woolen Mill where I was Supt &designer of a 14 set mill & when I was leaving this mill W. F. Oler Volunteered & gave me this other letter from W. Foler April 5" 1883 goes to confirm their opinion of me when the Trustees of the Lauren Woolen Co offered me the management of their mill at Laurence. But which I declined the printed slip is a cutting from the "Commercial Bulletin" & the recommend from Albert E Smith both tell their own on story Mr. Smith is the Senior partner of two mills the Valley and Cehappell Mills. Please return these papers after reading them. I hope that your decision will be in my favor & soon. Your truly
Robt P. Grant

East Brookfield Mass July 10, 1901
Yount Woolen Co
Yountville, Ind
Gentleman
Yours received some few days ago & this if might be well to write you although I have nothing especial to add to my letter of application Except that I am, Since receiving your letter more than Ever Satisfied I could meet your Every requirement as Super. Some few years ago at least 20 I went to a Small custom mill to take Entire charge of it for a New York party the mill was only 1 of 40" card1 set of 24" custom Roll cards. I only saw the Proprietor once a year it was owned & the Estate of the late Geo N Patmer a Millionaire of New York & the Mill was at Palmer Falls Saratoga NY & was built as a means to an End the End was to get a large Water Power developed in the market & this small mill was the beginning. As agt of the Water Power Co I got a Pulp to Paper Co to build a Mill there & which after running about 5 year both the Entire Estate selling the Woolen machinery though Mr Meantinig I had run the Mill catering to the brants of the Horse Market & Some where of ones I had increased the Mill from 1 to 4 sat and paid for *all* of this increase out of the Earnings of the machinery in about 6 yairs. I made plain & fancy Cassimere. Flannels. Dress goods, Blankets, and Lumber men Flannels & I also traded our wool & Selected out & sold Every yard of goods the Mill. I think I would Just hint you & let you know I have had a through training & Experience in just such a mill as yours & repeat that I should like to go to your mill when you are ready & should be glad to hear from you at your convenience
Truly Your
Robert P. Grant

Figure 3.9. Letters to and from Robert P. Grant, Mill Supervisor, 1901. Transcribed from Yount Woolen Mill Papers, Rotary Jail Museum and Tannenbaum Cultural Center, Crawfordsville, Indiana.

must be sober since the present mill operator had a problem with alcoholism. The mill representative, probably Andrew, asked Grant about his age and health. The mill representative also asked if he could apply himself to all the tasks of a mill. The mill representative described the mill as small "only a 3 set 40 cards 10 broad looms drying and finish machinery" and close to Crawfordsville.

In response, Grant described himself as fifty-eight years old and said that he could direct all the work in a small mill and that he has had good experience, growing up as boy and a man in a mill of which his father was a mill superintendent. He was temperate and suggested a six-months trial at "the same salary as you are now paying & at the end of that time if my services are not entirely satisfactory to you I shall leave your employ but if they are satisfactory then the salary question to be fixed as we can agree, we will both be more interested & know each other better then." Grant described his abilities working with labor and said that he could give notice of less than a week. He referred to his references, including a bank president, and described past positions where he worked himself up from boy weaver to designer to superintendent. He also explained that a competing mill wished to hire him. He was quite eager for employment and followed his letter with a second one in under a fortnight in which he explained that at one mill he saw the owner only once a year. The problems of attracting talent by mail, interviewing, soliciting references, and offering a job without face-to-face contact were formidable. For Grant, moving to the Yount Mill presented a possibility of starting over. In 1901 Grant accepted a job as the Yount Mill Supervisor.[51] The job was enticing, and people keep applying and sending references for the supervisor job for the next two years.

When Andrew made it to the end of 1901, he wrote, "OK Paid Out" in big letters across the bottom third of the page of the great leather book with gold lettering on the cover to celebrate the successful conclusion of the year.[52] The pants plant was a 1902 experiment the following year that did not seem to last the year.

Daniel's children and grandchildren reorganized the mill as a stock company called Yount Woolen Company, with son Andrew at the helm, but Daniel Yount's 1903 probate meant that Andrew had to part with company assets to send money to heirs. This left the company weak, cash-starved, and not able to be flexible for coming changes. To add insult to injury, Andrew had to pay fuel costs for coal and oil to run the dynamo and the steam plant in the once all-hydropower mill that Daniel had built, and the aging plant required repairs.[53] In addition, Andrew faced rapidly mounting fees from Moore and Morgan, the Lafayette, Indiana, express company. Shipping bills of over $200 and $300 per month came to Andrew during May, June, and July of 1903.[54] Facing all of these financial demands, Andrew borrowed money from Mr. Elston's bank in Crawfordsville, Indiana, in 1895, 1896, 1899, 1903, 1904, and 1906.[55]

In 1903 Andrew examined wool samples from the South Bend Woolen Company.[56] These rainbow-colored silk and wool textured threads dazzled the eye with their shine, and Andrew could imagine them made into festive clothing, upholstery, or curtains. Here was a product that was a world apart from the brown, black, grey, and dark blue of the Yount Mill with which he had grown up; these were colors for a new century. Andrew's goals included getting this company's business, exploring the possibilities of a partnership, or getting an offer to buy the Yount Mill. South Bend countered that the mill needed to make improvements before it would be interested. Andrew examined more wool samples and a business proposal with no result, and he faced another closed door. There was nothing quaint about lost jobs, declining facilities, and a few options. A rural location was not attractive to investors.

The state inspector reported that for three hundred days thirty-seven employees worked at the Yount Mill, with a total of twenty-three males and fourteen females. By 1870 the census reported both the reading and writing but not cyphering abilities of the mill workers (see Chapter 5). The employees worked in good, sanitary conditions, but they were not unionized. The workers used water, motor, and horse power to do their jobs. The business did not align with any other businesses. The inspector issued thirty orders, and Andrew complied with five orders from the previous inspection.[57] The mill used half the wool in October that it had in previous months, but the mill's workers still made dress goods, cashmere, and flannel by the yard, skirts by the dozens, blankets by the pairs, and yarns by the skeins.[58] Andrew was past due on a debt to Mr. Baker, and the 1903 Assessor's Plat Book for Ripley Township, Montgomery County, Indiana, shows seven buildings at the Yount Mill site.

The Montgomery County Assessor's Plat Book's showing the owners of the mill sites, starts in 1891 and ends in 1932 (Table 3.7). In 1891 Daniel and Andrew Yount owned the land, valued at $750, and the improvements

Table 3.7. Ownership of the Mill Site, 1891–1932

Year	Owner	Value of Land	Value of Improvements	Value of Land and Improvements
1891	Yount Daniel & Andrew	$750	$8,150	$8,900
1895	Yount Woolen Mills Co.	$700	$8,300	$9,000
1899	Yount Woolen Mills Co.	$700	$8,300	$9,000
1903	Yount Woolen Mills Co.	$700	$8,300	$9,000
1911	Yount Woolen Mills Co.	$500	$3,500	$4,000
1915	Yount Woolen Mills Co.	$500	$3,000	$3,500
1919	J. Clarke Smith	$900	$3,000	$3,900
1922	Hoosier Hotel Resort Company	$1,200	$5,000	$6,200
1925	Hoosier Hotel Resort Company	$700	$4,000	$4,700
1928	Hoosier Hotel Resort Company [marked out] Homer Steele	$700	$3,500	$4,200
1932	Thelma Bohanan	$300	$1,400	$1,700

Source: Data compiled and transcribed from the *Assessor's Plat-Book for Ripley Township, Montgomery County, Indiana,* Marian Morrison Local History Collection at the Crawfordsville District Public Library, Crawfordsville, IN.

are listed at $8,150. By 1895 the owner is listed as the Yount Woolen Mills Co., and the land's value had declined $50 dollars, but the improvements grew to $8,300. In 1911 the ground declined to $500 and the improvements slide to $3,500. By 1915 the improvements had declined by $500. In 1919 J. Clarke Smith owned the property and the land was valued at $900, with the improvements holding at $3,000. In 1922, under the Hoosier Hotel Resort Company, the land's value rose to $1,200 and the improvements rose to $5,000. By 1925 the land fell again to $700 and the improvements dropped to $4,000. In 1928 Homer Steele acquired the property with the same land value but improvements falling by $500. In 1932, during the Great Depression Thelma Bohanan owned the property, then valued at $300, and the improvements were valued at $1,400. The tax records display the process of deindustrialization and the resulting plunging tax valuation of the property. After long years of stability the mill property changed hands frequently.

Between 1904 and 1908 their traveling sales man opened 118 accounts with store customers in nine states in order to sell Yount Mill products. Most stores were in Indiana, but Illinois, Ohio, Kentucky, Michigan, and Missouri were represented along with Pennsylvania, New York, and Connecticut. The mill made a major commitment to setting up new accounts and marketing their products.

One of the mill's largest changes was its targeting of larger towns and cities compared to its historic client base of local and small communities for its goods. From 1904 to 1908, the major expenditures tracked by the company (Figure 3.10) included financial services in categories including Bills Payable 1904–1907, Bills Receivable, Discounts, Insurance, Interest, Losses and Gains, a Plant Surplus Fund, and Stock. Other items tracked were costs of doing business including costs for Dye, Fuel, Machinery, Manufacturing Expenses, Merchandise, Oil, Soap, Wool Expenses, and Wool for 1904, 1905, and 1908 (these were the years the mill attempted to buy wool for production). Still other items seemed to deal with personnel: Commissions, Expense (Accounts), Labor, Salesman No. 1 T. A. Scott (the mill's only salesman, who traveled and tried to arrange new accounts), Rent, and Salary. Unfortunately, the expenses of running the company did not diminish, because there were new accounts. The account books filled with expenses.

Between 1904 and 1909 the mill paid some dividends to stockholders but also suffered from overdrafts.[59] The company continued to fail when

Stock
Plant Surplus Fund
Loss and Gain
Bills Payable 1904–1907
Bills Receivable
Machinery
Rent
Commission
Wool Expense
Discount
Soap
Oil
Manufacturing Expenses
Merchandise
Dye
Labor
Salesman No. 1 T. A. Scott
Fuel
Wool 1904–1905, 1908
Interest
Insurance
Expense
Salary

Figure 3.10. Yount Mill Ledger, Major Categories of Entries, 1904–1908. Transcribed from Rotary Jail Museum and Tannenbaum Cultural Center, Crawfordsville, Indiana.

there was a great rush of consignment orders returned between 1904 and 1905.[60] The stockholders reorganized the mill in order to stop the outflow of cash, but the company continued to limp along as a corporation. Andrew consistently took short-term loans to keep the company afloat—a habit acquired since his father's death. Some of the heirs were either waiting for their inheritance or had loaned the company money to try to keep it solvent.[61] The company seemingly owed money to everyone. At the end of 1904 Cunningham Bros. Woolen Co. of St. Louis gave notice of their bankruptcy and returned two orders to Yount Mill (Figure 3.11); the desperate Yount Mill demanded full payment, half of it in cash. There is no indication

St. Louis Dec. 1, 1904 Cunningham Bros. Woolen Co notice of bankruptcy.

Cunningham Bros. Woolen Co. Dec. 14 1904
Yount Woolen Mills
Yountsville, Ind.
Gentlemen:
Please make a note that we refused to receive goods covered by the following
    invoice, for reason as explain in our circular letter
Nov. 18th 78.85
Nov. 23rd 148.41
Yours truly,
Cunningham Bros. Woolen Co.

Figure 3.11. Notice of Bankruptcy, Cunningham Bros. Woolen Co., 1904. Transcribed from Yount Woolen Mill Papers, Rotary Jail Museum and Tannenbaum Cultural Center, Crawfordsville, Indiana.

that it was satisfied. There was no way to insulate the mill from other companies dissolving and leaving the Yount company hanging.

In 1905 Peter Hammelshein wrote to the Yount Mill Company (Figure 3.12) looking for work as a mill superintendent. As a German immigrant he had been a superintendent in Connecticut, New York, and Illinois and had worked for fifteen years at two different mills. The company checked his references and found them to be solid; it offered him the position. The mill still looked attractive to outsiders who wanted to work there. The deindustrialization process was still unfolding.

Former Yount Mill supervisor Robert P. Grant sent the mill a letter of introduction in 1906 (Figure 3.13) suggesting that Yount Mill sell all of its textile inventory with the new company Freeman and Fox of Hartford, Connecticut. This seemed like a wonderful opportunity to generate some fast cash from the mill's large inventory. Freemen and Fox wrote (Figure 3.13) to say it was creating samples to send out with salesmen for clothing orders and it wanted wool cloth shipped by railroad as soon as possible. It seemed too good to be true, and it was. Rather than being a wonderful opportunity to sell the Yount inventory, the promise was empty.

On February 7, Freeman and Fox placed a large order (Figure 3.14) for five different types of Yount wool cloth and clarified the price, which seemed to be a typographical error from a past price list, but they asked that they have sixty days to pay for it. While they may have been overly optimistic,

Topeka, Kan., 11/27 1905
Mr. Andrew Yount , Treas
Yountsville
Dear Sir.

I wish to offer my service as Superintendent and Designer. If the matter is of interest to you, I would add that I have had 34 years experience on Cassimere of all grades and have during that time, filled position as Superintendent Designer in some of the best mills, both in Germany and in this country. I am thoroughly competent to oversee all department of a woolen mill.

I am 55 year of age, married, sober, industrious, capable and want only a steady position where good work is appreciated. I can give the best of references.

Enclosed is a stamped return envelope; please favor me with your early reply.

Yours respectfully,
Peter Hammelshein

Oakland, Kansa 12 /5–1905
Mr. Andrew Yount , Treas.
Yountville, INd.
Dear Sir.

. . . In answer would say that I leave learned the trade in the old country, visited a singlet weaving stead, and keep the position there as super. As a young man only 24 years old About 30 years ago I came to this county and was Spt. And Designer at the Broad Brook Company in Broad Brook Conn (16 sets) at the old Home Woolen Mill Co. In Beacon falls, Conn (18 sets) the Stacey Satescoke Woolen Mills in Satescoke New York (12 sets) Prom Ram these & came west to the Hanover Woolen Mills in Hanover Illinois (8sets), where I been the position as Sup. & designer for 15 year. Fr there I came here to the Topeka Woolen Mills in the same capacity but on account of some trouble amount the stockholder this mill was sold few mouth ago and the parties who bought the same and engaged me as there manager fail to start it the same year and as they are in the law suit at current telling of the will There is the reason why I am out a position

Enclosed you will find a copy from the recommendation form Hanover and also from Sceles. You also will find letter of recommendation from the east and from South–Bend, Indiana which you please will return at your earliest convenience as I may be would need them in the case that I could not make any arrangement with you I don't have the least doubt that I would not be able to make money for you as the Hanover people would not keep it me 15 year and the south Bend People would not offer me a situation for 13 year with a salary of 3000 dollars a year in the company that I did not understand my business. As your mill is small I cannot expect any higher wages and as I am looking for a steady position I would be satisfied with reasonable payment let me know what you can do about these maters praying to hear soon from you gentleman
Your truly
Peter Hammerlsheim
Oakland, Kansas

[One-line note from Andrew Yount]
Peter H has good references

The Home Building Association
Byron R. Russell, Secretary
Crawfordsville, Ind Dec. 12, '05
Mr. Hammelsheim,
Topeka, Kas
Dear Sir:
Replying to your letter of Dec. 5, 1905 at a meeting of our board yesterday we concluded to ask you upon what term you would come her and take charge of the mill as superintendent on trial for a short period. Pleas state the length of time and salary you would think reasonable to demand for the trial. Awaiting your reply., we are—
Yours very truly.
The Yount Woolen Mills Co., by

Figure 3.12. Letters from and to P. Hammelshein Regarding Mill Superintendent Job, 1905. Transcribed from Yount Woolen Mill Papers, Rotary Jail Museum and Tannenbaum Cultural Center, Crawfordsville, Indiana.

Room 524
Conn Mutual Building
Hartford Conn Jany 17 /06
Dr. Luis Bischof
     Crawfordsville Ind
My Dear Mr. Bischof
I have just written Mr. Andrew Yount to the effect that a new firm been in business less that 3 months as to thier responsibility and I don't know yet but they appear prosperous and doing a good business and are will spoken of & 3 or 4 houses that I have inquired from. This firm Freeman and Fox wants the Yount Woolen Mills Co. to send them samples and list (as to amount or quantities) of each style of dress wools and Cassimere they have on hand & their price for the same. On all goods they have of 3 yards or over. More I think this is an opportunity to dispose of all your goods at the Mill. This house is Mr. Freeman and Father is a
Consisted farm mfr in Leeds Eng his is an English Hebrew & Mr. Fox I think is a human Hebrew. Both gentlemen 35 to 38 yrs old & I think understand their business. Now . . . know how samples have been sent out of this mill. Without making any criticism or than point *will you please* see that the samples are cut uniform and neat so the good will show to good advantage & oblige yours with best wishes & regards
Yours truly
Robert P. Grant

Freeman and Fox Mfg. Co
Hartford , Conn Jan 30, 1906
The Yount Woolen Mills Co.,
Yountville, Ind. Dear Sirs:
    Yours of the 26th inst with sample through American Express Co., to hand. Out of your lot we have select the following as per enclose order which you will note that it closes out some of the styles, some of the other styles we are not fully decided about until we see the garment made up, then if they meet our expectations we will order further other of the styles we cannot use at this time but will let you now about them a little later.
    Kindly ship these goods at once via the Big Four, New Your Central & New York New Haven & Hartford Railroad terms 60 days. This being our first transaction and not being known to you we enclose you statement of our financial standing, and if you desire references we can finish same from large house we are doing business with. You can also refer to your Mr. Robert P. Gant, of this city, who has visited our place of business several times.
    Trusting you will find everything satisfactory to ship the goods at once, as we are now making up samples for our travelers, and we want to include your good among our samples, we are ,
Your very respectfully, A. Rosen

Freeman and Fox Mfg. Co

Figure 3.13. Letters to and from Freeman and Fox Mfg. Co., 1906. Transcribed from Yount Woolen Mill papers, Rotary Jail Museum and Tannenbaum Cultural Center, Crawfordsville, Indiana.

Hartford Conn Feb. 7th 1906
Messrs. Yount Woolen Mills Col,
Yountsville Indiana
Dear Sirs:

Yours of the 3rd last to hand, replying to same please ship order #2–3 and 4 at once on receipt of this, same routing as order #1 by Big Four and soforth We have some large orders for your style #309/2 and other colorings of this style. Some of these orders are not for immediate delivery. You may if you care too in addition to orders 1, 2, 3, and 4 add order #5 of Ten piece of style #309 /2 if you will date the bill February 26th 60 days as we do not care to have the bill mature before that time. There is no doubt about our being able to use all you have of this style, but we do not care to have any more shipped at present until we give you further notice. In regard to price we are in error in our #3 order of this style #309/2 it should be 55 cents, and not 60 cents. We thank you for calling our attention to the error which was a clerical one. We cannot say anything future about clearing out the smaller quanities of the different styles until we receive the goods new ordered, we shall do our best to close them out.

Trust you will ship these goods at once, we are in need of same, we are,
Yours truly,
ASR

Figure 3.14. Request for Merchandise, 1906. Transcribed from Yount Mill papers, Rotary Jail Museum and Tannenbaum Cultural Center, Crawfordsville, Indiana.

they may, in fact, have been disingenuous. In the end Freeman and Fox left Yount holding the bag. Also, that year two pieces of bad news from lawyers within just a couple of months of each other (Figure 3.15) revealed that the mill's attempts to collect a debt of $50 was futile. The attempt to collect from the Jacob Peters estate resulted in failure; he had dispersed his assets prior to his death. Blessedly the court ruled that Yount Mill deserved a small settlement from the Peters estate, and the second letter on this topic, after removing $3 for the attorney fees resulted in their receiving a check for $5.11. The lawyer did not promise redress, and the fee added insult to injury. The mill continued to go down the drain.

The mill superintendent quit, and in that year James Shaw wrote (Figure 3.16) to negotiate terms for employment at the mill. Shaw had worked in England and had turned a mill around in Louisville. He said he was willing to work on commission or salary for a year. But he never showed up to work. The mill was looking for a miracle, but the miracle never came.

In 1905 Andrew negotiated with agent William A. Reade and Company to sell the mill real estate (Figure 3.17). Reade and Company boasted

May 3, 1906
Does not recommend suit trying to recover $50.00
William Cummings Lawyer

Penwell & Lindley Lawyers
July 10, 1906
...in the estate of Jacob C. Peters, bankrupt, Peters managed to get rid of all of his assets before his creditor file the petition in bankruptcy

August 3, 1907
Yount Woolen Mills Co.,
Crawfordsville, Indiana
Gentlemen:
     Answering your favor of the 2nd. With reference to the J. C. Peters bankruptcy matter. There will be a very small dividend, and it ought to be paid before long. Close the estate. Will report as soon as the court makes the order.
Very truly yours,
Linley, Penwell & Lindley

January 1908
Yount Woolen Mills Co,
Yountsville, Indiana
Gentleman:
IN RE your claim vs. Jacob C. Peters.
We have collect the first and final dividends of $7.11
We deduct fee minim fee $2,00
Balance enclosed by check $5.11
Very truly your.
Linley, Penwell & Lindley

Figure 3.15. Letters from Lawyers Regarding Attempts at Debt Recovery, 1906, 1907, and 1908. Transcribed from Yount Mill Ledger, Rotary Jail Museum and Tannenbaum Cultural Center, Crawfordsville, Indiana.

Figure 3.16
P.O. Box 8 Stockton
Calif—May 8th 1906
Mr. Yount
Yountsville INd
Dear Sir
I understand that Mr. H. your super had quit—I was at your place last
Feb but did not have the pleasure of meeting you I was brought up in
Hudd—England had had charge of J. Fairbanks factor in Leeds—also
of Fisher Shaw *& Fisher Leeds—in this county run a small factory in
Dallas—Or. My last situation as super was in Louisville KY at the Falls
City Woolen Factory. I was there over three year and I completely built
the pace and business up again for them, as they were in a most de-
plorable situation when I took hold. I set them on their feet—I enclose
you a copy of testimonial they gave me.

   I will take, and run your place for one year without salary but on a
commission to be agreed, on between us—but I must have full charge or
if you would rather pay a salary please to say what you will give—shall be
pleased to hear from you.
Yours truly
James Shaw

Figure 3.16. Letter from James Shaw Requesting Employment as Mill Supervisor,
1906. Transcribed from Yount Mill papers, Rotary Jail Museum and Tannenbaum
Cultural Center, Crawfordsville, Indiana.

about how successful they had been selling this type of property. By the next
year, the mill had not sold, and all Andrew had was a couple of letters filled
with excuses about how difficult it was to sell this type of property.[62] Reade
moaned that only one person had responded to their advertisements, and
that person was not be persuaded to come and look at the property. Andrew
countered that they would still honor the terms of the sale as long as Reed
and Company provided a customer to purchase the mill. Turning to the real
estate company also proved to be a fruitless effort. It did not even get a nibble.

   Andrew sold raw material, made-up goods, machinery, tools, office
fixtures, cash, and debts to Freeman and Fox, but no check came. The wool
products sold to Freeman and Fox had not been paid for, and Andrew

William A Reade & Co.
402 Chamber of Commerce Building. Cleveland, O.
April 25th, 1906
Mr. Andrew Yount, Prest.,
     The Yount Woolen Mills Co.,
     Yountville, Ind

Dear Sir: –
. . . regret to inform you that we have been unable to get more than one inquiry so far to our circular letter and advertisements which we place in the Sunday editions of the Chicago Record Herald and Hitchcock's Lists. The inquiry we received was from the Allen-Lane Company, #49 Leonard Street, New York. We took the matter up thoroughly with them but failed to get them interest enough to warren a personal inspection of the property. . . . We find woolen mills are one of the hardest proposition we handle, and are very had to dispose of. However, we have not give up hope of interesting some one in your property, and will continue our efforts in your behalf.
Your very truly,
Wm. A Reade & Co.

Yount Woolen Mills Co
Mfg. Pure Woolens
Dealers in Wool
Yountsivlle, INd June 6th 1906
Wm A Reade & Co
Cleveland
Ohio
Gentlemen.
     Yours of Apl /06 in reply to our enquiry of the 24th (Apr) was Duly received. The contract entered into between your selves and the Yount Woolen Mills Co. Jan 12/06 giving you from this date until May the 1st /06. The exclusive right to sell the entire manufacturing plant of "the Yount Woolen Mills Co." the time having expired as named an agreed on, in said contract, we hereby withdraw any further extension of the exclusive right as agreed on in said contract executed Jan 12th and 13th/06. The property is still for sale! And if you can furnish a bonafide purchaser on terms acceptable to our company and sale fully and satisfactorily consummated, We will give you the percent agreed on in said contract of Jan 12th and 13th /06. This proposition to hold until written notice is given of the independent disposition of the said plant either through other agencies or our own individual corporate efforts. Hope you may favorable consider this proposition an soon secure us a purchaser,
Respectfully
The Yount Woolen Mills Co.

Figure 3.17. Letter from William A. Reade and Company Regarding Failure to Get Ads, 1906. Transcribed from the papers of Allen and Barbara Brooke White, Yountsville Mill, Yountsville, Indiana.

Aug. 26th/ 06
Augustine Sonergau
Hartford
Conn.
Dear Sir

In Cotton and wool reporter of Aug 8th we saw an advertisement wanted to purchase a small 3 to 5 sett woolen mill.—we have a small 3 sett woolen mill for sale is now in operation the business maintained here in 1840 by Daniel Yount and has had and still maintains a good business and no doubt but the business could be profitable enlarged by a practical and competent man or party should be pleased to give you all possible information in regard to the property if desired but would prefer that you visit and examine this property as to situation business and condition. If you are open for a deal and not objection to location out west we should be pleased to hear from you by return mail, Respectfully

Figure 3.18. Response to Interest in Purchasing a Mill, 1906. Transcribed from Yount Mill papers, Rotary Jail Museum and Tannenbaum Cultural Center, Crawfordsville, Indiana.

brought a bankruptcy suit against Freeman and Fox to recover his goods.[63] Andrew charged that the company engaged in fraud to take the goods from Yount Mill, sell them, and use the money to cover other debts without intending to repay the Younts ever.

The directors of Yount Mill received a letter (Figure 3.18) from Augustine Sonergau of Hartford, Connecticut saying he wanted to purchase a mill. In desperation they offered him Yount Mill. The effort went nowhere, but it did provide a brief flicker of hope. The mill's western location seemed to be a detriment.

On March 23, 1906, the board hired a Mr. Househesaine to act as the superintendent of the mill for one year for $100 per month. They also hired Frank Denise as a traveling salesman with a salary of $75 per month and traveling expenses.[64] In November of 1906 the board rented a room in Crawfordsville to serve as a showroom for the mill's goods.[65] Unfortunately, in May of the next year Mrs. Ben Myers was injured when her horse was startled and bolted, seemingly on account of a display of merchandise on the sidewalk in front of the company store.[66] The board decided to pay for the doctor but not to honor any other claim from her.

Russell & McCluer
Attorneys at Law
Loans and Abstracts of Title
Crawfordsville, Ind.
Jan 9, 1909

Mr. Matthew Robertson
Campbellsburg, Ind.

Dear Sir:
    The Directors of The Yount Woolen Mills Company, and after considering the report of the committee sent to examine your land, at a meeting here today, direct that the following offer be made to you.
    They will convey the woolen mill property to you and give ten thousand (10,000) dollars in cash, for your Washington County land, provided you furnish an abstract showing a clean and complete title, and provided further that they be given time to negotiate a loan of ten thousand dollars with which to make said cash payment. This would require but a short time in our opinion, after approval of the title. Very truly yours,

The Yount Woolen Mill Company,
Benjamin R. Russell Sec.

Figure 3.19. Lawyer's Letter Regarding a Land Swap, 1909. Transcribed from the Yount Woolen Mills Co. Minute Book No. 2, Rotary Jail Museum and Tannenbaum Cultural Center, Crawfordsville, Indiana.

On January 30, 1908, there was resolve to reorganize the mill and try to reopen, and later in July the board determined to get fire insurance and hire a watchman.[67] In 1909 the board agreed (Figure 3.19) to give $10,000 and the mill lands for a parcel of land in Washington County if clear title was provided. The next attempt to make a profit for the company was a land swap. It also went nowhere since there were no good options that would allow the directors to trade to their advantage.

At the December 15, 1909, meeting of the board a discussion of the finances of the company revealed a dismal financial picture and the board decided to take the property of the company to its creators to settle the company liabilities.[68] On January 7, 1910, the closed plant was offered for sale to J. S. Fields of Charleston, IL.[69] There was no interest. On February 9, 1910, the old company was dismembered, stock was sold, a new company formed, old stock was redeemed, and new stock was issued.[70]

At the January 9, 1912, board meeting, Mr. Isaac C. Elston reported on his attempts to sell the property. He had received several propositions for exchanges, but those who inquired were all so heavily encumbered in debt that he preferred the Yount property, which was free from liens.[71] Crawford also reported that he had a small amount of cash on hand, which included some rental receipts. He might have enough money to meet the first tax installment. He also reported that his trip to examine land in southern Indiana allowed him to look at 700 acres in exchange for Yount Mill, but he found that it was poor, rough, and broken land, heavily encumbered in debt, and of doubtful title, so a deal could not be considered.[72]

On May 24, 1913, the board sent a R. M. Allen to examine the possible cash value of land located in Sherman County, Texas, and the feasibility of an exchange for the Yount Mill.[73] In 1913 the Yountsville Woolen Mill of Yountsville, Indiana, was listed as for sale or rent, with three sets and ten broad looms and power provided by water.[74] It was now a large, mostly vacant albatross.

On October 14, 1916, the board accepted the offer of J. Clark Smith of Newport, Indiana. The Yountsville Woolen Mill Company was to receive a property near Clinton, Indiana, and a property at Ashley, Indiana, with a note secured by a mortgage aggregation for $6,200 for its mill property.[75] By 1917, J. Clark Smith owned the property.[76]

People continued to purchase stock in the Yount Woolen Mill Company until 1918.[77] On February 9, 1918, the stockholders elected Isaac C. Elston president of the board of directors, C. M. Crawford as Treasurer, and Andrew Yount as Secretary. On January 8, 1918, the board reported that the sale to J. Clark Smith had been accomplished. The Yountsville Woolen Mill Company accepted a house and lot at Clinton, Indiana, and a house and lot at Ashley, Indiana. The latter was encumbered by a mortgage. J. Clark Smith gave back to the Woolen Mill Company a mortgage for $6,200, which had fallen due the *previous* July, but he failed to pay any part of the principal balance or the interest up to September 1, 1916. He had made a payment on that date, but no payment had been made since then. The mortgage was placed in the hands of attorney Chase Harding, and foreclosure was to be instituted.[78]

Chase Harding then reported that the Ashley property was encumbered beyond its real value and the company had been fortunate to avoid the liability and the cost of getting it off their hands. He had contracted a sale of the Ashley property for $1,000 on time payment of $10 dollars per month to the present occupant, Louis Wally—a good sale. J. Clark Smith had an account to him for the rent to November 1, 1917, and the taxes were paid.

Mr. Harding and Andrew Yount made a full report of a proposition to lease the mill property through a Mr. Cowan by the superintendent of J. Capps and Sons of Jacksonville, Illinois, and Howard and Jones of New York. They gave little encouragement that any lease or operation of the mill property would result and that the foreclosure proceedings would have to go through to sale.[79]

On March 5, 1920, the Yount Woolen Mill Company sold the mill site, land, buildings, water rights, equipment, and products and went out of business forever.[80] The proceeds from the sale after paying all debts went to the stockholders as a dividend. The mill went to sleep in a peaceful, cool valley and dreamed of the days when the mill had shaken with manufacturing might and people swarmed over the valley in trade and manufacturing.

The process of industrialization and deindustrialization in Yountsville ran its course. The next part of the story was a test of adaptive reuse. In 1922 the tax rolls showed that the Terre Haute–based Hoosier Hotel Resort Company purchased the property for a fleeting interest, an amusement park and hotel, a fizzle, and nothing developed from those dreams. The company did not even fully capitalize before it collapsed, but the brick mill annex was demolished during this time. In 1922 a photo showed the remains of the dam and a wall that came off the still-standing turbine house in front of the annex footings. Looking upstream toward a nearby covered bridge, the mill had a solid-looking masonry platform on the west side of Sugar Creek that was the annex. Emerging from the annex platform and a sandbar upstream from the timber cribs, boards and timber for the foundation of the dam extended one-third of the way across Sugar Creek.[81] The dam remnants consisted of logs notched to interlock and held together with metal pins.[82] All windows were out of the frame mill, and the frame store was between the two mills on a hill. There was no damage to the second- or third-floor windows of the brick mill and no sign of the present south door on the first floor.

After the Hoosier Hotel Resort Company departed, people continued to find the mill fascinating. But while the public started to pay more attention to the mill, the property itself went sliding down the banister of eco-

Figure 3.20. Yount Mill from the North Side. This picture was taken on a hill overlooking the mill. From the Marian Morrison Local History Collection at the Crawfordsville District Public Library.

nomic distress. In 1930 Forrest Grimes purchased the property but lost it in 1937 due to the Great Depression. The Winkler family owned the property until O. Ray James purchased it and moved there in 1942. In 1958 the Grimes family purchased the property again. Photographers documented (Figure 3.20) the slate roof's disintegration, the loss of the first-floor windows, and the loss of a first-floor door.

By 1964 vines had eaten the mortar from between the bricks (Figure 3.21), the fascia and soffit boards had crumbled, and a hole in the first level gaped on the south side of the sandstone foundation. On July 11, 1965, the Montgomery County Historical Society erected a marker at the site as part of the centennial of the Civil War.

By 1983 the window frames, sashes, and glass had failed, allowing the elements to pass freely through the building. The turbine driveshaft and gears stood defiantly, and the driveshaft reached hopefully toward it. The drive wheel hung onto the side of the building with its hexagonal support and wooden frame. In 1987 the John Hardwick family began the major job of cleaning, scraping, roofing, and restoring the boarding house at the mill for use as a bed and breakfast.

Figure 3.21. West Side of Yount Mill, 1964. The photo shows the ivy covering the front and side of the building. From the Marian Morrison Local History Collection at the Crawfordsville District Public Library.

By 1993 the mill had a new composite shingle roof, but the windows were gone, making the building a toothless parody of the past vigor of the mill. Two couples, Dr. and Mrs. Leech and Mr. and Mrs. Ward Bop, operated the inn as a bed and breakfast, but they lived offsite before Keith and Jerone Collier operated the inn as a bed and breakfast. The Colliers bought the inn from the two couples. In 2009 Alan and Barbara White purchased the boarding house to use as a bed and breakfast. The path of the mill (Figure 3.22) passed from industrialism under Daniel Yount to deindustrialization with his descendants. Following the dissolution of the company, the site entered a phase of adaptive reuse.

Surprisingly, after a hundred years of use there were still some Yountsville Wool Mill blankets that were carefully guarded by collectors in the Crawfordsville area (Figure 3.23). They had easily passed the test of time and were still serving their owners. The blankets looked every bit as good as

November 3, 1807	Daniel Yount was born.
1818	Daniel Yount worked in his father's mill near Dayton, Ohio.
1840	Daniel took possession of what was known as the Snyder grist mill, situated on Spring Creek.
1843	Daniel and Allen bought Abijah O'Neal's land and water rights and built a carding mill.
1849	Daniel and Allen built a spinning and weaving mill.
1857	Allen Yount sold his interest in the property for $8,000 to Arthur Russell, who was also an inlaw of Daniel and Sarah's first child, Rhoda (Yount) Gilkey.
January 1, 1858	Russell died of typhoid the day he expected to take possession of the mill. Daniel bought his share at auction for $6,000 and became the sole owner.
1864	Daniel built a brick mill.
1875	Daniel Yount and Sons formed between Daniel, Andrew, John, and Wycliff C. Whitehead.
November 29, 1876	John M. was killed in a railroad accident.
September 30, 1890	Daniel Yount died. Yount's Woolen Company was formed.
1930	Forrest Grimes purchased the property.
1937	Grimes lost property in the Great Depression.
1942	B. R. James owned the property.
1958	Grimes purchased the property again.
July 11, 1965	Montgomery County Historical Society erected a marker at the mill.
1969	Walter Bowman owned the mill site.
1987	The Hardwicks began the major job of cleaning, scraping, roofing, and restoring the boarding house for use as a bed and breakfast.

Figure 3.22. Timeline of Yount Mill, 1807–1987.

May 20, 2014 RVM observed blanket owned by Bob and Donna Mills

December 5, 1989
White woolen Blanket
    An all white, double sized (two double beds long, one wide), woolen blanket made at the Yount Woolen Mill was purchased from Marietta June (Dowd) Boone and Ralph M. Boone on December 2, 1989. The blanket is in excellent condition; only evidence of use is the worn edging.
    Per Mrs. Boone, her great-grandmother Margaret Catherine Davidson, born 1843, received the blanket at the time of her marriage in 1862 to Abram Washington Houser. The marriage was at Pleasant Hill Church, near the Turkey Run Cemetery Wingate. The church is now gone. The blanket came to Mrs. Boon through her Great-Aunt, a daughter of Mrs. Davidson who was childless. (Collection of Allen and Barbara White)

May 22, 2014 RVM observed Olive Gray blanket 61 by 76 inches blanket stitch around edge, tight heavy weave, one side smooth, the other rough, looks new except for old stain. (Collection of Allen and Barbara White)

May 24, 2014 RVM observed 3 blankets belonging to Mr. and Mrs. Mel Kelly
1. Scarlet blanket yellow blanket stitch—fine and thin
2. White blanket with white blanket stich—very fine
3. White blanket with indigo blanket stich—very fine—center seam 78 × 69

May 25, 2014 RVM observed Wabash Archives blanket of Benjamin Marshall Mills (Caleb Mills' son) dark stripes across top and bottom US drawn on it. Stripes have same weave pattern that White family blanket has. Greenish/grey cast—fiber looks mixed.

May 22, 2015 RVM observed Montgomery Historical Society blankets:
1. Fine light beige 13 stripes at ends (1 solid, 2 pins, 2 solid with single in the middle, 2 pins, 2 solid with single in the middle, 2 pins, 1 solid) fan stich at ends 77 × 70
2. Fine light beige 5 stripes at ends (thick stripe in the middle) × stick at ends one thread dark brown and one thread beige 77 × 69
3. Fine beige fringe at ends, line at each end, wide center line, line at the ¼ and ¾ marks (maybe more faint lines) 122 × 55

Figure 3.23. Five Accounts of Yount Mill Blankets, 1989 and 2014. Found by the author.

comparable-sized woolen blankets made in the twenty-first century. The blankets ranged from hard, dark, and heavy blankets to soft, colorful, and smooth ones. They ranged from thin, elegant weaves in cream with a rich indigo blanket stitch around the edges to a bold scarlet blanket or a heavy olive that might have been the very popular sheep's grey. They ranged from rough to soft, and some of them had stripes at the ends. None of the plaid or flowered blankets seemed to have survived, which is not too surprising. When they were made they were just another factory commodity important for the service they rendered to a farm woman's family. No one could guess they would one day be prized by collectors.

From the beginning to the end of the mill, the Yount family was central to its operation. The quality of the merchandise was a source of pride for the family, and they enjoyed providing valuable goods for the community. Factory production reflected the character of the owners and their determination to remain relevant in a changing wool business.

FOUR

The Yount Family

On November 3, 1807, Daniel Yount was born to Andrew and Eve Yount of Warren County, Ohio; he was one of eight children.[1] At age eleven Daniel started working with his family at their father's mill near Dayton, Ohio; Daniel's brothers Allen, who was one year behind Daniel, and John, who was six years behind Daniel, also worked in the mill. In 1827 Daniel, Allen, and John settled with their parents in Tippecanoe County, Indiana, on the Wea Creek five miles south of Lafayette. While Daniel was there he married Sarah Price in 1830, and they had five children, starting with Rhoda and progressing to Mary, Andrew, John, and Anna.[2] From 1835 to 1839 Daniel followed his brother John to Attica, Indiana, where they started a wool mill.[3] Next Daniel tried farming for a year, but after farming he never again left milling. He was comfortable with the excitement and change of industrialization. Only two members of the family appeared in the 1840 census. The two brothers appear as heads of households.

Daniel attempted to create not only a successful industrial community but also a successful social community where he would practice his values. Daniel described his place in the community when he mused, "Our business involves a system of exchange with the farmers around us. They bring their wool to us; we supply them with goods, which represent the labor and wages of our employees, who are their own children, and thus the money and the products are all kept in the country."[4] Dan's description sounds like a cooperative venture from which everyone benefits. The Yount family had been Quakers, but when they came to Yountsville Daniel became a leader in the Methodist Episcopal Church. More important than dogma was the practice of a good quality of life among people who lived in harmony. From the beginning he was both a class leader and a trustee, and by the end of the year he habitually closed the gap between the giving of the congregation and the expenses of the church. Daniel seemed to relish taking the lead in everything that he did, and in the small Yountsville community people looked to him to provide that leadership.

Community members recognized Daniel Yount's philanthropy, including giving the land for the parsonage for the Methodist Church or, at a time of no personal banking services, granting multiple loans both from his own resources and from the mill—some of which were never repaid. He made many loans, and many were paid back with six percent interest; he was, after all, a businessman, and at a time without banks, companies and wealthy members of the community served their peers by providing personal credit. Daniel never refused a request for assistance.[5] In the fall of each year he said to his clerk, "James, if you know of any poor families in the neighborhood needing clothing or blankets send them enough to supply their wants."[6] During the Civil War Daniel manifested benevolence, character, and patriotism when he donated hundreds of blankets to soldiers. When Governor Oliver P. Morton sent out the call to equip regiments for federal service, Daniel took the call seriously. "He sent similar contributions to flood sufferers."[7] In the last painful days of Daniel's life, he instructed one of his workers to collect cloth and flannel remnants from the store to send to the Orphans' Home. Many children had lost their fathers during the Civil War, and Indiana established an orphanage for them south of Knightstown. When Daniel heard that his son Andrew had completed that task, he commented, "Very well" in contentment that his son had performed a Christian service, as was his own custom.[8] He gave generously during his life to help people in his community who were in need, and he responded to people who asked for help. In addition, he spent time looking for people to help. Needless to say, his employees looked to him as a friend, and the community depended on his sage advice and commitment to manage and protect their common interests.

In politics he was temperate, reading the *Indianapolis Journal*, a pro-Republican daily newspaper that arrived with the morning mail, and favoring Benjamin Harrison for president because of the Republican support for protectionist tariffs on imported wool.[9] Daniel enjoyed the support of the transportation enhancements of the Republicans and their support for corporations. He stated, "I am a Republican of course but I have never been an active politician or a party worker."[10] Of course, he did not need to actively engage in politics because in the small local network of the county everyone would have known of his views.

The Younts appear in the guardian records of the county (Table 4.1). Soon after Allen came to the county in 1841, he and his wife agreed to serve as guardians for James A. Lincoln, age three. On the same day, Daniel Yount served as sureties for James and Samuel Minor, ages nineteen and seventeen, in order for them to live with their father, Stephen Minor. Daniel Yount also served as sureties for his grandchildren upon the death of their father so they could live with his daughter Rhonda Rhodes. In 1862, when their father, Arthur, died, Daniel served as a guardian for Bryan and Lindia Rusell.[11] Illness claimed many lives in the antebellum period. Daniel was an important source of support for the family.

Speaking in the 1930s, Dr. William Reser remembered Daniel in this glowing story:

> The following statement illustrates this unselfish man's practical application of the principle of the Golden Rule. At the beginning of the Civil War, the price of wool was very low and as soon as it began to rise everyone wanted to sell. Dan Yount had enough foresight to know that to buy then was a display of business sagacity. So he bought, manufactured, and stored all the wool offered until he had a stock of probably 75,000 to 100,000 pounds. In the meantime the price kept going up and continued to rise until eventually his stock of wool was worth enough in the open market that by selling he could have realized a dollar a pound over and above the average price paid. He could have sold his entire stock of wool, closed down his mill and retired with far more wealth than he ever acquired. But Dan Yount did not do that because profiteering was not an element in his make-up. Know[ing] that his faithful employees would be thrown out of work and the cost of living was rising, he refuse[d] to sell beyond the needs of this consumption by keeping the mill working. He kept his employees working and sold their product on a declining market, as he well knew would be the case. It was not his nature to profiteer at the expense of his fellow men.[12]

Table 4.1. Yount Family Child Guardianship

Date of Letters	Names of Guardians	Names of Wards and Ages	Names of Sureties	Page Number
August 10th 1841	Allen Yount	James A. Lincoln age 3 years heir of Thomas Lincoln deceased	Abijah O'Neal	30
August 10th 1841	Stephen	James D. Minor aged 19 years Samuel G. D. Minor aged 17 years Minor heirs of Stephen Minor	Daniel Yount	30
April 29th 1858	Rhonda Rhodes	Alice Gilkey Allen Gilkey minor heirs of James W. Gilkey deceased	Daniel Yount	155
October 9th 1862	Daniel Yount	Bryan R. Russell and Lidia J. Russell minor heirs of Arthur Russell deceased	Abijah O'Neal	175

Source: Data compiled by and transcribed from the Montgomery County's Guardian's Docket located in the Montgomery County Clerk's Office, Crawfordville, IN.

While Daniel did make multiple good decisions, this story seems to be celebrating the past by attributing the good businessman with almost superhuman qualities. This story is colored by the experience of World War I and the propaganda against war profiteers; moreover, Daniel probably expected wool supply costs and wool cloth prices to remain high. He and his relatives probably realized only in retrospect that they had missed an opportunity of a lifetime after the closing of the mill. Further, the language of "his faithful employees would have been thrown out of work" reflected the concerns of a 1930 community witnessing the Great Depression unfolding in front of them. As companies failed, factories closed and people became desperate. Looking back across forty years, the steady and steadfast qualities Daniel exercised made him look like a luminary.

By the 1930s Dr. Reser remembered Daniel in another story, as follows:

> With his advancing years the duties of conducting the business became arduous, and he began negotiations for selling the business. A purchaser had been found, terms had been agreed upon, and with the physical property was to go the firm's name along with its good will. For the completion of the detail of the sale, the interested parties of both sides of the proposed transfer had retired to the store room where Dan Yount was busily engaged in reading in preparation to signing the contract of sale. Meanwhile a bystander among those assembled around the stove asked the purchaser about the prospective working or operating policy under the new management. In reply, [the future buyer] stated, that in order to compete with other like concerns he would insert a thread of cotton in the yarns and some in the cloth, but, of course, not enough that it could be readily detected by the average purchaser. Dan, at that time, had just finished signing one set of papers and looking up thought he heard the remark as stated. He immediately ask[ed], "What is that?" The statement was repeated, where upon Dan picked up the signed contact of sale, opened the stove door, and consigned [the contract] to the flames, saying. "No one shall ever use the Yount name in practicing deceit." And the sale was never consummated.[13]

The elements of truth in this story confirm that Daniel produced only high-quality goods and valued his reputation. Since he was so generous, he did not need to cheat anyone in business; in a small community, word would have spread quickly of his disingenuous qualities. His reputation's

being intact was more valuable to him than anything he could have pro-
cured through deception, and trade at his store and wool sales would have
been jeopardized. One element does not ring true: if Daniel had really
wanted to part with the company, he could easily have sold the firm without the use of the family name. He could have sold the clients, contacts,
real estate, machinery, and stock to someone who promised not to associate
his name with the business.

His son-in-law vanished from the firm, and Daniel Yount and sons
became Daniel Yount and son. Does the story, told as heroic virtue, contain
the seed of the separation between Daniel and his son-in-law, or did the
split with his son-in-law prompt this attempt to sell the mill? There is one
cryptic letter in the files of someone who felt he deserved a share of something and had not been treated fairly by Daniel. Was this the son-in-law?
Considering how difficult finding a buyer for the mill proved to be, this
great virtue may have been a foolish missed opportunity. At the time of
Daniel's death, his son Andrew searched in vain for a new owner for the
mill, and even when he used an agent, there was no one looking for an old
woolen mill with outdated equipment. As it was four miles from a rail
head and a major population center, it was hard to keep viable.

Daniel tried to think of everything. He knew he was dying and wanted
to make sure that he provided for his children and grandchildren. He gave
his daughter Mary Troutman the Troutman mill property, and he gave his
grandsons and John's widow the fifty-eight-acre farm where they were
living. He gave his granddaughter Alice Drake $500 in cash, and released
his grandson Allen Gilkey from his debt and gave him $154. After paying
all his debts and expenses he divided his property into fifths: one part went
to Andrew, another to Anna Whitehead, a third part to Mary Troutman,
one part to his grandchildren (the children of John), since he had prede-
ceased Daniel, and another fifth to Andrew so he could establish a trust
fund to generate an annual income for the use of Rhoda Townsley.[14] In addition to the mill, part of the estate was 160 acres that Daniel owned in
Starke County.[15]

When Daniel died he had an old bedstead and bed springs plus chairs
around a chipped marble-topped table (Table 4.2). He lived a simple and
unpretentious life. In a bookcase and stand he kept well-worn books, and
on the walls he displayed the framed pictures gathered across a lifetime.[16]
He put his assets into the business. His personal possessions were not as
valuable to him as ownership of the mill.

Table 4.2. The Personal Property Estate of Daniel Yount, 1891

Quantity	Description	Cash
1	Marble top table (damaged)	$1.00
4	Chairs	$1.00
1	Bookcase and stand	$3.00
1	Lot books old and damaged	$8.00
3	Pictures and frames	$1.50
1	Old bedstead	$.75
1	Bed springs	$1.00

Source: Data compiled and transcribed from the Montgomery County Clerk's Probate Files, Crawfordsville, Indiana.

People in the community called him "Uncle Dan," and the Yountsville Methodist Episcopal Church had the funeral.[17] He demonstrated his success in business by accumulating a large estate, and at the time of his death he gave it all away to his heirs. In business he could not be replaced, and the people at the mill did not realize that with his death their lives would forever change. The community he had worked so hard to create was unraveling.

The Yount family lived a simple life, but they were comfortable as they attained education and experience. Daniel lived long enough to see his grandson Andrew Gilbert Yount graduate from Wabash College as a Minister of the Gospel in the Methodist Episcopal Church. Given Daniel's leadership in the church, this made him very proud. Daniel Yount Lozier also graduated from Wabash five years after Daniel's death.[18] Even though many of Daniel's children were buried in Crawfordsville, Indiana, the grandchildren left Yountsville to find economic opportunity. They did not come from privilege, but they did come from a very stable community. Members of the Yount family availed themselves of the benefits of a common-school education, and the next generation explored higher education, usually at Caleb Mills's college. They received the benefits of economic change transformed into educational opportunity and created a future for themselves.

YOUNT FAMILY TIES

Allen and Daniel Yount were present in Ripley Township of Montgomery County in the 1840 census, but their families are not reported as being there. By 1850 forty-two-year-old Allen was there with his thirty-year-old wife, Mary, plus their three children: eight-year-old Anny, six-year-old Isabel, and two-year-old Albert. Seventeen-year-old William was living with his uncle and aunt. At forty-three Daniel headed his household with his Maryland-born wife, Sarah, age thirty-eight. Their four children were present: fourteen-year-old Mary, twelve-year-old Andrew, ten-year-old John, and five-year-old Anna. The members of the Yount family seem to have had more assets than their neighbors.

By 1860 the mill community looked much different. Allen's family had moved away, and Daniel owned $10,000 of real estate property and $15,000 in personal property. His wife, Sarah, lived with him, as did the last of their two children, twenty-year-old John and fourteen-year-old Annie. At the same time, in the boarding house, Daniel's daughter, twenty-six-year-old Rhoda Russel, owned $300 of personal property and was raising eight-year-old Byron and Lidda. She was also raising seven-year-old Alice Gilkey and five-year-old Allen Gilkey, the children of her first marriage. Andrew Yount, now twenty-two, was living in the boarding house. In their own home twenty-six-year-old William Yount was married to twenty-five-year-old Sarah. He had $300 in real estate property and $100 in personal property. Their children lived with them: six-year-old Clara, three-year-old Charles, and one-year-old Allen.

By 1870 Daniel's nephew William P. Yount, age thirty-six, had $800 in real estate property and $200 in personal property. His wife, Sarah A., was one year younger than he and had been born in Pennsylvania and worked in the factory. Their daughter Clara was sixteen, Charley H. was thirteen, Allen C. was eleven, Nettie B. was six, Andrew G. was three, and Walter was eleven months. After a life of service to the mill, William succumbed to death. His life reflected the family values that described other members of his tribe (Figure 4.1).

Daniel and Sarah, who were now sixty-two and fifty-eight, respectively, were worth $45,000 in real estate property and $50,000 in personal property. Thirty-two-year-old Andrew was listed as a wool manufacturer like his father. Annie was twenty-five and living at home. Lydia Russell, who should have been sixteen now, was living with her grandparents. She had $500 in real estate and $1,000 in personal property. The boarding house also had big changes. John M. was now married to Mary M. Yount, and they managed the boarding house. He was a thirty-year-old woolen

PIONEER OF THE COUNTY IS DEAD
WILLIAM P. YOUNT DIED SUNDAY AT HIS HOME
HERE AFTER LONG ILLNESS WAS HEAD
OF YOUNT MILL HALF CENTURY
Mr. Yount Was One of Best Known Men in County,
Having Lived Here Since Youth

William P. Yount, aged eighty-one, died at his home 511 Crawford street, at eleven-thirty Sunday morning after a long illness which had become of a serious nature only a few days ago. Last Thursday the aged man commenced to weaken and he sank rapidly until his demise Sunday. He had been suffering paralysis for some time.

Mr. Yount came to this county with his father, Allen Yount and his brother, Daniel Yount, while he was a youth and the three started the Yount woolen mill at Yountsville. For a half century the deceased was superintendent of this mill. In 1900 his health began to weaken and he retired from the work, coming to this city to live. Sixty years ago, Mr. Yount was married to Miss Sarah Walter at Yountsville, whose death occurred thirty years ago. He was later married to Miss Ella Burkshire of Rising Sun, Ohio, who survives him. He is survived by two daughters and three sons by his first marriage, Mrs. Harry Lebo, Crawfordsville; Mrs. C.Y. Stubbins, Indianapolis; Rev. Andrew J. Yount, Cincinnati; L.D. Yount, Olney, Ill., and W.V. Yount, New Market.

The deceased was one of the best known men in Montgomery county and he was recognized everywhere for his strength of character. he was prominent as a church worker and for more than a quarter of a century was superintendent of the Sunday school at Yountsville. Funeral services will probably be held from the late home at two-thirty Wednesday afternoon. The services will be in charge of Rev. C. B. Stanforth, pastor of Trinity M.E. church, and Rev. Williams, former pastor of that church. Burial will be in Oak Hill cemetery.

Figure 4.1. William Yount Obituary, 1915. *Crawfordsville Daily Journal*, Monday, May 24.

manufacturer with $1,500 in real estate and $300 in personal property. They had two sons, four-year-old Daniel M. and one-year-old Freddie. One of the boarders was Byron R. Russell, who was now twenty-one and a student of law. Another boarder was Albert R. Yount, son of Allen and nephew of Daniel, who was now back in Yountsville, was twenty-one years of age, and worked in the woolen factory.

In 1880 William's son and Daniel's grandnephew, Allen, was a twenty-one-year-old spinner in the factory and married to Nora. All of them lived within sight of each other. William was listed as a mechanic at the mill, but he and Sarah A. Yount were still married and lived in their own home. Their son Charles was the twenty-three-year-old clerk at the mill store. Nellie was sixteen. Twelve-year-old Andrew and ten-year-old Walter worked in the woolen factory. The last of their children, Lozie, was six. In the boarding house, Albert and Eva Yount had three-year-old Arthur along with their new boarders. Also living within sight of the boarding house was seventy-two-year-old Daniel Yount, who had been born in Ohio and was listed as the proprietor of the mill and a widower. Born in Indiana, Allen Gilkey, Daniel's twenty-six-year-old grandchild, was living with him. Living next to his father, forty-two-year-old Andrew Yount, who had been born in Maryland, was listed as the proprietor of the mill. His twenty-seven-year-old wife, Lydia, had also born in Maryland. Their two children, Edison R., age six, and Mary, age four, were both born in Indiana.

In 1900 Allief C. Yount was a forty-one-year-old merchant from Indiana. Also living on the hill was William P. Yount from Indiana, who at age sixty-six was the boss weaver, along with his forty-eight-year-old wife, Ella B., who was also from Indiana. Also living with them was their twenty-year-old Indiana niece, Elizabeth Hopping. On the same side of the hill was Allen R. Yount, who was fifty-two years old and the boss carder from Indiana. Eva, his wife, was twenty-four and from Ohio. They lived through a time of rapid industrial change, and by the turn of the century their generation had common-school educations.

The Walter Family

Sarah Walter was Daniel Yount's first wife. In 1850 Allen Yount's family boarded seventeen-year-old Sarah Walter of Indiana. The next record of the

Walter family occurs when the 1870 census documents "Aaron Walters" as a forty-two-year-old boot- and shoemaker from Pennsylvania who boarded with the Yount family. He had real estate property of $1,200 and personal property of $2,500. There was a gap in the records, but in 1900 forty-one-year-old Scott Walter from Scotland was the supervisor at the Yount Woolen Mills, while Bertha Walter, his twenty-six-year-old wife, was from Canada, which was then part of the British Empire. The mill family really was a family, with multiple branches of relatives weaving in and out of the life of the mill.

The Lebo Family

The Lebo family was also intertwined with the Yount family. In 1850 Pennsylvanian carder William Lebo worked at the mill. In 1890 Mrs. Harry Lebo, a daughter of Daniel Yount, lived in Yountsville. Ten years later, thirty-nine-year-old Henry Lebo was the loom boss. His wife, Nettie B., was thirty-six and, like him, was from Indiana. Of their children, William F. was eight, Ruth seven, Mary five, and Lois M. one.

As in many other family businesses, everyone worked in the business as children and sometimes across multiple generations. Everyone worked in the mill or worked to support the operation of the mill doing all of those jobs that had to be done. The Yount home seemed to be open as a place where young members of the family could get started and find a place to board on their own away from their parents. They got experience, put some wages in their pockets, and looked to different opportunities to create their own futures. It was a very common experience for members of the Yount family to bring boarders into their homes in addition to the boarding house. All of the members of the families left Yountsville eventually, carrying away their memories and experiences. While theirs was not the typical story of pioneers living on farms in log cabins, the lives of this family were hard and not at all what people think about if they read about Laura Ingalls Wilder.

The Yount Family worked and lived every day with people they employed in a small community devoted to wool manufacture. Their employees and coworkers were not German, but reflected the British Isles. The workers were not part of a faceless mass but rather were people who knew the Younts in their daily and professional lives.

FIVE

The Lives of the Workers

With the coming of industrialization and the spread of the factory system, the labor of workers underwent a transformation.[1] The experience of working in a mill would be a difficult adjustment for anyone used to working outdoors or even working indoors in a small workshop.

Work in textile mills was fast-paced, loud, and difficult work. The workers monitored the machines closely for problems that, if they went uncaught, could significantly affect the quality of the work. Workers in the textile mill could monitor only a few machines per person, but each of these machines required constant attention to repair breaks and maintain efficiency.[2] This meant that workers were constantly on their feet, walking across the factory floor monitoring machines and repeating the same process all day.

In addition to the tedious nature of observation, the mill itself would often be an uncomfortable environment. The floors vibrated; there was constant loud noise, and often dust and other particles filling the air.[3] In a study of the Boott Cotton Mills in Lowell, Massachusetts, archaeologists and historians noted that working in textile mills was dirty work. The machines were covered in grease that got on the workers as they maintained

---

This chapter was written with the assistance of J. B. Bilbrey, Jessica L. Clark, and Mark D. Groover.

them, the temperature inside the mills was kept hot to improve the quality of the product, and the process of making cloth filled the air with lint. This lint stuck to the skin, hair, and clothes of the workers, covering them by the end of a workday.[4]

The switch from the task-oriented work of agriculture to the time-oriented work of the factory system was a difficult transition for most. Unlike small workshops, textile mills attempted to impose on their workers a regular discipline revolving around a clock. A factory bell would tell workers when to start, when to stop for lunch and dinner breaks, and when to end work for the day. The reliance on this bell greatly limited the control workers had over their days.[5] Few workers at the time had personal clocks with which to verify that the bell was being rung at the right time, and therefore the manufacturers would often ring the factory bell twenty or twenty-five minutes after the workday was technically supposed to end.[6]

Since the mill relied on the power of the water turbine or steam engine and the machines, workers labored at a steady pace throughout the day, with limited breaks. Despite these innovations in labor, in the first half of the nineteenth century many textile mills were still dependent on water supply (until the switch to steam engines), the flow of the markets and delivery of goods, and the light of the sun (until the widespread use of electricity in the mills).[7] These factors slowed the transition of labor from small workshop to industrialized factory in textile mills until the middle of the nineteenth century.

As the industry evolved, not all workers were content to allow manufacturers to take advantage of them. In addition to procuring personal timepieces to verify the time at which the factory bells were rung, there were several instances of workers' going on strike to protest unfair practices.[8] Strikes began to occur in the early 1850s, increasing to widespread strikes in 1857 and 1858 at mills on the East Coast, particularly in Massachusetts. The causes of strikes were varied but generally involved management's either decreasing pay or refusing to increase pay despite increases in production.[9] The influx of immigrant labor, or mill employees' need for work resolved the strikes; in both cases the mills prevailed. Large-scale organization and the success of the strikes would not occur until the early twentieth century.[10]

Despite these instances of resistance, it was far more common for workers to simply leave a mill than to resist. In the first half of the nineteenth century, there were high rates of turnover for factory workers and also increased migration, illustrating that in most cases workers chose to leave an unfair situation rather than fight it. The strikes noted above were occurring in the middle and second half of the nineteenth century and on the East Coast, which reflected the changing values of the culture because of the Industrial Revolution, the increase in urbanization, and the development of large cities.[11]

Unlike mill workers at mill towns on the East Coast, the workers at Yount's Mill had few choices, because the rural setting gave few alternatives for workers than to live at the boarding house and take their meals there for $3.00 a week.[12] The Yountsville mill offered workers a place with good wages and working conditions. If they were married and had children, their families could work with them, and they could be together.[13] If workers were single, they had the sociability of the boarding house and the possibility of being independent wage earners. This was a respectable possibility for women in rural Indiana, and if they had children, it allowed them to provide for their families. While it was not the usual life in rural agricultural Indiana, there was excitement at living in close proximity with people in the boarding house and the mill and working in community. Women were not supposed to have children out of wedlock. They were supposed to be married or living with a father, brother, or brother-in-law in rural Midwestern communities during the Victorian period.

For the mill workers, life in the boarding house had a routine. They woke before sunrise and tossed aside the sheets, blanket, comforter, bedspread, feather pillow, and pillowslip from the straw ticks or mattresses of their bedframes. Their feet hit the carpeted floor, and they passed the stand and chair in their room as they raced for the washstand with its pitcher, bowl, soap, soap dish, and towel.[14] As they got ready for the day, so did the other mill hands; when they finished their morning tasks, they headed down the hall and stairs. Other people had been up before them: those milking the cows, preparing breakfast, or preparing the mill for the day. Only bad weather or Sundays varied the routine.

In the double parlor, the clock ticked next to the lamp on the parlor table, and there were two stoves flanked by two rocking chairs and four sofas on pattered carpeted floors. The blinds on the windows controlled the early morning light that reflected in the mirror on the wall.[15] A pair of side tables, two freestanding tables, and a wardrobe were scattered around the room. There would be time for conversation, games, reading, and writing in these rooms later in the day after work. The boarding house did not encourage late hours, especially for those who were tired from the exertions of the day. The mill closed only on Sundays, and people had that day to visit family or friends or to worship as their consciences dictated.

Passing the double parlor, the workers entered the dining room with a long table covered with a tablecloth and lined by twenty chairs on top of a rag carpet. A lamp hung suspended over the table, giving a flickering light for breakfast, and the stoves sat along a wall. The shades on the windows allowed people to eat without the glare of the sun in their eyes during the afternoons on Sundays.[16] The mill workers engaged in light conversation around the table and heard the latest news repeated before starting their day. After breakfast, people grabbed their aprons, hats, or wraps from the wooden pegs mounted to boards on the walls where they had left them as they were coming back from the mill the previous evening. Then they walked down the hill to the mill to be at their jobs by sunrise.

In the kitchen, the gasoline stove hissed under the pancakes cooking and bacon crackling next to the flour bin. The cook had been up for a while making sure everything was ready for the meals of the day, as she had a younger helper. These two depended on the mill for their livelihood, but they spent their lives on food preparation. The lamp flickered yellow on the old-fashioned extension table next to the cast iron cook stove, and the kitchen utensils were moved to their respective places. A pump brought wash water from the cistern.[17] The nearby cow and heifer provided their contributions to the dinner table.[18] Tucked into a corner of the back porch near the firewood were tubs and washboards, a washing machine and clothes wringer, and a clothes basket waiting for laundry. The inventory completed at the time of Daniel's death (Table 5.1) gave a comprehensive picture of what life was like inside the boarding house. It listed the furniture and carpets used by the workers in the mill.

THE MILL

When Lee Nevitt worked at the Yountsville mill he witnessed customers bringing wool from as far away as Illinois. With farmers bringing in a steady stream of wool, the workers had plenty of business (Figure 5.1).

Table 5.1. Copartnership of Daniel Yount and Andrew Yount,
[Inventory, Including] Miscellaneous Wood, etc., 1891

Quantity	Description	Cost
116	Boards common rough wood	$132.16
5	3 lbs. soap @ $.90	$4
4	Short Montgomery County Fair stock	$50
1	Stove and pipe in office	$10
1	Fire proof safe in office	$50
1	Cow	$25
1	Heifer	$20
10	Cords wood	$25
1	Parlor table	$5
1	Clock	$3
2	Stoves	$4
1	Washstand	$1
2	Rocking chairs	$2
1	Mirror	$1.50
26 yds.	Carpet	$10.40
9 yds.	Carpet	$1.80
1	Stove	$2
1	Saw	$.50
24 yds.	Carpet	$9.60
1	Wardrobe	$2
30 yds.	Carpet	$6
1	Table	$1
1	Lamp	$.25
1	Stove	$2
1	Gasoline stove and can	$10
7	Bedsteads (old)	$7
1	Stand	$1
1	Lamp	$.50
40 yds.	Carpet	$4
4	Sofas	$3
20 yds.	Carpet	$4
3	Stoves	$3
4	Washstands	$1
2	Stands	$.50
1	Lamp	$.25

Table 5.1. Copartnership of Daniel Yount and Andrew Yount, [Inventory, Including] Miscellaneous Wood, etc., 1891 (*cont.*)

Quantity	Description	Cost
4	?	$1
7	Chairs	$1.75
58 yds.	Rag carpet	$4
5	Chairs	$.75
1	Table and cover	$1
6	Straw ticks	$3
2	Straw mattresses	$.50
10	Blankets (old)	$10
12	Feather pillows & cases	$6
6	Comforts	$6
12	Sheets	$3
8	Bed spreads	$4
10	Towels	$1
4	Bowls, Pitchers & Soap dishes	$2
1	Stove	$1
1	Extension table, old style	$2.50
2	Tables	$2
20	Chairs	$5
1	Washing machine	$2
1	Clothes wringer	$1
2	Side tables	$1
2	Tubs and washboards	$1
1	Flour chest	$1
4	?	$1
1	Cook stove	$5
1	Set kitchen utensils	$3
7	Table cloths	$3
4	Table cloths	$2
1	Lot window shades	$4
1	Blinds	$.25
1	Clothes basket	$.25
	Horse feed at stable corn & hay	$5

Source: Data compiled and transcribed from the Montgomery County Clerk's Office Probate Files.

Figure 5.1. Men Sorting and Grading Raw Wool Fleeces, American Woolen Company, Boston. From American Woolen Company, *The Manufacture of Woolen Textiles*, 1912.

The first steps in processing wool got the workers covered in lanolin. The mills tended to be dark and dirty, and there was plenty of lint in the mill to be recaptured and woven into blankets. Sorting the wool into the proper grade (Figure 5.2) ensured that it was used for the best purpose. Yount saw the customers bring it in, and the workers sorted the fleece and weighed it before taking it to the mill, where they placed the wool into vats or tanks. Sorting the wool resulted in its being sent on different paths, to become either wool blankets or clothing. This was work machines could not perform because it called for judgment.

The workers washed or scoured the wool, usually with lye soap, before rinsing it. After one rinsing the workers dyed the wool blue, light blue, or black before they rinsed it again.[19] The workers who did this labor-intensive job finished the day filthy, with their aprons and dresses spattered with wool, soap, and dye.

Figure 5.2. Women Sorting Wool, American Woolen Company, Boston. From American Woolen Company, *The Manufacture of Woolen Textiles*, 1912.

In the South building, Lee described placing the wool on drying screens, where large fans circulated hot air.[20] The workers thoroughly dried the wool, because moist wool tangled in the machines. During the summer, workers found this to be hot steamy work in the moist Sugar Creek valley; however, during the winter months it was a more pleasant task. Because wool holds so much moisture even when it feels dry to the touch, this task took a considerable amount of time. This quality of feeling dry when it is holding moisture was a great quality for cold-weather clothing.

Lee remembered taking the wool to the third floor of the North building, where workers picked and carded it. In the not-too-distant-past, workers had performed this process, but now the workers used the power of the mill to accomplish it. The workers fed the wool into the mechanical picker, which used rotating cylinders and hooked teeth to effectively remove the burrs and other foreign material from the wool missed in the washing process. Next the workers fed the wool into the carding or "cording" machine; the carding

Figure 5.3. Man Carding Wool, American Woolen Company, Boston. From American Woolen Company, *The Manufacture of Woolen Textiles*, 1912.

machine (Figure 5.3) took the free and loose wool and aligned the fibers into loose bundles about an inch in diameter. [21] This work, too, had once been completed solely by hand, but now the machines did the work of multiple laborers. The machines needed to be carefully loaded to prevent jamming.

The workers fed this rope or "cord" onto spools that were about ten inches in diameter.[22] Workers had once had this job of hand carding wool, but now workers kept the machines running and harvested the wool ready for spinning. The workers applied their specialized technical knowledge to keep the product flowing from the factory.

Younger or less-skilled workers moved the various wool products around the mill. Workers took the spools of wool to the spinning jacks or "mules," which held several large spools (Figure 5.4).[23]

The new spinning machinery owned by the competition made the Yount Mill old-fashioned. More modern machines needed less attention from workers. Lee noted that the spinning jacks held the same number of

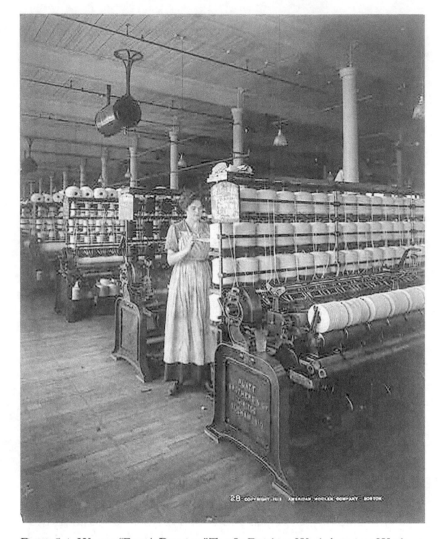

Figure 5.4. Woman "French Drawing," That Is, Finishing Wool, American Woolen Company, Boston. From American Woolen Company, *The Manufacture of Woolen Textiles*, 1912.

bobbins directly in front of the spools lined up in rows, illustrating that it took a complex machine to replicate a simple human process (Figure 5.5). The worker had to keep moving to stay on top of all the machines working at the same time. "These bobbins traveled back and forth at a very high speed, twisting the yarn to the size of a thread."[24] The finished wool was almost ready for shipment. The fabric was used in many types of clothing.

Figure 5.5. Spinning Wool, American Woolen Company, Boston. From American Woolen Company, *The Manufacture of Woolen Textiles*, 1912.

Bobbin boys or girls replaced the filled bobbins with empty bobbins on this technical marvel. It was neither specifically hard nor dangerous work, but it did require the worker to be attentive. Underfilling a bobbin wasted bobbins. Overfilling bobbins was much worse, because of the danger of the thread tangling on the machine and then the workers having to untangle it. Inspecting the product (Figure 5.6) meant that no flaws made it to the consumer. The mill's reputation was one of its most important attributes.

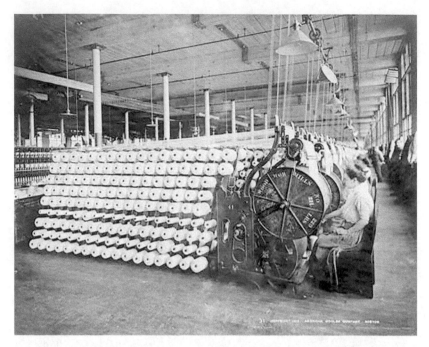

Figure 5.6. Woman Inspecting Wool Thread, American Woolen Company, Boston. From American Woolen Company, *The Manufacture of Woolen Textiles*, 1912.

The automated looms in the mill at Lowell, Massachusetts, worked at full speed. Workers tended the machines to replace bobbins, fix broken threads, and remove the finished product.[25] Workers took the filled bobbins to the South building, where Mr. Dansmore, Harry Shanklin, or Claude Stonebreaker wove the threadlike wool into cloth on one of the three looms. The men lived in dread of a shuttle malfunction causing a common flaw in the material that resulted in their losing production time. Repairing a shuttle often required a man to spend half the day just to retie the warp. Since each operator earned money by the yard, time for repairs meant that there was less money to take home to his family at the end of his pay period. The Younts sold no damaged goods in their store.

After weaving the cloth, a worker wound it on drums and returned it to the basement of the North building. All material was subject to inspection, and the workers allowed only high-quality cloth to leave the Yount Mill. Lee remembered that the cloth passed over rollers for inspection by women who picked lint from the cloth with tweezers before placing the cloth on bolts. This was the last chance to catch problems before the cloth went to the store. After workers placed the cloth on bolts, it could go anywhere via railroad.

Lee recalled workers taking the bolts of cloth to the first-floor tailor shop, where head tailor Tom Harp cut and sewed it into suits of clothes for the men and women who brought the wool to the mill. To cater to changing consumer tastes, the Younts added this service to the mill. For customers to gett clothing produced at the factory using wool provided to the factory seemed advantageous. Offering fitted clothing, but not having to do that in the customers' homes was also advantageous. Since the Younts added cotton to the merchandise offered in their store, they also made shirts to accompany the suits.

Lee recalled that the suits went to the pressers, who steam-pressed the articles of clothing for the customers. The Younts tried this innovation to meet changing consumer demands in the clothing industry. Workers equipped a room with sheet-metal walls and ceilings so that the steam would not damage the structure of the building. In addition to the metal sheeting, technical changes included adding a steam line to bring steam from the boiler. The workers steamed the garments on forms representing the shapes of the bodies of the consumers to help the garments hold their shapes and fit across time. Wet finishing by steaming the cloth made for a much more tailored fit for the wearer. For the worker it was hot work, with the danger of burns (Figure 5.7).

The Younts bought the remainder of the wool cloth and received a share of the finished wool cloth for sale in their store. They made money when customers exchanged raw wool for processed wool in the form of a share or when they sold the woolen products from their store. They also could make some money when they sold their goods to other stores in the region. And they did business directly with customers through the mail. On a commissioned item, such as a suit, there would be another possibility for charging for this service.

The workers swept the lint from the looms that settled on the floor, walls, machines, and window ledges for reprocessing through the carding machine and spinning jacks. Having a shorter fiber would tend to make a thick and fluffy texture. Lee called this processed lint "shoddy," and the workers wove it into blankets.[26] Neither the workers nor the customers thought of this as poor-quality material. Unscrupulous war profiteers gave the word its present connotation. The loom the workers used for these

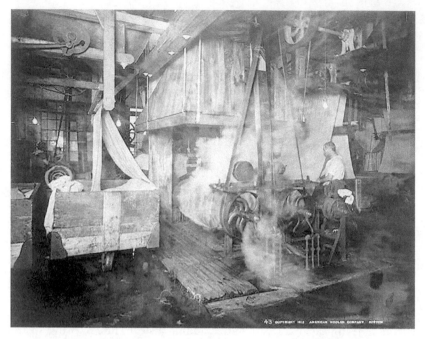

Figure 5.7. Man Wet Finishing, That Is, Steaming Cloth, American Woolen Company, Boston. From American Woolen Company, *The Manufacture of Woolen Textiles*, 1912.

blankets was a special large loom located in the South building, and the workers wove many floral designs, including rose or lily patterns, into the blankets.

Lee recollected that when he worked at the mill during the Spanish-American War Yountsville prospered. The US Government ordered the light and dark-blue cloth for uniforms for the servicemen.[27] Unfortunately, no primary sources can support this claim for the Civil War. There are no documents from either Indiana or the federal War Department or Office of the Quartermaster. A third party with a contract for the government might have purchased fabric and made it into uniforms, or individuals might have purchased cloth for their uniforms, just as Caleb Mills purchased a Yount's Mill blanket for his son to carry into the Civil War. It seems hard to believe that neither Lew Wallace, working as Governor Morton's adjunct general in Indianapolis, nor Senator Henry S. Lane would have gotten a wool-mill contract for their constituents working four miles from the politicians' homes.

Because of the long workday, the workers were often hungry before their shift ended.[28] During the summer, there could be sun from 5:00 a.m. until 10 p.m., which made for a long day, and a diet high in starch would leave them hungry long before they could break their fast. They would have been hungry not from cruelty or want of food, but because of a lack of knowledge about good nutrition that was pervasive in that region during that period.

GRAFFITI IN THE MILL

When there was extra time during the day, it was a common practice for employees of Yount's Mill to graffiti the walls of the mill with their names. Shortly after the 1864 brick millhouse was completed and put into operation, the mill workers began using the white-washed plaster interior walls as a canvas for graffiti. The name of the company is proudly drawn on the wall (Figure 5.8) in a Fraktur script reflecting the Yount family's background.

Figure 5.8. "Yount Woolen" Written on a Millhouse Wall. Photo taken by Mark Groover, Department of Anthropology, Ball State University, Muncie, Indiana.

Other signatures graced the walls from later times. Consisting mainly of workers' names, dates, tallies, and a smaller number of sketches, the workplace graffiti continued from shortly after the new mill-house opened in 1864 until the mill closed in the early 1900s.[29]

Graffiti was categorized into two main context groups, locational context and functional context. Regarding general locational context, three main graffiti categories were represented by landscape-, home-, and work/occupation–related locations. Landscape graffiti occurs in areas away from peoples' homes or workplaces. Tags on train cars in the twenty-first century illustrate mobile landscape graffiti in the modern era. Another locational context for graffiti was homes, such as marks created by children in classical-period cultures. Perhaps the most prevalent locational category of graffiti was represented by work- and occupation/institutional–related graffiti. Graffiti drawn by laborers at public buildings, as well as marks drawn by inmates, soldiers, students, or hospital patients illustrate occupation/institutional–related graffiti. This category was prevalent because people spent much of their time at their work-places, and they were more inclined to create graffiti outside of their homes as a form of collective communication.

In addition to the category of locational context, graffiti was also categorized by the function of the content. Memorialization graffiti, social commentary, and belief-related graffiti were three underlying content categories. The most prevalent function of graffiti was focused on memorialization, with people seeking to be remembered or memorialized via graffiti. Through the act of making graffiti, they were making small marks that survived them and to some degree preserved their names—their existence—for others to see in the future.[30] This was a sentiment that seemed to be restricted not to a time period or a medium of graffiti but rather to be an underlying universal cultural characteristic of humans— the tendency to mark places that people visited or inhabited. The act of inscribing one's name on a surface memorialized one in that time and place and set the stage for the interaction of that inscription with generations of people who came into contact with it.[31] The quality of the man's face in Figure 5.9 looks as if it had been traced on the wall with midcentury muttonchop whiskers and the name "Shaffer" written across the drawing. It could easily have been a portrait of one of the workers.

In the well-preserved graffiti of Pompeii, individuals took the spoken word and imbued it with "a presence which would last beyond the corporeal presence of the writer."[32] Inscriptions carved into the stone walls

Figure 5.9. Profile of a Man's Face: An Example of the Category "Image Graffiti." Photo taken by Mark Groover, Department of Anthropology, Ball State University, Muncie, Indiana.

of the Tower of London were interpreted as prisoners' "defense against anonymity"—their way to escape the ultimate punishment of being forgotten in death.[33] It was the essence of human existence that was preserved in graffiti—United States Civil War soldiers from Wisconsin, hospitalized in Virginia, wrote their names on the ceiling; Soviet conscripts in mid-twentieth century Germany filled the cellar walls of barracks with not only their names but the cities and towns that they called home—thus making sure that physical markers of their lives remained, regardless of the perils that awaited them in war.[34]

In addition to memorialization marks, graffiti related to social commentary was another functional graffiti type noted in the previous studies. Interestingly, this type of graffiti was often, but not always, functionally the opposite of memorialization marks. Social commentary graffiti was usually anonymous and was intended to serve as a form of social discourse or criticism related to specific topics. The topics related to social commentary graffiti were often political or social in nature or were related to sexuality or occupational hierarchies. In addition to being anonymous since the content was often inflammatory, social discourse graffiti was also usually marked in public places and was meant to be viewed by the masses.

Finally, a third functional type of graffiti consisted of belief-related marks. Archetypally illustrated by cave art, this type of graffiti had a specific context and culturally related meaning, was often inscribed in private or belief-associated spiritual spaces, and was based on icons or symbols rather than being expressed via written or text statements. Whereas text-based memorials or social commentary statements were more readily interpreted by modern scholars, belief-based symbols drawn by pre-literate cultures were enigmatic, difficult to understand with certainty, and in the final analysis perhaps unknowable.

These categories provided a lens for understanding the graffiti at Yount's Mill. In terms of location, the graffiti was work-based and placed on walls in high-traffic areas (Graph 5.1), one of which was the entrance to the workplace. Functionally, the graffiti at Yount's Mill fell within the memorialization category. The markings, while in a public space, did not relate to social commentary or beliefs. A majority of the markings were names; individuals carved their identities into the walls of a building where they spent most of their days, inscribing themselves so that future generations could know that they were there.

Enoch Lawton was one of those workers. Enoch first started working at the mill as an adolescent, replacing the spools of thread on the looms. His hands, unlike those of the adults who worked at the mill, could reach into the loom to change the spools. When he was twelve years old, he signed his name on the millhouse wall along with the date, 1878. Enoch worked at Yount's Mill for the rest of his life. When he retired, he lived the remainder of his days on the mill property. Throughout his life he signed his name and the date several times on the millhouse walls. Many names appeared on the walls of Yount's Mill (Figures 5.10 and 5.11). They were almost an inventory of the workers there.

Daniel Yount signed his name, next to that of worker John Sullivan, with equations and dates nearby. In some places the walls were nearly full. The graffiti of Enoch and the others who worked at the mill took place on the first floor, the second floor, and the stairway.[35] The graffiti was located in general workspaces that were clearly visible to the rest of the workplace, not hidden as if they represented unsolicited acts.[36] Since the mill walls were a very public, employment-related space, there were not examples of

Graph 5.1. Graffiti in the Yount Mill, by Category

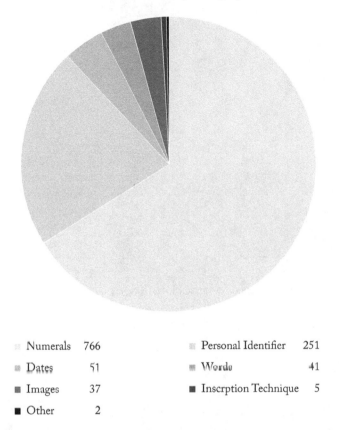

Numerals	766	Personal Identifier	251
Dates	51	Words	41
Images	37	Inscrption Technique	5
Other	2		

Source: Jessica L. Clark, graduate student.
Note: Functional categories of all identified instances of graffiti in the Yount Mill.

protest or social commentary–related content or sexually oriented content. The "public consumption" nature of the mill graffiti illustrated its function in a work-related public space. Graffiti by function categories identified numbers as most prevalent, followed by signatures, images, words, and dates made up the last sixth of the pie graph seen in Graph 5.1. Males eagerly wrote their names on the walls. Women were more hesitant to claim the real estate, even if unidentified, and men tended to sign the mill walls more frequently than did women (Graph 5.2).

Spatially, the graffiti signatures clustered on the first floor in the northwest corner of the mill near the west door, which served as a main

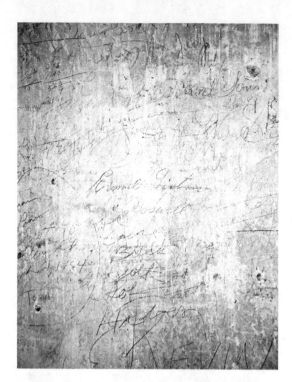

Figure 5.10. Name Graffiti Inscribed on a Mill Wall by Workers at the Yount Mill. Photo taken by Mark Groover, Department of Anthropology, Ball State University, Muncie, Indiana.

Figure 5.11. Signature of Daniel Yount, Mill Owner, among Those of His Employees on a Mill Wall. Includes date inscriptions and addition figures. Photo taken by Mark Groover, Department of Anthropology, Ball State University, Muncie, Indiana.

Graph 5.2. Name Inscriptions in the Yount Mill, by Gender

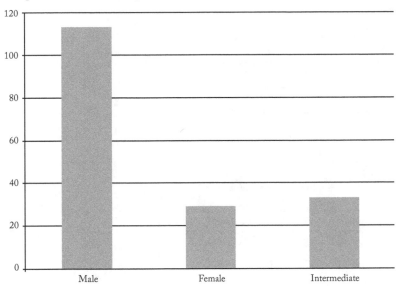

Source: Jessica L. Clark, graduate student.
Note: Sex determination based on name identification, cross-referenced with Yountsville census records (where available), 1850–70. "Indeterminate" indicates an undecipherable first name, a first initial solely, or a set of initials.

entrance to the building.[37] Managers, owners, and employees signed and dated the main graffiti panel next to the west door. The number of marks in this area suggested that the northwest corner of the first floor was an informal registry, perhaps a worker tradition, as an initiatory gesture upon new employment. Workers may have continued the behavior when they changed work stations or floor assignments over time. The graffiti was scattered across two floors and all four walls. It appeared neither on the ceiling nor the floor. On the first floor the graffiti tends to be located on the northwest wall. The other three walls were about equal in terms of graffiti (Graphs 5.3 and 5.4).

Enoch was one of many workers and individuals to inscribe his name onto the wall of Yount's Mill multiple times. The walls were never painted, and there was no indication that this act was one of degradation by any mill worker. Yount's Mill was a community of individuals who lived and worked together in shared space. The graffiti on the walls of Yount's Mill was an example of the communal atmosphere that Daniel Yount cultivated.

Graph 5.3. Inscription Distribution in the Yount Mill, by Location

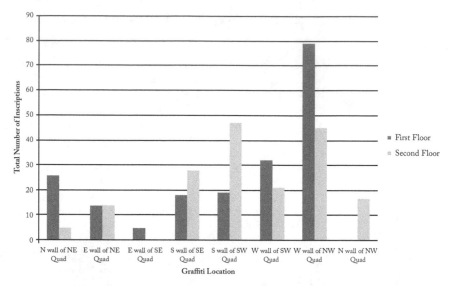

Source: Jessica L. Clark, graduate student.

Graph 5.4. First-Floor Graffiti Distribution, by Quadrant

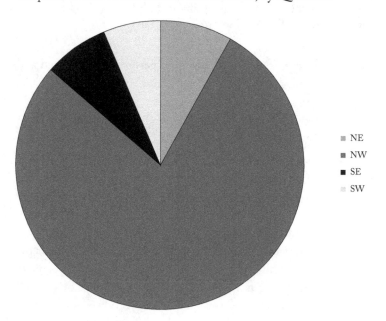

Source: Jessica L. Clark, graduate student.

THE WORKPLACE

For Jennie Hays Murray and the other mill girls, talking to other workers for pleasure was probably not an option during the sunrise-to-sundown year-round six-day work week. Once the engineer turned on the mill for the day, the turbine transferred power through gears to the line shaft, and the line shaft passed mechanical energy to each machine. Jennie used a canvas or leather belt to bring her machines onto the line shaft, and by looking at just one machine Jennie saw what happens when a mechanical loom operated. The loom shoots the shuttle from one side of the loom to the other through the shed, then the heddle slams down the row of cloth the shuttle just left before the harnesses move the shed and the process repeats itself.[38] Since it is an automated machine, this process happens more quickly than it takes to read this sentence before the shuttle flies through the shed again and the process is repeated. All of this sounded like a toaster falling down a flight of stairs, but when the mill was running at capacity, the three floors magnified the sound and the entire building, including Jennie, would shudder and vibrate. The crashing of the machines drowned out all other sound, leaving Jennie to endure the vibration, headaches, and hearing damage that were parts of millwork.

When employees were not at work, the boarding house rules were very strict, keeping the men separated from the women.[39] The Younts' Victorian Methodist morality and the desire to prevent time lost from work due to pregnancy contributed to the separation, as did the length of the workday. Men and women each had their own tasks, and if they were together, they were not working. In a rural community, the mill and boarding house had to keep a good reputation or workers would not come or stay. The managers efficiently controlled the mill.

LEISURE TIME

On some occasion around 1870, Daniel's son and part owner of the mill, Andrew Yount, had his photo taken with Jennie and four other women from the mill in a formal studio setting (Figure 5.12). Andrew had a beard, no mustache, hair on the side of his head, a wool suit, a metal pin clasping his tie, legs crossed at the knees, and hands—one over the other—in his lap.

Figure 5.12. Andrew Yount with Five "Loom Girls" Who Worked at the Mill, 1870s. One woman (far right, front row) has the following note written over her image: "Mother Jessie Hays Murray." She is not listed in the census records. From the Marian Morrison Local History Collection at the Crawfordsville District Public Library, Crawfordsville, Indiana.

He was surrounded on either side by women, all seated, and three women standing behind them. To the right of Andrew sat Jennie Hays Murray, with her hands folded in her lap, and to the left of Andrew sat a woman who had a bracelet on her left hand, which was resting on the chair arm, while her right hand was laid across her lap. The woman standing on his right had an arm on Murray's shoulder, and the woman standing at the left had her hand on the shoulder of the woman seated in front of her. All the women have their hair pulled back and curled, their dresses all go from high necks to their wrists and the floor. Four women are in lace collars, three women have ribbons around their necks, and three have large bows at their necks.

At roughly the same time, but not on the same day, Andrew Yount posed for another formal studio photograph (Figure 5.13). This time he was in the front row on the left side with six women. He was wearing a wool suit and vest, and his hands were folded in his lap. The woman next to Andrew had her left hand in her lap and her right hand behind her.

Figure 5.13. Andrew Yount with Six Mill Girls, 1870s. From the Marian Morrison Local History Collection, Crawfordsville District Public Library, Crawfordsville, Indiana.

The woman in the center had her head resting on her right hand and her left hand in her lap. The woman at the right end of the front row had her arms crossed, and the women in the back row had their arms down at their sides, though the one in the middle had her left hand on the shoulder of the woman to her right. Of the six women, four were in dark dresses, the one in the center of the back row had a light stripe in her dress, and one was in a light-colored dress. Five of the women had decorations in their hair, four wore bows at their necks, and at least three wore earrings. All six women had lace collars, ribbons around their necks, and their hair pulled back and curled.

The formal photos contrast with an informal photo of people taken in front of the mill (Figure 5.14). There were thirteen men pictured, two in coats, one with a hat and the other with a tie. Two men were in shirtsleeves showing suspenders, and all of the others were wearing vests. Two boys

Figure 5.14. Mill Workers in Front of the Mill, c. 1882. This picture shows twenty-four men, women, and children standing in front of Yount Mill. From the Marian Morrison Local History Collection, Crawfordsville District Public Library, Crawfordsville, Indiana.

with vests were in the middle of the photo, while two other boys in shirt-sleeves sat in the open fourth-floor window of the brick mill with both sashes gone. Nine women or girls were in the photograph; five of them wore stained aprons. The lower sashes of the Annex were open, and two windows of the frame mill were visible and open.

The mill was dark, dirty, and very crowded. It seemed impossible for people to move through the space. Another informal photo of the second-floor interior of the Annex shows five women standing, each wearing a dress with an apron (Figure 5.15). At least one power loom was visible, and the power transmission system was visible from the belts on the ceiling and the belts running from floor to ceiling. There were many tools on the walls and on the posts. The room had a cluttered, tightly packed look; it did not look as if there was much space to move between the machines. Workers needed to move carefully between them to make sure they did not entangle themselves in the mill workings.

MILL FAMILIES

The 1850 census documented not only the Yount family, but also other families, clustered by residences (Table 5.2). It showed Allen Yount's family

Figure 5.15. Yount Woolen Mill Interior. From the Marian Morrison Local History Collection, Crawfordsville District Public Library, Crawfordsville, Indiana.

with boarders and Daniel's family living in their own home. And fortunately the census records gave life to the mill workers, who were faceless to us. They had no names, families, jobs, ages, or places of origin without the census to list them. The mill families were neither anonymous nor forgotten, but it was hard to tell why mill workers came or stayed during the changes that came with industrialization. "Most of the work is done by the piece, the most skillful earning, in the palmy day of the trade from $8 to $15 per week."[40] This was certainly a better wage than could be found at many locations during this time and reflects the demand for wool products during the Civil War. This also contrasted with the wage of a Union soldier, who made $13 per month. The mill drew good people to the community. "It has naturally attracted working people of the very best class, the sons and daughters of the neighboring farmers."[41] No mention of immigrants was made, and the silence about nonlocal people was probably indicative of how they were viewed by the local folk. Maybe between public school and life at the mill they felt they were hedging their bets against the future.

Table 5.2. Yount Mill Families, 1850

Last Name	First Name	Age	Notes	Location of Birth
Yount	Allen	42	manufacturer	OH
Yount	Mary	30		OH
Yount	William	17	manufacturer	IN
Yount	Anny	8		IN
Yount	Isabel	6		IN
Yount	Albert	2		IN
Smith	Phoebe	24		OH
Smith	Amelia	19		OH
Find	Mary	19		IN
Lebo	William		carder	PA
Walters	Sarah	17		IN
Yount	Daniel	43	manufacturer	OH
Yount	Sara	38		MD
Yount	Mary	14		IN
Yount	Andrew	12		IN
Yount	John	10		IN
Yount	Anna	5		IN
Smith	Hanna	30		OH
Stott	Alfred		manufacturer	England

Source: Data compiled from the United States Census, 1850.
Note: Horizontal rule separates households.

The Smith Family

In 1850, the Smith sisters from Ohio, thirty-year-old Hanna, twenty-four-year-old Phoebe, and nineteen-year-old Amilia were boarding with Allen Yount's family. Ten years later, Phoebe Smith and her sister Amilia were living at the boarding house, but Polly Smith was twenty-five, and another sister, Rebecca Smith, was taking care of eight-year-old Robert Lee. By 1870, Phoebe A. Smith was listed as forty but had $2,000 in personal property, and fifteen-year-old Mary C. Smith, of Ohio, also worked in the woolen factory. In the next census, fifty-four-year-old Phoebe Smith was still boarding and working in the woolen factory. Phoebe was truly a spinster, and according to the census, as she reported it to the census-taker, her age changed across the years, perhaps for job security. The family seems to have had a positive relationship with the Yount family, and the Younts always seemed to have room for another Smith to work at the mill.

The Chaffer Family

The 1860 census really told a lot about the lives of the mill workers and their families; it included birth locations and the amount of property each family had (Table 5.3). In that census, forty-four-year-old William Chaffer, a laborer from Yorkshire, England, had fifty dollars in personal property. He had met his thirty-seven-year-old wife, Elizabeth, in Pennsylvania, and they had nine-year-old Annie, seven-year-old Mary, five-year-old Martha, four-year-old Jane, and three-year-old Jackson while they were in Pennsylvania. Ten years later, William's personal property was valued at $600 and his real estate at $1,000. Mary E. worked at the wool factory. William and Elizabeth also had a thirteen-year-old son, John M. Ten years had passed, and now William Chaffer was sixty-four and working in the factory with his children May and John. William's wife, Elizabeth, worked at home.

The Dean Family

Some people appeared just for a moment in the census records, and some were probably never captured in the census records. The Dean family may at one time have consisted of a mother and daughter or granddaughter. In 1860, Levi Dean appeared in the census and showed up as being from Connecticut, and in 1900 May Dean appeared as a twenty-one-year-old weaver from Indiana.

The Fink Family

In 1860, in the area, but not at the mill, were thirty-seven-year-old Rueben (wrongly spelled "Rewben" in the census), and his twenty-nine-year-old wife, Lucinda Fink. They had met in Ohio, where he had learned to be a carpenter. When they came to Indiana, they had thirteen-year-old Isadora, eleven-year-old Irwin, nine-year-old Cyrus, seven-year-old Commodore, and four-year-old Willard (wrongly spelled "Williard" in the census), along

Table 5.3. Residents of Yountsville, 1860

Last Name	First Name	Age	Notes	Real Estate Property	Personal Property	Location of Birth
Yount	Daniel	53	clothier	$10,000	$15,000	OH
Yount	Sarah	48				MD
Yount	John	20	domestic			IN
Yount	Annie	14				IN
Russel	Rhoda	26			$300	IN
Russel	Byron	8				IN
Russel	Lidda	6				IN
Gilkey	Alice	7				IN
Gilkey	Allan	5				IN
Yount	Andrew	22	laborer			IN
Smith	Pheobe	32	domestic			IN
Smith	Polly	25	domestic			IN
Robinson	Luiza	25	domestic			IN
Vaughn	Annie	23	domestic			IN
Price	Manerva	21	domestic			IN
Smith	Amelia	28	domestic			IN
Smith	Rebecca		domestic			IN
Lee	Robert	8				NY
Mathewman	Nathan	41	clothier		$50	Hudersfield, England
Mathewman	Grace	43				Parsley, England
Mathewman	David	11				PA
Mathewman	Benjamine	5				PA

Table 5.3. Residents of Yountsville, 1860 (cont.)

Last Name	First Name	Age	Notes	Real Estate Property	Personal Property	Location of Birth
Yount	William	26		$300	$100	IN
Yount	Sarah	25				IN
Yount	Clara	6				
Yount	Charles	3				
Yount	Allen	1				
Love	Samuel	25	laborer		$300	PA
Mathewman	Enoch	33	laborer		$300	Yorkshire, England
Dean	Levi	33	laborer			PA
Marshall	Mary	18	domestic			IL
Henry	William	18	machinist		$200	Yorkshire, England
Henry	James	45	machinist		$200	County of Kildore, Ireland
Henry	Briget	45				County of Kildore, Ireland
Henry	Mary	16				Yorkshire, England
Henry	Catharine	12				MA
Henry	Jane	8				OH
Love	Eli	32	laborer			DE
Chaffer	William	44	laborer		$50	Yorkshire, England
Chaffer	Bitty	37				PA
Chaffer	Annie	9				PA
Chaffer	Mary	7				PA
Chaffer	Martha	5				PA
Chaffer	Jane	4				PA
Chaffer	Jackson	3				PA

Table 5.3. Residents of Yountsville, 1860 (*cont.*)

Last Name	First Name	Age	Notes	Real Estate Property	Personal Property	Location of Birth
Not at mill:						
Stubbins	Samuel	21	Potter	$250	$100	IN
Stubbins	Nancy	21				IN
Fink	Rewben	37	Carpenter	$600	$200	OH
Fink	Lucinda	29				OH
Fink	Isadora	13				IN
Fink	Irwin	11				IN
Fink	Cyrus	9				IN
Fink	Commodore	7				IN
Fink	Williard	4				IN
Fink	Francis (female)	2				IN
Fink	Mary	2 mo.				IN

Source: Data compiled and transcribed from the US Census, 1860.
Note: Horizontal rules separate households. Households associated with the mill are listed first.

with their two-year-old daughter Francis and two-month-old May. Rueben had managed to acquire $600 in real estate and $200 in personal property. Ten years later, the Fink family continued to be in the community;
Reuben J., the carpenter, had real estate valued at $5,200 and $320 in personal property. His son Ivan was a schoolteacher, Cyrus was a farm laborer,
fifteen-year-old Commodore worked in the woolen factory, and thirteen-
year-old Willard was the tollgate keeper. Ella M. was nine; Floyd was
seven, daughter Adda was five, and Clarence was two. By 1900 Catherine
Fink, forty-three, was a farmer from Indiana, but her son, twenty-one-
year-old Edson, was a farm laborer from Indiana. Carrie E. was a twenty-
three-year-old bundler at the woolen mill, and at the same time Ethel
(Fink) Elliott was living in the area.

The Love Family

In 1860 thirty-two-year-old Eli Love, a laborer from Delaware, boarded
with Henry and Bridget James. At the same time twenty-five-year-old
Samuel Love from Pennsylvania boarded with William Yount. By 1870
Samuel had married twenty-nine-year-old Hoosier Minerva Love, and
they had two-year-old Allen Y. while living in Indiana. Samuel worked in
the woolen factory and had $600 in real estate, and $205 in personal property. By 1880 Allen worked in the mill. Eva, their eight-year-old daughter,
was born in Missouri, but their six-year-old son James A., was born in Indi-
ana. By 1900 Allen Love was a dyer; his wife, Mary E., was from Indiana.
Their daughter Alisha was six years old, and Lein H. was one month old.
Melissa Hayworth was Mary E.'s Indiana mother, and Jeru Stalmaker was
Allen's Indiana niece. They all lived together, but at the same time, Samuel
Love was the boss dyer and still lived with Minerva. Andrew Love was a
twenty-six-year-old spinner at the woolen mills and was from Indiana, and
Lula Grace was his twenty-six-year-old boarder, also from Indiana.

The Mathewman Family

In 1860 Nathan Mathewman, a forty-one-year-old clothier, came from
Hersfield, England, with his forty-three-year-old wife, Grace, from Pars-
ley, England. As a clothier, he had $50 in personal property, which he had
accumulated, perhaps while his two sons, eleven-year-old David and five-

year-old Benjamin, were being born in Pennsylvania. At the same time, thirty-three-year-old Enoch Mathewman, from Yorkshire, England, owned $300 of personal property.

The Stubbins Family

By 1860 Samuel Thomas and Nancy Stubbins, both twenty-one, and both from Indiana were not at the mill then, but they were in the area. He was working as a potter with $250 in real estate and $100 in personal property, but by 1870 and thirty-years old he gave up pottery to work in the woolen factory. Their situation had declined, he had personal property of $200 and to support his family he had gone to work in the mill. They had six-year-old Martha D. and eight-month-old Joseph E. At the same time the Stubbins brothers, twenty-four-year-old Alex and twenty-two-year-old James M., were both from Indiana. Alex worked in the woolen factory and James clerked in the factory office. By 1880, Alex had left the area, James M. married Clara, and at thirty-two and twenty-six, respectively, they have two-month-old Floyd.

The Price Family

In 1860 Manerva Price was twenty-one and lived at the boarding house, and in 1870, sixteen-year-old Mary M. Price from Indiana boarded with the Love family. They could have been sisters or cousins, or Mary could have been Manerva's daughter.

The Clements Family

In the spring of 1866, twenty-four-year-old Henry Clements came from Armagh, an area in Northern Ireland known for growing and weaving flax, to work in Yount's Mill. Life was good, and he summoned his brothers and parents to join him in Indiana.[42] In the 1870 census, Henry had $100 in personal property, and his twenty-two-year-old wife, Mary, was from England. When they got to Indiana, they had one-month-old James. The family stayed in Indiana along the banks of Sugar Creek, continuing to make a living from the power of the fast-flowing water even in the twenty-first century.

The Campbell Family

The 1870 census (Table 5.4) showed a much larger workforce than the mill had employed ten years earlier, and it also showed how workers crowded the boarding house and lived with other families. The Campbell family appeared in the 1870 census, when John Campbell was seventeen, had come from Ohio, and worked in the woolen factory. The next mention of the family occurred in 1900, when Talbot Campbell was a twenty-one-year-old spinner who had been born in Indiana. Joan Campbell, his eighteen-year-old sister, was also a spinner and had been born in Indiana. The Campbell family represented the draw of migration from within the nation and the opportunity the mill provided immigrants to put down roots and become Hoosiers.

The Sullivan Family

Michael and Mary Sullivan had come from Ireland in 1870; he was forty-six, worked in the woolen factory, and had $300 in personal property. She was thirty-four. Their children were all born in Indiana, including nine-year-old Johannah, eight-year-old Margaret, seven-year-old John, five-year-old Mary, two-year-old Catherine, and four-month-old Timothy. A decade later, twenty-year-old Johannah had consumption, a hazard of working in textile mills, but seventeen-year-old Margaret, fourteen-year-old Mary, twelve-year-old Catherine, and ten-year-old Timothy all worked in the woolen factory. Michael Jr. was six, Ellen was one, and Lawrence was three months old. John was not present. By 1900, Michael was being called Harshall Sullivan, and at seventy-five years old he was still working as a wool sorter. The mill workers chose to come to Yount's Mill and liked it enough to stay, some for a short time and others long enough to raise a family. These families lived through the rapid changes in industrialization and school reform.

The Hall Family

In 1870, James W. Hall, fifty-five, was the clerk in the woolen mill office; he held $800 in personal property. He and his thirty-three-year-old wife, Clare W., had both been born in Ohio, and ten years later, they were still married.

Table 5.4. Residents of Yountsville, 1870

Last Name	First Name	Age	Notes	Real Estate Property	Personal Property	Location of Birth
Worl	Atwill	58	farmer	$500	$910	KY
Worl	Martha	47	can't write			OH
Worl	Lizzie	22	works in woolen factory			IN
Worl	Harriett	18				IN
Albertson	William W.	50	wagon maker	$2000	$395	OH
Albertson	Rhoda M.	46				IN
Albertson	A. T. (male)		blacksmith		$400	IN
Albertson	Wallace	20	can't read or write			IN
Albertson	Thomas W.	17	works in woolen factory			IN
Albertson	Lew M.	8				IN
Yount	William P.	36		$800	$200	IN
Yount	Sarah A.	35	factory			PA
Yount	Clara	16				IN
Yount	Charley H.	13				IN
Yount	Allen C.	11				IN
Yount	Nettie B.	6				IN
Yount	Andrew G.	3				IN
Yount	Walter	11 months				
Walters	Aaron	42	boot & shoemaker	$1200	$2500	PA

Table 5.4. Residents of Yountsville, 1870 (*cont.*)

Last Name	First Name	Age	Notes	Real Estate Property	Personal Property	Location of Birth
Miller	George S.	60	works in woolen factory		$100	KY
Miller	Nancy	64				NC
Stubbins	Samuel Thomas	31	works in woolen factory		$200	IN
Stubbins	Nancy J.	30				IN
Stubbins	Martha D.	6				IN
Stubbins	Joseph E.	8 months			IN	
Hall	James W.	55	clerks in woolen mill office	$800		OH
Hall	Clara W.	33				OH
Yount	Daniel	62	wool manufacturer	$45,000	$50,000	OH
Yount	Sarah	58				MD
Yount	Andrew	32	wool manufacturer			IN
Yount	Annie	25				IN
Russle	Lydia	25		$500	$1000	IN
Chaffer	William W.	54	woolen factory	$1000	$600	England
Chaffer	Elizabeth	47				PA
Chaffer	Mary E.	17	woolen factory			PA
Chaffer	John M.	13				PA
Hirst	Edward T.	25	woolen factory			England
Hirst	Hannah	19				PA
Crampton	Thomas W.	23	painter			England

Table 5.4. Residents of Yountsville, 1870 (cont.)

Last Name	First Name	Age	Notes	Real Estate Property	Personal Property	Location of Birth
Lawton	George	39	works in woolen factory		$100	England
Lawton	Amelia	39				England
Lawton	William	6				PA
Lawton	Enoch	4				PA
Lawton	John E.	2				IN
Clements	Henry	26	works in woolen factory		$100	Ireland
Clements	Mary	22				England
Clements	James	1 month				IN
Sullivan	Michael	46	works in woolen factory		$300	Ireland
Sullivan	Mary	34				Ireland
Sullivan	Johannah	9				IN
Sullivan	Margret	8				IN
Sullivan	John	7				IN
Sullivan	Mary	5				IN
Sullivan	Catherine	2				IN
Sullivan	Timothy	4 months				IN
Love	Samuel	35	works in woolen factory	$600	$205	PA
Love	Minerva	29				IN
Love	Allen Y.	2				IN
Price	Mary M.	16				IN
Brown	Eliza	63	retired housekeeper			NJ

Table 5.4. Residents of Yountsville, 1870 (*cont.*)

Last Name	First Name	Age	Notes	Real Estate Property	Personal Property	Location of Birth
The following is a boarding house:						
Yount	John M.	30	woolen manufacturer	$1500	$300	IN
Yount	Mary A.	28				IN
Yount	Daniel M.	4				IN
Yount	Freddie	1				IN
Ballard	Sue C.		cook in boarding house			Foreign
Fleshar	Mary M.	19	waits on tables			OH
Smith	Mary C.	15	works in woolen factory			MA
Rutledge	C. W. (male)	15	works in woolen factory		$400	OH
Smith	Phebe A.	40	works in woolen factory		$2000	IN
Hays	Nancy A.	20	works in woolen factory			IN
Rhodes	Alice	20	works in woolen factory			IN
Powers	Eliza B.	35	works in woolen factory			IN
Dewert	Alice D.	20	works in woolen factory			IN
Miller	Mary E.	22	works in woolen factory			IN
Clark	Annie E.	22	works in woolen factory			IN
Clark	Edith	4				IN
Russell	Bryon R.	21	student at law			IN
Harlan	William	21	works in woolen factory			IN

Table 5.4. Residents of Yountsville, 1870 (*cont.*)

Last Name	First Name	Age	Notes	Real Estate Property	Personal Property	Location of Birth
Stubbines	Alex	24	works in woolen factory			IN
Stubbines	James M.	22	clerks in factory office			IN
Campbell	John	17	works in woolen factory			OH
Yount	Albert R.	21	works in woolen factory			IN
Swenney	Christopher	25	works in woolen factory			NY
Fink	Reuben J.	49	carpenter	$5200	$360	OH
Fink	Lucinda	40				OH
Fink	Ivan G.	21	school teacher		$350	IN
Fink	Cyrus	18	farm laborer			IN
Fink	Commodore	15	works in woolen factory			IN
Fink	Willard	13	toll gate keeper			IN
Fink	Ella M.	9				IN
Fink	Floyd	7				IN
Fink	Adda (female)	5				IN
Fink	Clarence	2				IN
Denman	Julia	20	retired housekeeper			IN

Source: Data compiled and transcribed from the US Census, 1870.
Note: Horizontal rules separate households.

The Hays Family

In 1870 Nancy A. Hays was twenty, had come from Indiana, and worked in the mill. At the same time, Jennie (Hays) Murray appeared in a photograph of mill workers. It was unusual to be documented by photo at this site, and Jennie was not documented by the census. Jennie and Nancy may have been either sisters or cousins.

The Hirst Family

In 1870 Edward T. Hirst was a twenty-five-year-old wool sorter and from England, and Hannah Hirst was from Pennsylvania and nineteen. Ten years later, they had a family; Pearly was ten, John W. was eight, and Winferd T. was six. At the same time, twenty-seven-year-old Charles Hirst, born in England, worked in the mill, but Mary, his twenty-three-year-old wife, had been born in Indiana. In 1900 Edmond Hirst, at fifty-seven, was a wool grader from England, and his fifty-nine-year-old wife was from Pennsylvania. Their son J. William, twenty-eight, was also a wool grader, and fifteen-year-old Mae was from Indiana, as was her brother.

The Lawton Family

In 1870 George and Amelia Lawton were both thirty-nine and had come from England; he worked in the woolen factory and had $100 in personal property. They had come through Pennsylvania, where they had had six-year-old William; they had had four-year-old Enoch and two-year-old John E. when they got to Indiana. Ten years later, both worked at the factory, as did their sons William and Enoch, and Sarah A.—a new addition to the family—was seven. In 1900, Will M. Lawton was the boss finisher at the woolen mill.

The 1880 census (Table 5.5) showed even more notes about how people were employed. The 1890 census burned, depriving scholars of insights as to how the mill looked near the time of Daniel's death.

The Miller Family

In 1870 Mary E. Miller was twenty-two, from Indiana, and worked in the mill. At the same time another family included sixty-year-old George S.

Table 5.5. Lives In and Outside of Yountsville, 1880

Last Name	First Name	Age	Notes	Location of Birth
Lives in Yountsville:				
Hirst	Edward	38	wool sorter	England
Hirst	Hannah	29		PA
Hirst	Pearle	10		IN
Hirst	John W.	8		IN
Hirst	Winferd T.	6		IN
Stubbin	James M.	32	clerk in woolen mill	IN
Stubbin	Clara	26		
Stubbin	Floyd	2 months		
Lawton	George	53	works in woolen factory	England
Lawton	Mary	50	works in woolen factory	England
Lawton	William	17	works in woolen factory	PA
Lawton	Enoch	15	works in woolen factory	PA
Lawton	John E.	12		IN
Lawton	Sarah A.	7		IN
Yount	Allen	21	Spinner in factory	IN
Yount	Nora	19		IN
Sullivan	Michael	55	works in woolen factory	Ireland
Sullivan	Mary	44		Ireland
Sullivan	Johanna	20	consumption	IN
Sullivan	Margaret	17	works in woolen factory	IN
Sullivan	Mary	14	works in woolen factory	IN
Sullivan	Catherine	12	works in woolen factory	IN
Sullivan	Timothy	10	works in woolen factory	IN
Sullivan	Michael Jr.	6		IN
Sullivan	Ellen	1		IN
Sullivan	Lawrence	3 months		IN
Yount	William	47	mechanic	PA
Yount	Sarah A.	45		IN
Yount	Charles	23	clerk at woolen mill store	IN
Yount	Nellie	16		IN
Yount	Andrew	12		IN
Yount	Walter	10		IN
Yount	Lozie	6		IN
Hall	James W.	65	Works in woolen factory	OH
Hall	Clara W.	43		OH
Yount	Albert	31	works in woolen factory	IN
Yount	Eva	21		IN

Table 5.5. Lives In and Outside of Yountsville, 1880 (*cont.*)

Last Name	First Name	Age	Notes	Location of Birth
Yount	Arthur	3		IN
Berkshire	Ella	28	boarder works in woolen factory	IN
Garland	Anna	28	boarder works in woolen factory	IN
Smith	Phoebe	54	boarder works in woolen factory	OH
Shaffer	William	64	wool sorter	England
Shaffer	Elizabeth	57		PA
Shaffer	Mary	25	woolen factory	PA
Shaffer	John	22	works in factory	PA
Love	Samuel	44	works in woolen factory	PA
Love	Minerva	41		IN
Love	Allen	12	works in woolen factory	IN
Love	Eva	8		MO
Love	James A.	6		IN
Yount	Daniel	72	proprietor of mill, widower	OH
Gilkey	Allen	26	grandchild	IN
Yount	Andrew	42	proprietor of mill	MD
Yount	Lydia	27		MD
Yount	Edison R.	6		IN
Yount	Mary	4		IN
Hirst	Charles	27	works in factory	England
Hirst	Mary	23		IN
Ridge	Charles		carpenter	PA
Ridge	Mary			KY
Hornbaker	Thirza		boarder works in woolen mill	IN

Lives Out of Yountsville:

Last Name	First Name	Age	Notes	Location of Birth
Copner	Joseph	51	laborer	OH
Copner	Susan	51	keeping house	OH
Copner	Calvin S.	26	laborer	OH
Copner	Flora B.	23	works at woolen mills	OH
Copner	Sarah A.	18	does house work	IN
Copner	Grant	15	works on farm	IN

Source: Data compiled and transcribed from the US Census, 1880.
Note: Horizontal rules separate households.

and sixty-four-year-old Nancy Miller were from Kentucky and North Carolina respectively. He worked in the woolen factory and had $100 in personal property.

The Fruits Family

In 1900 twenty-eight-year-old Edger Fruits worked as a weaver and was from Indiana, but at the same time Michael Fruits was sixty-seven and a miller in the grist mill and was also from Indiana. His wife, Mary, was sixty-two and from Indiana; their daughter Gertrude M. was seventeen, and John A. Fruits, forty-three, was a day laborer and from Indiana.

The Shanklin Family

In 1900 Myrtle Shanklin was a twenty-one-year-old boarder of William P. Yount; she was from Indiana and served as a seamstress. Harry Shanklin was one of the last mill workers, and Myrtle and Harry could have been siblings, cousins, or married.

The Stonebraker Family

In 1900 William Stonebraker was a thirty-one-year-old wool washer from England who boarded with the Fruits family, and at the same time, Hargoog Stonebraker, born in Indiana, was thirty-three and a wool mixer. His thirty-four-year-old wife was also from Indiana, and their nine-year-old daughter, Margaret, was born in Indiana. At the same time, Claude Stonebraker also worked in the mill.

The Graham Family

In 1900 Eton Graham was a twenty-seven-year-old spinner from Indiana, and his wife, Bela, was twenty-two and from Indiana. At the same time, Duclos Graham was a twenty-five-year-old carder from Indiana. The Graham family represented the stability the mill offered where both marriage partners were Hoosier-born.

IMMIGRANTS WHO WORKED AT THE MILL

Immigrants lived through rapid changes in their lives, and these immigrants seemed to follow industrialization.[43] As the educational reform laws tightened, their children had less access to the mill and spent more time in school, but compulsory education was enforced weakly until the 1920s, after the mill was shuttered. There is no way to tell how many children of immigrants got to go to school, how much education they had, or if the education they had came from Sunday schools. Relatively few immigrants came to Yountsville (Table 5.6), and those who did came from places that reflected the immigration to Indiana. The places they came from probably offered hydropower, wool, or textile jobs, which meant that they had experience when they applied for the mill jobs. They tended to join relatives employed in the mill. The number of immigrants changed very little across time, with England and Ireland the predominant homes of all until 1900, when immigrants from Scotland and Canada arrived. Families came to Yountsville for jobs in the mill, and individuals came to the mill at Yountsville and found families.[44] Immigrants lived and worked in both the boarding house and the mill. Immigrants continued to occupy the site consistently across the decades.

THE BOARDING HOUSE

In the 1860s, Rhoda Russel, a daughter of Daniel Yount, lived in the boarding house with her four children. Her brother Andrew also lived there. For boarders to have children was an unusual situation, but one mother had two children with her in the house. The boarders were usually single women

Table 5.6. Immigrants at Yount Mill, by Country of Origin, 1850–1900

	England	*Ireland*	*Scotland*	*Canada*
1850	1			
1860	6	2		
1870	5	3		
1880	4	2		
1900	3	3	1	1

Source: Data compiled from the US Census, 1850–90.

who worked in the mill. Most of the women were in their twenties, except for thirty-two-year-old Phoebe Smith.

Ten years later, John and Mary Yount and their two children were living at the boarding house. Sue Ballard was the cook, and Mary Fleshar waited on tables. Sixteen single boarders lived in the house, and one was a child, four-year-old Edith, the daughter of boarder Anne Clark. Half of the boarders were female, and all of them worked at the mill. All but one of the men worked at the mill; the exception was Byron Russell (Daniel's grandson), who was a law student; James Stubbins had the title of mill clerk. Most of the boarders were around twenty, except for forty-year-old Phoebe Smith, whose census record showed that she had aged only eight years in a decade.

In the 1880 census, twenty-eight-year-old Ella Berkshire and Anna Garland were boarders who worked in the woolen factory. While some people stayed long enough to connect with the community, others stayed only long enough to be captured by the census taker, while others were passing through, leaving no record of their presence. By 1900, Allen and Mary Love operated the boarding house with their two children, Alish and Lein, Allen's mother-in-law, Melissa Hayworth, his niece, Jeru, and the fourteen-year-old servant, Kate Lefer. There were six boarders, and only one was female. Peter was the mail carrier, but the others all worked in the mill.

The boarding house was not the only place where single people could live. In 1900, Mary Hopping was nineteen and a seamstress who boarded with the Meyer family, who were from Indiana. People who worked in the mill did not tend to live in Alamo or Crawfordsville; nor did they live in the township in rural locations; they tended to live in Yountsville.

Yount Mill was a prosperous factory located along the west bank of Sugar Creek near present-day Crawfordsville in Montgomery County. The mill was owned by Allen and Daniel Yount, brothers whose family had originated in Germany. Located approximately an hour west of Indianapolis, the site of the Yount Mill along the Sugar Creek watershed was well suited to powering mills due to the size and grade of the creek. Yount Mill was one of several textile mills located in the western half of Indiana. Unfortunately, the industrial landscapes associated with many of the mills from this era have not survived to the present time. However, Yount Mill is a well-preserved example of a textile mill complex from the period. The industrial area of the mill is well preserved, and the residential landscape is also extant, which offers a unique and detailed example of nineteenth-century industrialization in the region.

SIX

Landscape Reconstruction at Yount Mill

The quality of historic preservation at Yount's Mill provided a unique opportunity to reconstruct the past cultural landscape of a wool mill in west
central Indiana from the 1800s to the early 1900s. The primary goal of
landscape reconstruction was recreating the appearance of a historic site,
including the locations and appearances of dwellings, nonresidential buildings, and other improvements. In addition to basic landscape reconstruction, archaeologists often attempt to use a phasing approach in which different periods in the life history of a site are identified and the periods
were, in turn, linked to landscape and site events related to specific households and site owners.[1] The existence of Yount's Mill was divided into four
phases: the Abijah O'Neal Ownership Period (1840–42), the Early Yount
Period (1843–1859), the Middle Yount Period (1860–90), and the Late
Yount Period (1890–1921).[2]

The mill complex experienced consistent change over time and provided
an interesting opportunity to track landscape changes at a well-documented
wool mill. The rapid changes on the site corresponded well with the educational reform efforts in the state. The most dramatic of these changes took
place during the Yount family's ownership of the mill, especially during the

This chapter was written with the assistance of J. B. Bilbrey, Mark Groover, Colin
MacLeod, and Stephen Lacey.

latter period of the mill's operation by the Yount family. Landscape analysis identified two distinct functional areas and four specific periods in the landscape history of the mill complex. The two functional areas consisted of a residential area and an industrial area. The residential area was located on an upland feature and contained the historic boarding house, Daniel Yount's house, and at least two other historic structures. The industrial mill complex was located at the base of the bluff that the creek ran down, on the floodplain of Sugar Creek.

The nine-to-five work of the field school participants on the Yount Mill sites started in the second week of May 2014 and progressed to the second week of June. Five days each week, the research team explored the site. The first week was spent exploring the site with probes to confirm oral tradition as to the locations of all the structures. All sites indicated on the Sanborn Maps were located. Two sites invisible to the probing prompted the use of ground-penetrating radar one afternoon to locate those two sites.

At most sites of this sort it is known where the captains of industry lived; however, at this site the boarding house was still standing, but the owners' residences were missing. Ground-penetrating radar also revealed a significant structure near the mill, but the second-week test pits yielded a major discovery. This fine feature reflected the technology of an early twentieth-century cement sewer connection. Work was discontinued due to large quantities of rain, with no artifacts retrieved. The swamplike conditions created by the rain led the students to explore two levels of the inside of the mill for graffiti.

A drier third week allowed the students to move to the top of the hill to explore the site of the owner's house. They started a series of test pits that revealed a brick foundation for a modest frame house, and brick steps led to a vaulted brick cellar. The site burned in the 1940s and had been bulldozed, and most of the artifacts discovered were a variety 1940s bottles for food, medicine, and hygiene. Across the fourth and fifth weeks of the study the rest of the residence site was uncovered. The next five weeks of lab work involved sorting, cleaning, and labeling the artifacts.

The research team used several data-gathering methods to reconstruct the landscape history of the mill complex, consisting of primary archaeological investigation and remote sensing (including information from ground-penetrating radar [GPR] and LiDAR, an airborne recording system that creates three dimensional images of the surface of the Earth). The

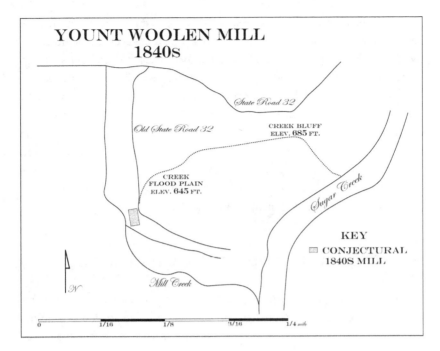

Figure 6.1. Yount Woolen Mill, 1840s. From Jessica L. Clark.

team also reviewed primary historical records and interviewed local informants, which resulted in a comprehensive understanding of the periods of development on the land. Yountsville was not the expected idyllic rural Midwestern agricultural community.[3] The ownership by period provided a way to explore the context of the site at specific intervals.[4]

THE ABIJAH O'NEAL OWNERSHIP PERIOD

In 1840 Abijah O'Neal owned the property that would later be developed into Yount's Mill. When O'Neal owned the site, the configuration of the land was simple. Only one structure was on the site (Figure 6.1). Abijah O'Neal leased his land and water property rights along Sugar Creek to Silias Write. Silias established the first mill on the O'Neal property. It was probably a log mill built by Silias. Upon termination of his lease, Silias moved the mill to a new location. There was also an indication in the

historical record that a Sugar Creek race had existed prior to Yount ownership that, if true, Silias had constructed it. One race was clearly identifiable
by LiDAR imagery; however, this race had two distinct traces, one going to
what was the mill pond and one going to what was the dye house. The diversion of the race to the mill pond undoubtedly originated with Yount;
however, the other lobe of this race may be the remnants of a race that had
originally been constructed in pre-Yount times and then repurposed by the
Younts while they operated the mill. No archaeological evidence of this era
or owner was recovered, but this was not unexpected, as the material movement and the industrial footprint of the mill during later decades was considerable and potentially destroyed much of it.

THE EARLY YOUNT PERIOD (1843–1859)

The Early Yount period began with the acquisition of the land by Allen
and Daniel Yount in 1843. This period was characterized by small mill improvements and a moderate increase in both mill and residential structures
(Figure 6.2), including the brush dam and the frame mill, which was
probably for wool carding and the sawing of lumber (1843), the frame mill
(1850), the boarding house (1851), Daniel's house (1843), and the sleeping
house (1843). The brush mill dam was near the first mill in the Early Yount
period, and the brothers constructed it the year they purchased the land.
Little evidence exists regarding the location of this structure other than
that it was positioned along Mill Creek.

Allen and Daniel started some of the major transformations of the
land. In addition to structures, they created a dam and a sluice to power the
mill. According to surviving records, the frame mill (1850) was a wooden
frame mill with a vertical waterwheel. This structure was central in the
early mill era, and though it was no longer standing, it left a tremendous
impact on the land in the form of a depression for the water wheel. Upon
the completion of the standing mill in 1864, this structure was repurposed
and used for storage and wool drying. The boarding house was still standing and was the residence of the current property owners. The exterior of
this structure was relatively unchanged. However, late twentieth-century
owners remodeled much of the interior for habitation. The boarding house
was the residence of the mill managers.

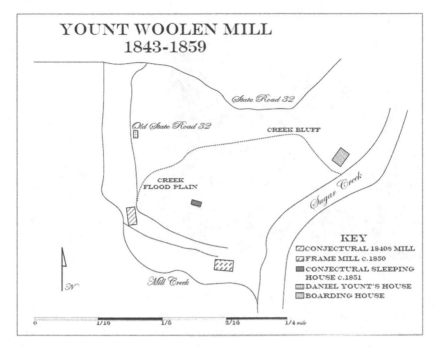

Figure 6.2. Yount Woolen Mill, 1843–1859. From Jessica L. Clark.

The Frame Mill

The mill was off the main road, accessed by an aggressive grade that stretched out like a serpent in the morning sun. The frame mill was a three-story structure with the decaying and ancient water wheel standing as a sentinel against time.[5] The Yount family used the frame mill for wool drying and storage, and the old frame mill had a cement floor across the basement.[6] At another time it was used as the receiving and weighing department for the mill.[7]

The Residential Area: Daniel and Sarah Younts' Home

Using thick description, an ethnographic interpretation process, allowed for study of the architectural exterior and interior spaces through an ethnographic recreation of the land that both the family and the workers inhabited and used for commercial purposes.[8] Daniel and Sarah lived in a comfortable brick house on the hill away from the floods of Sugar Creek

Figure 6.3. Daniel and Sarah Younts' Home. From *Atlas of Montgomery County*, Yount Mill Collection, Marian Morrison Local History Collection, Crawfordsville District Public Library, Crawfordsville, Indiana.

and the noise of the mill. They also lived away from the boarding house. Allen and Daniel built brick homes near each other. Daniel surrounded his home with a sawn board fence. The unostentatious one-story, five-bay brick house with chimneys in the east gable was a comfortable residence. Daniel equipped it with a center door with two tall panels on top and two short on the bottom, and on the east side he created an L with a chimney poking through the roof. He continued his L with a frame containing a window, two panel doors, and two chimneys. Allen's house was similar. An illustration (Figure 6.3) shows a fashionably dressed woman in the yard and a well-dressed man attending to a horse and retractable-top carriage next to the fence. This remained Daniel's home for the remainder of his life.

The two dwellings were denoted on the property plat map for the mill. It was also depicted in a lithograph illustration of the mill complex from the county atlas. The results of a systematic shovel test pit survey suggested the general location of the house, based on the plat map and the illustration in the county atlas lithograph. A subsequent GPR survey conducted by Jarrod Burkes revealed several subsurface radar anomalies that corresponded to the suspected dwelling location. The GPR results suggested the remains of the house's foundation, a cellar, and a cistern in the house's assumed location.

Subsequent excavation indicated that the house had an L addition. It was a single-story dwelling, as depicted in the county atlas lithograph. The Yount family constructed it of brick with a limestone foundation. Excava-

tion units confirmed the size of the dwelling, and the field school participants sampled the cellar and cistern contents, which dated to the early to
middle twentieth century. As depicted in the county atlas lithograph, Daniel Yount's house was the first observable structure for visitors to the mill.
This mill was a family-operated business. Consequently, due to the public
nature of the mill entrance, where Daniel Yount's house was located, the
Yount family maintained the yard surrounding the dwelling. The systematic shovel test pit survey and excavation units recovered some artifacts deposited in the yard during the period of the Yount ownership. However, a
densely deposited midden was conspicuously absent in the yard area, indicating that the owner had probably made a conscious effort to keep the
yard clean. He was apparently not depositing refuse on the domestic lot
surrounding the house. There was a community refuse dump in Yountsville,
so it is likely that community members deposited refuse from the mill at
that location. Fire destroyed Daniel Yount's dwelling in the first half of the
twentieth century, and the ruins stood until the middle of the twentieth
century, when new property owners used a bulldozer and pushed the wall
remnants into the open cellar hole.

The Sleeping House

During the Early Yount period, the family constructed a "sleeping house"
or guest house for mill visitors. The sleeping house provided a place for
people selling wool to spend the night. It encouraged trade with Daniel,
and he offered them basic hospitality. While most customers probably appreciated this service, the prospect did not please all customers. One customer brought his "wool to the mill on one occasion [and] they let him
sleep in a barn like building with straw on the floor. He was awakened
during the night by a snake crossing his legs. He got up, packed, and swore
he would never stay there again."[9]

THE BOARDING HOUSE

In 1851, Daniel Yount built a large brick two-story Greek Revival dwelling
that served as a boarding house for mill managers. The boarding house stood
on top of the hill, away from the bottom-of-the-hill business activities. It

caught more breeze there and had fewer bugs during the summer. Daniel was able to keep it well supplied. For the spring, he needed four new screen windows; four yards of rope, perhaps for clothesline; six yards of netting for sleeping without mosquitoes; tacks for laying seasonal carpet; and screen-door hinges. To update the kitchen, he got a teakettle for Albert, a granite kettle, four pot lids, a china plate, and a child's high chair. He also purchased a chair bottom to replace a seat that wore out of one of the chairs. A visitor described the boarding house as having, "all the comfort and cleanliness of a well ordered home. . . . There are cheerful rooms, good and abundant food, a pleasant parlor for the social inclined."[10]

The boarding house was away from the noise, flies, and dust of the road. Unfortunately, there was no water on top of the hill, so the roof provided the important function of collecting rainwater. Tucked into the L Daniel placed an exterior door and a wooden, partially enclosed, single-flight exterior staircase. On the south side of the west wing of the L, he had one window per floor and a door, and on the east wing of the L he had three openings, with the one closest to the L being a door. On the east wall of the west wing he arranged for a door on the first floor and a window and a door on the second floor. He covered part of this with a two-story shed roof supported by two large square posts that also supported a porch and reinforced it with simple scallop-edged diagonal braces connecting the corners and the posts. He installed a wood floor on the second story of the porch. He located the staircase under the porch to provide access to the second story of the porch, exterior access to the second floor of the boarding house, and exterior access to a bedroom only through a door there.

The Interior of the Younts' Boarding House

On entering Daniel and Sarah's boarding house, one found that the nine-foot-wide center hall ran from the front door to the back of the house through a mixture of Federal and Greek Revival finishes. The simple home included a plane baseboard, plaster wainscoting, and a molded lip and simple cornice chair rail. There were transoms over all the doors off the center hall. Wide surrounds of black walnut were built around each door, and headers were positioned to overlap the vertical boards, leaving corner tabs. The cherry stairway rose on the west side, starting with octagonal base newel posts that morphed into a bulbous vase before encountering the stair reel, tapered, or urn-shaped balusters. On the sides their steps ended with arched brackets.

Before the stairway, Sarah brought visitors to either the east or the west of the central hall. When she brought them to the east, she hosted them in the double parlor with random-width tongue-and-groove flooring, a molded upper-edge baseboard, and an eight-foot opening between parlors with folding wood-paneled doors. Her parlor included Greek Revival door and window surrounds with shouldered architrave moldings and a plaster ceiling. With so many boarders, there were always people in the parlors downstairs, lingering or passing through the central halls, camped in the dining room, or visiting in the kitchen. The house was always buzzing with activity.

When Sarah invited visitors to the west of the house, they entered the thirty-foot-long dining room, where mill workers received meals. She entered onto the oak random tongue-and-groove flooring and surveyed the plane baseboards, door surrounds, window moldings, and plaster walls and ceilings. Sarah might step away from her guests for a moment to check on the cook in the kitchen behind the dining room to determine if food was available for a snack. Upon entering the kitchen, she would see the two-by-six poplar flooring and the simple surrounds. She might go outside below the kitchen to retrieve some apple cider for her guests.

The Second Floor

When Daniel and Sarah entertained visitors for the evening, Sarah might invite them to spend the night. She would escort them up the stairs to the U-shaped hall where the stair rails surrounded the stairwell with oak random-width boards to one of the seven bedrooms. She could show them the three bedrooms to the east with their three heating stoves and chimneys, but exclude the rooms for family on the west, which had the same layout as the guest rooms. She would not show them the exterior porch and back stairs, or the fourth western bedroom, which was accessible from the exterior only, since that was most likely occupied by the cook.

THE MIDDLE YOUNT PERIOD (1860–1890)

The Middle Yount period began in 1860 and was characterized by a substantial increase in mill production. During this period the mill expanded to its greatest capacity. Large contracts allowed for a dramatic increase in

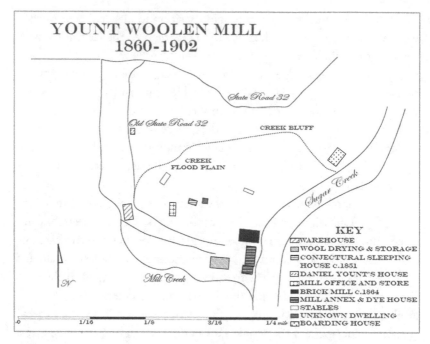

Figure 6.4. Yount Woolen Mill, 1860–1902. From Jessica L. Clark.

labor and infrastructure. People spent their days migrating from the residential hill to the industrial valley and back again. This period witnessed the construction of the standing mill in 1864 (the structure for which the property was best known), the Annex and the dye house in 1868, and a host of smaller auxiliary structures (Figure 6.4). The increases in labor as well as the nature of the increased labor were well documented in the census records and tax records, as well as a graffiti inventory that was conducted by the research team.

The 1864 brick mill house is the most iconic structure in the complex today. The three-floor building built by the Yount family along the west bank of Sugar Creek used a horizontal water turbine to power the mill. The axle of the turbine still rested in the east wall of the mill at the time of the field school, and evidence of the distribution of the turbine power was still present on all levels. Evidence of this power distribution came in the form of belt slits and holes for the supports of auxiliary axles found in the floors and conversely in the ceilings of all levels.[11]

Several large-scale landscape projects also began at this time. These included the construction of the mill pond as well as an apparent deepening and definite redirection of the primary millrace into the mill pond. The research team gathered this information by synthesizing historical records, primary surveys, and LiDAR data.

The Sugar Creek Dam and Turbine

To power the new mill, Daniel needed a more powerful form of energy.[12] He constructed a seven-and-a-half-foot dam after installing a turbine and wheel shed; then he dammed Sugar Creek. That gave him a significant constant impoundment of powerful water. When Daniel crossed Sugar Creek to inspect his dam, he looked down the length of the dam to see his turbine shed siting in the water with the dam connected to it. He framed it to the water line, open under the roof but with stone under the dam on the south side. He detached the turbine shed and moved it to the center of his 1864 brick mill.

The 1864 Mill

The town of Yountsville consisted of the spired Methodist church, a flour and grain mill, a blacksmith shop, a physician's residence, a cooper's business, a schoolhouse, and several parcels owned by Daniel and other Younts in addition to the wool mill (Figure 6.5).[13] Other people also owned land and structures along the single road. Flush with contracts for wool cloth and blankets during the boom decades of the 1850s and 1860s, in 1864 Daniel Yount built a new red brick mill with American common bond brickwork (seven rows of stretchers with a row of headers), with a slate roof in the symmetrical Greek Revival style. His new mill sat on a one-story sandstone-faced rock foundation, followed by a course of limestone cap or water table. Two brick floors climbed from there to a low-pitch gable with a clean frieze, white entablature, and broad cornice returns partially overlapping the lintels of the fourth-floor windows—capped by a slate roof with four chimneys on the north and south sides. From the west-facing opening he welcomed visitors approaching by road through a double-door entrance with dressed stone lintels with a four-light transom for loading cargo flanked by two six-over-six sashes on the second and third levels. On

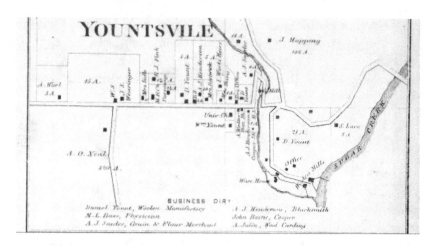

Figure 6.5. Yountsville, 1878. From *Atlas of Montgomery County*, Marian Morrison Local History Collection, Crawfordsville District Public Library, Crawfordsville, Indiana.

the fourth level, Daniel had two windows, also six-over-six panes that fit under the gable for ventilation. From the five sashes of the east wall, he could have overlooked Sugar Creek.

Daniel's eyes would have followed first the north and then the south wall to seven sashes on each side, with a proper limestone header and footer for each window and a wider space between the third and fourth windows from the west (Figure 6.6). On the east wall that faces Sugar Creek, his line shaft that carried power from the falling water behind his dam to his turbine and was geared into the line shaft on the first floor. Line shafts brought power to each workstation in the mill. The circular hex-supported wooden wheel took power by belt to the new mill addition to the south. This awkward-looking arrangement provided inexpensive constant renewable energy day after day for his workers.

In the figure, wool dried in the sun in the left foreground as empty transportation vehicles stood ready for pickup and ricks of wood were stacked against the far mill to provide fuel for the steam plant. The teams and loaded wagons stood ready in front of the two brick mills and the frame mill that was directly west of the brick mills. Daniel had all his teams of horses pulling his five matching wagons, all of which would be piled high with large bolts of cloth. He commissioned his matching wagon

"EXCHANGE WOOLEN MILLS, YOUNTSVILLE, MONTGOMERY CO., IND.
D. YOUNT & SONS, PROPRIETORS.

Figure 6.6. Yount Mill, 1878. This image, drawn from the northwest, shows the frame mill at left and the 1864 brick mill at right. From *Atlas of Montgomery County*, Marian Morrison Local History Collection, Crawfordsville District Public Library, Crawfordsville, Indiana.

boxes—painted with a curvilinear design to be easily recognizable as he delivered wool cloth to the railhead. The designs might reflect the patterns found in the Pennsylvania Dutch area or a faux grain painting. They seemed neither representational nor print. Just as Yount's mill cloth was known by people in the area, his wagon boxes reflected his brand when goods arrived at or departed from Yountsville.

In front of his brick mill, Daniel had five drying racks for wool textiles. Also in front of his brick mill, Daniel had constructed a wooden ramp rising to the set of double doors on the second floor. He lined his second- and third-floor front paneled doors on the west side with four light transoms, but did not include a transom on the first-floor door. He also placed a hoist like a keystone over each door lintel on the second and third floors. All these devices helped his workers move goods from one workstation to another.

On the north side of the first floor, third opening from the west, he placed another door without a transom. Furthermore, he inspected his four chimneys on the north and south sides from the visible roof access door, and from the ground on the north side, he observed the half-round scallops in the fascia board of the roofline. More substantive than decorative, on the fourth-floor west wall, approximately over each window, he set four iron star bolts to which workers could tie the bricks to the wooden internal frame. On the third floor, approximately over the center windows, he set two iron star bolts with which to tie the brick to the wooden internal frame. On the second floor, approximately over the center windows, he set two iron star bolts to tie the bricks to the wooden internal frame.

The Interior of the Mill

Upon entering the building, Daniel saw the four-inch boards that covered the floor, the whitewashed plaster walls, and the light-reflecting white-washed ceiling rafters. From the door of the second floor he looked down a colonnade of three matched square posts that were carefully tapered to octagons and carried the stress of the building, first on a six-foot ceiling support to the beams running the length of the building to support the weight of the floor joists, then to the crossbeams that connected the short width of the building with the masonry walls. Daniel built every part of the building to reflect durability and to withstand the stresses of the manu-facturing process. On the second floor he created an enormous wooden drum for transferring power to belts hanging just slightly to the west on the north wall ceiling. This transmission changed both the direction and the speed of the power coming to the machines in this area of the mill.

As he planned, Daniel found that the first floor looked similar to the other floors. He installed a wood floor, later replaced by concrete, and the wooden posts supported the floor in the same manner as on the second floor. He brought his line shaft into the building through the east wall. From a circular wooden wheel, covered with canvas, he allowed power to be pulled off the wheel with the assistance of belt drives. Power came into the mill from the line shaft on the east side of the mill and was transferred down parallel lines from east to west. In line with the line shaft and the cir-cular power belt on the east wall, eight hooks suspended from the ceiling cradled the line shaft on the south pillar side. Next, between the pillars on the south, Daniel observed three hooks from the ceiling that cradled the center line shaft. Also, between the between pillars but on the north side, the three hooks from ceiling cradled a line shaft. On the north side toward the pillars he saw the five hooks on the wall side protruding from the ceil-ing to cradle the last of the line shafts.

Daniel was particularly proud of the third floor with its four chimney flues each on the north and south walls and the absence of support beams, which made for one wide-open and uncluttered space. Four heavy iron bolts tied the crossbeams together, transferring the weight of the ceiling to the timber skeleton on the fourth floor. On both the north and the south sides, four additional iron bolts were used to link the ends of the beams to the fourth-floor beam framing, and four more iron bolts pulled the ceiling beams into the timber skeleton on the fourth floor. On the third floor, Daniel removed the most western window on the south side, where he added a connecting belt so that he could bring power to the third floor of the mill from the Annex. This was never a human passageway, as it was always a covered way to pass power from building to building on the third floor.

Daniel even found uses for the fourth floor under the unfinished roof, with a floor and two sash windows on the east and west gables and queen post trusses standing in the open space. Opening the gable windows during the spring, summer, and fall allowed warm air to rise through the building and exit with a crossbreeze across the attic. The slate roof also breathed naturally year-round. This helped the workers below at a time without air conditioning, and it was a great place to dry wool. Since the air circulated without the use of fans, workers needed to move wet wool onto the fourth floor, stir it periodically to encourage even drying, and remove the dry wool.

The workers finished cloth on the first floor of the brick mill; the second floor was where they carded the wool.[14] The third floor was where the workers picked the wool and spun it into thread, and the fourth floor was used for wool drying.[15]

Daniel's mill kept up with some of the changing technology to make the process of working with wool safer and more comfortable for the workers (Table 6.1). His brick mill had heat on the first floor, first heat from wood stoves, then steam heat from wood and coal, and finally steam heat from coal.[16] By the twentieth century, the first floor had a concrete floor, a dynamo for electric lights, and a steam jet to the picker room.[17] A two-thousand-gallon water tank in the attic of the building supplied pressure to the mill and the Annex, and thirty- and fourteen-foot hoses attached in the basement provided for fire suppression in addition to the distribution of barrels of water and pails in case of disaster.[18] Daniel had the original steel cleats in the walls and the ceiling reinforced the structure. The Sanborg maps, located at the Montgomery County Building Department in Crawfordsville, provide an excellent view of the changes to the mill through continuing industrialization. They also illustrate the process of deindustrialization.

Table 6.1. Yount Mill Building Notes, 1887 and 1892

	Title	Notes	Building A	Building B	Building C	Building D
1887	D. Yount & Son	No watchman Heat: Stoves "Exchange" Fuel: Wood Woolen Mills No lights Buckets Water wheel below dam Slate roofs A, B, C [Mill] Race goes through 8-inch pipe to Annex	Heats 1st	Stairs in NW corner of entrance section 2nd water tank	5 dye vats indicated	Cement floors in basement
1892	D. Yount and Son Exchange Woolen Mills	No watchman Heat: Steam Fuel: Wood & coal No light Buckets Water wheel in frame shed Dam Mill race goes underground 8-inch pipe to middle of Annex		2nd water tank	Concrete floor in basement	

Source: Data compiled from Sanborg Maps, Montgomery County Building Department, Crawfordsville, IN.

The Annex

When Daniel built an annex to the brick mill on the far south side of the mill, all three stories had panel doors, but set back to the east each of the three floors had four windows on each floor.[19] As in the brick mill, Daniel built each window with a stone header and footer over and under each window, and the six-over-six-pane sash windows allowed for light and air. Over the third floor he placed both between and over the middle windows, over the north window, and over the south window three-star bolts that protruded from the wall. Star bolts also protruded from the walls on the second floor, both over and between the middle windows. In the farthest section of the building to the north, star bolts protruded from the wall directly over the third-floor window. To provide for an entire year and be ready for the following year, Daniel piled two long stacks of wood to the top of the first-floor windows in front of the annex to keep the steam boiler going.[20]

Looking at the mill from across Sugar Creek (Figure 6.7), it hangs right on the edge of the stream. Rising above the dam to the right of the image was the boarding house. To the south of Daniel's mill was a brick addition with its sandstone foundation plunging straight down to the water line of Sugar Creek and three brick stories rising from the foundation. Daniel's design feature of having the stone foundation dip its toes into Sugar Creek would cause future maintenance issues, but he kept the factories close to the power supply. He designed its flat roof to slope toward Sugar Creek. He put eight windows down the east side of the mill addition on the first and second stories, but only three windows on the third story. On the south side of the addition, he put two windows on the second and third stories, but only one on the first floor.

Daniel's workers in the Annex used the first floor for a variety of functions, but most often they scoured wool there.[21] On the second floor, the workers wove the thread into cloth, and on the third floor, they dried the wool.[22] By 1887, Daniel had the race go through an underground eight-inch pipe to the middle of the Annex; this pipe was used until the millrace disappeared around the turn of the century, at which time the building had a concrete floor.[23] Daniel built the Annex with stairs in the northwest corner of the entrance area and a water tank on the second floor.[24] All of his brick buildings—the brick mill, Annex, and dye buildings—had slate roofs. Buildings A and B, as identified by the Sanborg Maps, held multiple

Figure 6.7. Yount Mill from Sugar Creek, 1878. The image, drawn by someone facing east, shows us, left to right, the dye house, built in 1868; the annex, built in 1864; and the mill and boarding house, with a turbine shed and dam in the foreground. From *Atlas of Montgomery County*, Yount Mill Collection, Marian Morrison Local History Collection, Crawfordsville District Public Library, Crawfordsville, Indiana.

textile production functions (Table 6.2). Building C acted exclusively as the dye house for the factory.

The Dye House

Working farther south, Daniel attached a dye house to the mill addition, putting one brick story on a sandstone foundation.[25] He placed two windows in the brick and one window in the stone and capped the building with two chimneys. From the west he could see one chimney and one north window, and over his dye house he saw his original 1849 frame mill. To the far north, he saw his boarding house cresting the northern hill. Just to the north of the brick mill and to the left of the boarding house, but set back in the distance, he saw only the gable end of his horse stable with a sawed board fence.

Daniel used the dye house exclusively for dyeing wool. The dye building had five dye vats. By 1902, the dye house got a concrete floor, and even though the mill was not in operation by 1913, the dye house had heating.[26]

Table 6.2. Yount Mill, Buildings A, B, and C, Uses by Floor, 1887–1913

| | Building A | | | | Building B | | Building C |
	Floor 1	Floor 2	Floor 3	Floor 4	Floor 1	Floor 2	Floor 3
1887	Heats	Carding	Spinning Picker		Finishing	Weaving	Drying Dye
1892	Heats	Carding	Picking Spinning		Finishing	Weaving	Drying Dye
1896	Finishing	Carding	Picking Spinning		Drying Wool Scouring	Weaving	Drying Dye
1902	Finishing	Carding Spinning	Picking	Scouring Room & Drying	Drying Wool	Weaving Stock Dye Dyeing	Drying Dye
1907	Finishing	Carding	Spinning	Wool Scouring & Drying Dyeing	Wool Weaving Stock	Weaving Stock	
1913	Finishing	Carding	Spinning Picker Room	Wool Scouring and Drying Dye			Dye house

Source: Data compiled from Sanborg Maps, Montgomery County Building Department, Crawfordsville, IN.

Table 6.3. Yount Mill Buildings D, E, F, H, and K, Uses by Floor, 1887–1913

	Building D	*Building E*	*Building F*	*Building H*	*Building K*
1887	Wool drying and storage	Storage of woolen goods Office	Warehouse	Horse shed	Horse shed
1892	Wool drying and storage	Office Storage of woolen goods	Warehouse	Horse shed	Horse shed
1896	Wool drying and storage	Office Storage of woolen goods	Warehouse	Horse shed	Horse shed
1902	Wool drying and storage	Office Storage of woolen goods	Warehouse		Horse shed
1907	Wool storage	Office	Warehouse		Horse shed
1913	Wool storage	Office	Warehouse		Horse shed

Source: Data complied from Sanborg Maps, Montgomery County Building Department, Crawfordsville, IN.

In addition to building new structures, Daniel modified the millrace across time. First he brought it from the dam on Mill Creek to the carding mill. Then he extended it to the frame mill, but later he ran it through an eight-inch pipe underground to the middle of the Annex. By the time the millrace was encapsulated by the pipe it was no longer being used for water power but was probably used to provide the dye house with water. Sugar Creek carried colloidal sediments that would make the dyes cloudy. The fresh water from Mill Creek, with its rocky bottom, provided a source of water that was ideal for dyeing. It was interesting to note how many structures were needed to support the functions of the mill. Multiple buildings provided for wool drying and storage and for the care of the horses and wagons (Table 6.3).

The Yount Store and Mill Office

There was a serious grade to the store (Figure 6.8), and no flooding of Sugar Creek despoiled the goods sold there.[27] Even though the illustrations gave the illusion of its being a large space, it was a densely occupied compound. Daniel built the gable end of the frame Yount store on a rise to face the road. He created a frame Greek Revival shotgun building sporting an entablature with two symmetrical windows with shutters flanking a

Figure 6.8. Yount Mill Office and Store. From *Atlas of Montgomery County*, Yount Mill Collection, Marian Morrison Local History Collection, Crawfordsville District Public Library, Crawfordsville, Indiana.

center door and two chimneys through the roof. He built the first chimney toward the front and the other midway back on the structure; his center door had two long panels on top and two short panels on the bottom. He met many customers there and concluded many business arrangements there with a handshake. His customers saw the front of the frame mill from the store, in the background to the left of the image.

At the mill office, customers sold their wool and selected products to take home.[28] The store was described thus: "Counter and shelves were piled with fine fabrics of his [Daniel's] manufacture, equal to the out put of Eastern mills, and here and there on the door and walks, were immense posters adverting the Blaine [a Republican politician] meeting at the battle-ground [Tippecanoe, where Benjamin Harrison's grandfather had earned his nickname]."[29] At the store, customers had a variety of possibilities for purchase, including collars, handkerchiefs, suspenders, and notions. The store also had yard upon yard of bed padding, blankets, bias fabric, bunting, calico, canvas, cashmere, denim, doeskin, drill, flannel, gauze, ginghams, lining, muslins, napkins, notions, quilting, sheeting, shirting, table linens, ticking, toweling, tweeds, worsted, and skeins of yarn. The customers stored their wool at the mill until it was ready for use. The workers used the original carding mill to warehouse raw wool, and the mill workers had two horse sheds and two outbuildings at their disposal.[30]

Archaeological evidence suggests a notable modesty in Daniel's lifestyle. This evidence, combined with primary documentation and local information, indicates that Daniel Yount invested his acquired resources into mill operation. Daniel was renowned for his modesty and philanthropy. He earned this reputation by both his individual acts of charity and his donation of blankets to soldiers. Local informants have also indicated that the large contracts fueling the surge in mill production during the 1860s may have been due to Civil War contracts with the Union Army. Research has been unable to find any evidence to support this claim; however, regardless of where the contracts were coming from, this period saw unprecedented growth in mill activity. The Sanborg maps show the full development of the mill site. The race brought clear creek water to the mill for washing and drying without the sediments of the fast-moving Sugar Creek.

THE LATE YOUNT PERIOD (1890–1921)

The Late Yount period began in 1890 with the death of Daniel Yount. The mill site was heavily developed by the time of Daniel's death, and all the structures were fully occupied. The land passed to his children, and in short order, mismanagement and falling demand forced the mill to downsize and eventually close in 1907. Daniel's children retained the land for approximately another twenty years (Figure 6.9); however, there is little evidence that they were occupying the land at this time. If his children did remain at the property, their footprint was light. This apparent absence was evidenced by what appears to be a stark decline in early twentieth-century artifacts from the site.

THE POST-YOUNT PERIOD (1921–PRESENT)

By 1921, many of the former structures left only archaeological footprints. However, the extant structures remained well maintained and retain their architectural integrity even today (Figure 6.10). Beginning in 1922 the Amusement Park period began with the acquisition of the Yount's Woolen Mill Complex by Hoosier Hotel and Resort with the intention of converting the property into a mill-themed amusement park. Like the Middle Yount period, this period saw another series of large-scale landscape renovations. These included a potential deepening of the mill pond, several subsurface features around the mill, and substantial ground movement around

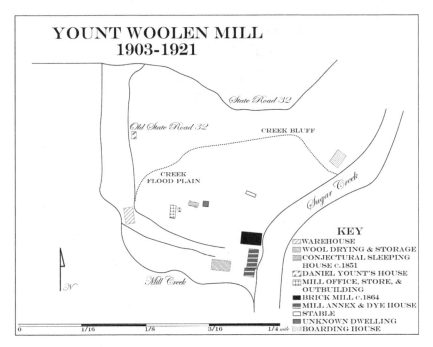

Figure 6.9. Yount Woolen Mill, 1903–1921. From Jessica L. Clark.

the standing mill. GPR investigation of the area immediately surrounding the mill indicated several subsurface features. The first of these was an oblong feature on the north side of the mill approximately 55 centimeters below the ground's surface that was trending in a northeast direction. Archaeological investigation uncovered moderate amounts of constructional material in a heavily disturbed matrix. This came as no surprise, as the test pits were near the mill. However, the test pits began terminating in level cement that appeared to have been introduced in approximately the early twentieth century. As the research team excavated more test pits, it was clear that this cement was a slab measuring approximately 3 by 3 meters. Further excavation in addition to a reexamination of the GPR data indicated that this northeast-trending feature was a septic field put in place during the Amusement Park period.

The research team initially interpreted the smaller, less well defined features identified to the south of the standing mill as possibly remnants of previous structures. However, further investigation revealed that this area

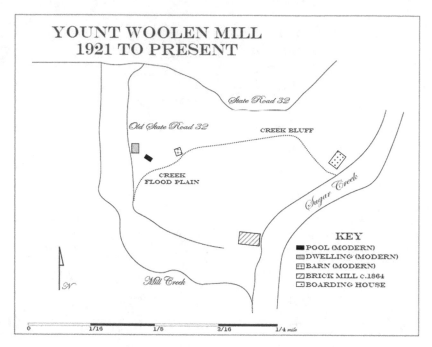

Figure 6.10. Yount Woolen Mill, 1921–present. From Jessica L. Clark.

was composed largely of homogenized construction rubble from both the Amusement Park period and the Middle Yount period, indicating massive ground disturbance during these periods, which had led to this homogenization of remnant debris.

A few short years after their acquisition of the property, the Great Depression caused Hoosier Hotel and Resort to file for bankruptcy and sell the property. The owners never completed or opened the Amusement Park.

The Post-Industrial Era

In 1932, following the collapse of the amusement park, the property changed to private ownership. During this postindustrial era, the property changed hands several times and fell into a state of disrepair. The only restorative projects by owners ensured that the mill structures still standing did not collapse. During this era, in the early 1940s, Daniel's house was struck by lightning and burned. A local resident informed us that her father used a bulldozer to push the rest of the ruined structure down and flatten the area, likely contributing to the mixing of mid-twentieth-century artifacts with the top layer of fill in the excavations of Daniel's House.

The Inn Era

Beginning in 1987, with yet another change in private ownership, the former Yount property began to see large-scale restoration and revitalization. Projects in this era, which ran until the present, included a complete structural overhaul and restoration of both the boarding house and the mill. Both structures were on the verge of collapse, and tremendous amounts of mechanical augmentation were required to stabilize and refurbish these impressive buildings.

The owners emptied the boarding house and started a restoration project. The original interior layout was lost because the intent of the new owner was to convert the building into a bed and breakfast. The mill saw mostly structural work, including repair of sagging support beams and water damage, as well as many cosmetic fixes, such as the installation of new windows and brickwork. The mill changed hands one more time, in 2009, to its present owners, who, after inheriting the impressive restoration work accomplished in the 1980s and 1890s, have done an excellent job of maintaining the property and currently operate it as a bed and breakfast featuring a "mill-themed experience."

The early period of Yount ownership of the land brought about development and settlement. Allen and Daniel built a frame mill and residential areas to establish themselves on the property in the 1840s and expanded their equipment in 1850 with the new frame mill. The Yount brothers were prosperous during this early period; they controlled the entire wool-making process at their mill and had profitable trade with local farmers. At the end of this period, Allen Yount sold his half of the business to Arthur Russel, who then married into the Yount family but died of illness shortly thereafter. Thus, at the end of the period Daniel Yount alone owned the mill and its assets and ran the mill himself. These early years of hard work would bring about a boom of business in the 1860s during the Civil War.

During the Middle Yount period, Daniel dammed Sugar Creek, built a new mill, and expanded the production and sale of Yount wool. The turbine in Sugar Creek provided power for the entire mill complex, and, combined with the construction of the brick mill, Yount Woolen Mill entered its most prosperous period. In 1875 Daniel Yount brought his sons into the business to form a partnership, and in 1887 Andrew Yount took over running the mill with his father serving as adviser. Daniel Younts died in 1890, and after that the mill began its slow decline.

Changes in industry and education meant that in the 1920s child labor ended in industry with stringent compulsory education laws. The mill did not exist as a company without family labor. As the archaeological study reveals, the Yount family sold the rights to the property in 1922, and there was a fleeting failed attempt at creating a mill-themed amusement park. As time passed, the land and its buildings repeatedly switched owners, falling into disuse and disrepair until its restoration in 1987 by the Hardwick family. Since that revitalization and despite the continual change in ownership of the land and its buildings, the property has been used as a bed and breakfast with its mill history on display.

The landscape history of Yount's Woolen Mill illustrated the life history of an industrial complex from the middle 1800s to the mid-twentieth century. The scale of the manufacturing complex was impressive considering that it was in a small rural community. Interestingly, due to the ample water power located along Sugar Creek, many mills were in this part of west central Indiana. However, none of the other mills survived. Consequently, Yount's Mill offered a fascinating glimpse of the built environment and architecture associated with an Indiana wool mill of the 1800s.

By the third quarter of the twentieth century, paralleling similar trends in much of the US manufacturing belt, Indiana experienced the transition from an industrial to a postindustrial society as twentieth-century industries declined due to global manufacturing shifts. Illustrating an important segment of approximately half a century, the ruins of twentieth-century textile mills in Indiana have quietly slipped into the realm of hidden history; their remnants can still be located on the rural landscape, but their overall historical, economic, and cultural significance has faded with time. Consequently, the neglected history, material characteristics, and social influence of early industrial life in Indiana during the second half of the nineteenth century intersect the material, social, political, and educational characteristics associated with Yount's Mill and its surrounding community during the second half of the 1800s.

SEVEN

Conclusions

In the same breath, the legislature passed the revolutionary Indiana school law of 1852 and elected Caleb Mills as the second superintendent of education of Indiana. The legislation required school reforms; among others, the civil township, not the school district, was to be the basic unit of education oversight, and the township trustees were in charge of buildings and teachers.[1] The trustees had the power to establish graded schools as needed; they also had the power to levy local property and poll taxes in addition to lengthening the school year.[2] The law required the Superintendent of Education to examine and license teachers, to create a board of education to advise the Superintendent, and to authorize textbooks for the schools.[3] Mills was also charged with making reports to the legislature; in his first report he called for graded schools.

In an image of the thin Caleb Mills, a painting (Figure 7.1), he sat in a chair and was wearing a dark suit, a white shirt, and a dark cravat knotted at his throat with the corners pointing to his shoulders. Mostly hidden by his jacket, a watch chain crossed his chest. His white shirt with collar lapels rose over his slightly pointed chin. A trace of a bemused grin lay on his thin, pursed lips, with wrinkles off to the sides of his mouth from smiling too much. The lines of his cheeks, which were starting to sag, flanked his thin, smooth nose. His bright eyes were visible behind wire-framed glasses, with crows' feet at the corners and topped by dark eyebrows. He had parted his silver, slightly recessed hair on his left, and it just touched the tops of his ears.

Figure 7.1. Caleb Mills.

Opponents of taxes appealed a case to the Indiana Supreme Court, and Justice Alvin Hovey wrote the majority decision blocking the use of local taxes for schools. His rationale was that state schools funded by local taxes would be locally controlled schools, but if they were state-funded they would be state-controlled. While Hovey's decision strengthened the cause of state funding, confusion over the decision resulted in the closure of some schools and in shortened school years.[4] Furthermore, the court was ruling only about taxes that paid for tuition because taxes can originate only in the Indiana House. Another suit, this time from Warren County and asking to use local taxes for school buildings, went to the Indiana Supreme Court. Judge Perkins, writing for the majority, stated that townships could use local taxes to pay for property and buildings.[5] The results of these two cases sent the education reformers reeling. They immediately looked for ways to reclaim the momentum in educational reform. The high court seemed to block the expansion of educational opportunities for students by the state.

AMENDING THE NEW CONSTITUTION

Since the 1850 constitution had been so successful in promoting the cause of education, Mills thought about the constitution as a way to regain the moral high ground with Indiana voters. He defended the proposal for a six-month school year as a constitutional minimum. He contended that it did not limit future expansions of the school year and that most children benefited from the tuition provided. He argued that the average citizen did not need a nine- to ten-month school. The state should not provide longer terms for youth, but the state should provide a minimum term.

Mills believed that citizens should be able to call on the commonwealth to provide for the educational needs of the masses. He thought that four-fifths of the children who lived in rural Indiana needed farm or domestic occupations. In school children developed a sound character that shaped their future mission as individuals at home. Children learned lessons of practical worth, industry, and obedience to parental authority. In the home circle they also acquired domestic training and employment favorable to the development of cultural and moral powers. Furthermore, the physical development connected with the industrious pursuits of the farm and household was as essential to children as the intellectual training provided by schools.

Mills also believed that students learned habits of observation and scientific principles from the plow, maul, ax, nail, and scythe. They learned concepts of physics and friction while using the corn sheller and the grindstone. They learned arithmetic and geography from determining the lines, angles, and distances of the split-rail fences, corn rows, wheat fields, and pastures. Students learned culinary arts in their homes, and the farms and workshops were important classrooms of practical knowledge. Therefore, Mills advocated for six months a year of symmetrical moral and intellectual development in the home and the school.

Mills acknowledged that the urban school year needed to be longer since there was not enough work in the towns and students required diversions in the towns to protect them from temptation. Just as the towns provided gas lights and sidewalks, and city government must provide education in urban spaces. This supplemental education relied on local men for tuition. While Mills conceded that students in urban areas needed additional schooling, he also warned of the lack of necessity of a year-round school. Even city students needed two months of rest and relaxation from school. He realized that teachers could not bear the draft of mental and physical activity for more than five-sixths of the year.

In his fifth report, ca. 1850, the superintendent of public instruction, with three quarters of all townships reporting, said that the average length of school for that year was three months.[6] Mills called for an investigation when he noted that the number of children enrolled in school in 1858 was inconsistent with the number of children in the previous three years. Nevertheless, Mills discerned that the state had spent two dollars per child to educate them for a six-month year of school. He did not charge malfeasance, but it does make one wonder where the money went.[7] The promised six-month school presented no danger of a wave of students flooding the resources of the state. Students enrolled but did not come to school. If they all came to school, there would still be enough space for them in the schools, and the teachers had the resources to teach them. Extra students did not require a huge school-building project across the state. Mills called for an amendment to the constitution to allow the legislation of six months of school. The amendment caused the Supreme Court to allow supplements to six-month school to lengthen the school year. A six-month school was preferable to other plans, and it was an excellent value for the taxpayer.

Mills determined that he needed to create a short list of reasons to get people to go to the polls and vote for a new constitutional convention that would support common school education.[8] His reasons revolved around the 1861 legislation's being blocked by the Constitution through the Indiana Supreme Court and being held hostage until 1865, which meant that local urban schools could not be open longer than six months. Antirevisionary people voting against a convention would postpone immediate action. He remained confident the people would elect delegates who would accept good policies. There would be no more effective action than that taken by the convention, which would end with satisfactory results. A vote for the convention would delay any uncertainty and produce speedier results. This was a nonpartisan proposal to adopt a convention for revision that Mills suggested to accomplish the work.

THE CIVIL WAR

The Civil War brought a substantial change to the common schools of Indiana. With large numbers of men fighting in the Union Army, a thriving economy putting men to work in factories, and the continued development of the American West, there were plenty of opportunities for an aspiring young man. In 1859 some twenty percent of the teachers were female, but by 1864 forty-two percent were women.[9] Intelligent, competent, and well-educated female teachers replaced men in the classrooms. Most of these women had attended the common schools where they received teaching positions, and some had even studied at the local academies. Township trustees administered exams to women and employed them to teach, frequently at lower salaries than those received by their male peers. The Civil War also changed school for the students. In 1863 fewer than half of the school-aged children enrolled in school, but by 1880 more than seventy percent were attending classes.[10] In a generation, Hoosier parents realized the importance and value of a common school education, and students took advantage of the opportunity.

By the end of Reconstruction, educators had lengthened the school term from 66 days in 1866 to 136 days in 1879.[11] As towns in Indiana grew, the citizens realized that their students needed more instructional time, and the voters were willing to support an enlarged educational opportunity. Changing attitudes toward education and burgeoning community pride in educational institutions reinforced the support for education. Manufacturing had grown significantly during the 1850s and exploded during the 1860s, creating multiple factory jobs that required a common school education. Unfortunately, neither the Civil War nor the end of Reconstruction meant that civil rights came to education in Indiana. Prior to 1869, public schools were for white children only, but separate schools for black students opened that year. However, when there were not enough black students for a school, they went to white schools.[12] Since Indiana did not have a large population of black people spread evenly over the state, this meant that most of the time black students mixed with white students. There were notable exceptions, such as in urban areas, areas with formerly free black communities, or, after the war, in places to which refugees from slavery migrated. More than twenty years before *Plessy* v. *Ferguson*, the Indiana Supreme Court ruled in 1874 that communities must provide separate schools for all students.[13] This important precedent required that black students receive a public-school education without exclusion from the system. All students were to receive a free education. In 1877 the legislature said that separate schools were possible, but where they were not practical, black children and white children could mix.[14] Though this was hardly a clarion call for equity, it closed a loophole that would have excluded black students from education. While hardly a bastion of progressivism, the state was consistent in creating laws for all children to attend school and receive instruction. Equality of education remained an elusive opportunity for all.

While the Civil War was being fought in 1861, voters selected the subjects for instruction in Indiana schools, and in 1865 they added US history and physiology to the curriculum.[15] These subjects were very limited. Unlike the South, which, of necessity, put all its resources into fighting the war, the North continued to develop commerce, education, and society while also conducting their part of the war. Furthermore, in an age that had seen noteworthy progress in the care and healing of wounded men and the consequences of gathering large numbers of men in camps, the subject of physiology was on the minds of many concerned citizens interested in public health. During the last year of the war, teachers officially used the Bible as a textbook to teach morals.[16] A society grieved by dead and wounded men, disrupted lives, and broken homes may have found comfort in religion. Certainly grieving families turned toward spiritualism or hopes of a happy, peaceful afterlife. In 1869 the curriculum continued to evolve to include arithmetic, good behavior, English grammar, geography, the history of the United States, penmanship, physiology, reading, writing, and languages that pupils required for further study, such as German.[17] In an industrial age with a need for factory workers, good behavior was highly desired so that workers could conform to the world of work. The patriotic and nationalistic fervor released during the celebration of the end of the war and the understanding of the United States as having a place in the world contributed to the inclusion of US history and geography. Handwriting was the key to accounting, recordkeeping, and correspondence, so possessing clear handwriting was valuable. Considering the large numbers of German immigrants in the Midwest, language was not a surprising choice for inclusion in the curriculum. In larger communities, teachers added drawing, vocal music, and elocution by the 1870s.[18] The flowering of the arts among people who had both time and disposable income was notable for those looking for culture and diversion. Unfortunately, education in Indiana was not a complete success. Some 7.5 percent of the population was still illiterate in 1870.[19] The change in attitude in favor of education encouraged people to vote on the subjects included in the curriculum that they supported with their tax funds. The relief from the war and the demands of industry had an impact on education. Changing tastes, additional time, and a growing leisure class promoted the arts in the schools.

Two more legal moves improved the public funding of education. In 1873, legislation allowed two or more districts to consolidate for graded schools, and in 1877 an act allowed for the consolidation of townships or counties if citizens petitioned for it.[20] This move gave areas greater flexibility in school organization and funding. This legislation was rarely used, but schools used it more in the twentieth century. The other move came from the Indiana Supreme Court. In 1885 the court reversed itself when it ruled that that local governments could tax citizens in order to support local schools for both tuition and buildings.[21] As stated earlier, communities had quietly ignored this mandate before this ruling. This was the last major obstacle to public funding of education from within state government. The judiciary would no longer bar the legislature from the concept of public funding by holding the strictures of the Indiana Constitution as an obstacle.

Mills asked for a lot from the Indiana General Assembly when he addressed it. His annual addresses were printed anonymously in the newspapers after he had delivered them in person before the General Assembly, in the same spirit as that of American political reformers going back to the Stamp Act. He provided the legislature with at least one solution to a pressing problem in each address. Usually he got a little, but rarely did the legislature grant his requests completely. Over the long term, most of what he asked for in creating a common school system for Indiana eventually passed. For the rest of his life he advocated for the creation of libraries in the public schools and for educational reform in neighboring states. Mills never understood the separation of church and state. In his mind education interlocked with his Presbyterian faith. In fact, his evangelical background probably prompted his fervency in advocating for the dissemination of education in Sunday School as well as the classroom. He remained vigilant in guarding his interests at Wabash College, and he never stopped lobbying for state support of private colleges. He also never completely gave up hope that once the state sold the state college at Bloomington to a sect, to be operated as a private college rather than a public college, the legislature would divide the money from that sale among the other colleges in the state. While his ideas spoke to the political sensibilities of the time and he was always trying to find something palatable for the legislature, his recommendations did not always resonate with the needs of twenty-first-century education. His commitment to education for all citizens was his enduring legacy.

Caleb Mills realized that the path both to work and to democratic participation followed from education, and his vision of an industrial society required workers with rudimentary education. He did not stand in opposition to a long tradition of family labor or the traditional community work skills based on apprenticeship, but he wanted it balanced with intellectual development for half of the year. In an interesting coincidence, Caleb Mills died in 1897 and the Indiana legislature passed compulsory education laws that same year and child labor laws in 1911.[22] Efforts at compliance and enforcement continued for several years.[23] Business decried these laws as interference with commerce. Some families argued that they needed the money their children earned. Indiana was moving students from the factory to the safety and limited hours of the classroom. This was the future for Indiana youth. These laws helped immigrants, poor children, and the youth of the middle class to make advances in education and opportunity.

INDIANA CHILD LABOR

In Indiana, children worked with their families on farms, in factories, and in service industries. Working under the supervision of their own parents or side by side with their parents provided an ideal education, enabling young people to learn occupations with their family members and to contribute as peers to their family economy. By 1867 the legislature put laws in place saying that children under sixteen could not work more than ten hours per day in wool factories.[24] The representation of children in this industry was strong enough to have specific protective legislation passed. Reformers continued to ameliorate factory conditions for children by mandating an eight-hour day for all children under twelve years of age in 1885. Legislators followed in 1893, requiring all children under fourteen years of age to work no more than an eight-hour day. As powerful as these laws sounded, they were unenforceable and roundly ignored until 1897, when the legislators required that children under age fourteen not work, that a fifteen-year-old who could not read or write in English not work, and that children sixteen years old not work more than ten hours per day and no more than ten hours per week. The 1897 law further required that inspectors be hired to visit workplaces, inform the community of infractions, and prosecute violations; Indiana workplaces started to conform to minimize child labor in factories. The same year, the legislators passed a compulsory school attendance law requiring that children from age eight to age fourteen attend a minimum of twelve weeks of school.[25] After this one-two punch against child labor, in 1911 the legislators passed a bill to completely end work in factories by children under age fourteen.[26] Labor supported the child labor reforms to stabilize wages so that jobs would not be undercut by the lower wages paid to children. The legislature continued to support the importance of the common schools by passing a 1921 law requiring fourteen- to sixteen-year-old children to finish the first eight grades prior to receiving work permits.[27] While some paper boys, agricultural workers on family farms, and children in family businesses still slipped through the cracks, child labor was regulated. The legislature made its intentions very clear: it expected children to attend and complete the first years of common school prior to entering the world of work. Indiana Children would learn to work in the schools and would form an educated workforce.

YOUNT MILL

Parents who worked at Yount Mill thought they were doing the best for their children by letting them work beside their family members. Children were under the supervision of the parents, they were learning skills and business that seemed to pay them a good wage, and they seemed to have a good future in the mill. Their lives were not significantly more subject than those of their neighbors to the scourges of illness, industrial accidents, unemployment, agricultural accidents, or old age. Then the unthinkable happened: the mill closed. At this time, the industry and most of the people vanished from Sugar Creek.

At the Yount Woolen Mill, Indiana children worked from first light to dusk six days a week, leaving little time for formal education. Four miles away, the prescient advocate for compulsory education, Caleb Mills at Wabash College in Crawfordsville, lobbied for children to be in school not solely in the factory or on the farm. His inspired leadership in providing public education included the children of immigrants who had been growing up working in factories with no options for education. Caleb Mills had to be aware of children working at Yount Mill and many other mills, factories, farms, and businesses in Montgomery County, and likewise many farmers, mill workers, factory hands, and business owners knew about the position Caleb Mills took. To businessmen, Mills's views might have seemed like unwelcome government interference in their lives or an unnecessary impediment to a family's ability to make money.

From the beginning of this book, Caleb Mills has been seen as in the vanguard of calling for change in public education. The state of Indiana slowly moved to funding public education and adopting a public common school system by the 1850s. Private colleges attempted to meet the needs for education of a changing population and realized they would need to provide the teachers for the common school movement. The interdenominational cooperation of sectarian interests contributed to securing public funding for common schools. Across time, Americans found the capacity to make a living and enrich community life through democratic participation.

In the second chapter we saw that the Industrial Revolution required enhanced engineering to build mill structures and stainable power sources, including hydropower and then steam; a continuous supply of high-quality raw materials such as cotton and wool; and an enhanced workforce that required a common school education to carry out mill-related tasks. The new Indiana Constitution provided an armature for public education and common school legislation. Public education changed with the needs of people to adapt to technology and commerce. In America, females and families worked in the mills to provide the labor in mechanical industrial settings. In Mills's and Yount's time and in the present, political and ideologic notions of economics impact citizens.

The Yount family started and operated the mill during its entire existence as a manufacturing venture, as described in Chapter 3. The family continued to adapt the business to the needs of the community and the changes in society. Business expanded across the 1850s and exploded in the 1860s as local women traded their raw wool for finished woolen products at the Yount store. The long, painful slide into insolvency showed the second generation scrambling to hang onto the assets created by the first generation. Across nearly a hundred years, Yount Mill played a role in the regional economy.

Daniel Yount was not the only member of his German immigrant family to work at the mill; the entire family was profiled in Chapter 4. Daniel was both the corporate face and the driving personality behind the mill. In addition to being philanthropic, he contributed generously to the community, played a role in the local church, and served as a de facto banker, lending money to people. The family members grew up working in the mill, and some spent all or most of their lives in the valley working in a variety of roles. One of Daniel's grandsons attended Caleb Mills's college to become a Methodist pastor, and another was a law student, demonstrating a transition from a labor-based to an information-based future. As immigrants they merged into mainstream American life, and they provided opportunities for other immigrants to integrate into American life as well.

As we saw in Chapter 5, British immigrants came to work for other immigrants who had just slightly longer affiliations with America. Many workers and working families worked together as a part of the mill at Yountsville, turning wool into cloth. Life at the boarding house changed as people had different configurations of families. Graffiti, photographs, and census records have given us ways to learn the names of the people who came to the mill to live and work. Families brought their textile skills to the mill until it closed, and then most of them moved, presumably to find their next textile jobs.

The site of Yount Mill provides a way to understand the bifurcated worlds of lived space on top of the hill and work space in the valley. The site has been described as Pre-Yount, Early Yount, Middle Yount, Late Yount, and Post-Yount, and Chapter 6 detailed the structures that existed and presently exist on the site. Descriptions of site features included residences, commercial buildings, and engineering structures. The major transformation of the site occurred when Daniel Yount decided to dam Sugar Creek and use it for power. With this dam the Yount family changed the geography of the mill site. After they left, people immediately valued the site for historic preservation purposes.

Nineteenth-century rural Midwesterners moving daily between work and social spheres imagined the future through the way they developed a relationship between education and industry, as illustrated by a case study of rural life that examined the transformation of work and school. The ruins on the land near a popular recreation venue, Sugar Creek, and visible from a state highway bridge incite people who pass by to ponder the past,[28] while it might just look like old buildings from the perspective of those taking an ideal canoe float downstream or like a ghost peering from the trees on a crisp winter morning with frost covering everything. But the landscape embodies a meaning for the present, representing the deindustrialization of the rural community. The mill also stands as a symbol of the success of waves of immigrants who were welcomed into the community as productive workers and neighbors who stayed to put down roots and call the land home.

CONNECTIONS TODAY

The study described in this book demonstrates that mill towns did exist in the Midwest. The community and the industry flourished for eighty years, managing change the entire time, and the immigrant owners brought their advantages to operate at the site. The workers and the owners lived and worked near each other. Immigrants from the British Isles populated this community and brought their skills with them as they searched for improved lives. The public school system helped people adapt to change during the industrialization and deindustrialization cycles of the past. The study presented here alerts present-day visitors to the site to the physical remains of the mill, which remind people today of values they cherish from the past.[29]

The Yount Woolen Mill represented an important and rapidly changing technological society. The uncertainty of the present created a desire for the security of the past; moreover, it was important to find something that seemed timeless and unchangeable. Modern innovation became obsolete in twenty years; computers were old in three years, and a new personal communication device arrived every year. Industry was rarely the subject of historic preservation, yet compelling stories and memories came from industrial sites and situations, including child labor, immigration, labor, and women's history. People dealt with the crucial elements of change, transition, and opportunity when considering the migrations from farm to factory that came with the transition from the nineteenth century to the twentieth.

Various groups still wrestle with the Indiana state legislature, supporting or denying the importance of public funding for education in the twenty-first century. Caleb Mills's vision of universal public education has been re-alized, and his dreams of publicly funded community libraries have been materialized in every Hoosier community. He demonstrated support of higher education in both public and private institutions. He was a vision-ary who saw a different future for Hoosier children. The need for all citi-zens in a democracy to have an education supplanted Caleb Mills's vision of higher education for men.

Some people still suggest that all some students need is a vocational education that will let them work in business. Mills would not have been pleased by the rise of parallel funding for private and charter schools. The scope of education expanded for students entering technology-heavy jobs. While Caleb Mills could not envision the highly technical world of the twenty-first century, he certainly understood that children in the future would need the knowledge, skills, values, and dispositions to adapt flexibly to a future dependent on knowledge. He also knew that those children would need educations to serve Indiana as leaders in education, business, agriculture, manufacturing, culture, and philanthropy.

In the twenty-first century there are renewed calls for students, or at least some students, not to go to college and just get jobs that will provide them with a good future. Though usually it is someone else's child and not their child that they are thinking of. There are a variety of proposals for in-ternships, co-ops, and apprenticeship programs that seek to minimize the value of public-school and public higher education. These proposals seek to reduce education to merely occupational training or job preparation for a great many students. While this may be good in the short run or for some-one seeking a first job, it does not seem to consider the rapidly changing economic, technological, industrialization, and deindustrialization of the job market in the twenty-first century. In a rapidly changing world, there is a need for highly skilled workers provided by a sound educational system with a variety of communication, thinking, and creative skills to solve the problems of today and tomorrow.

Yount Mill was important because people debated the persistent issues raised at that time in examining what defined a quality education. The idea of vocationalism, or the idea that students should get an education solely for the purposes of getting and keeping jobs, was a popular idea then and still is now. Should children receive an education for the jobs that exist today, or should they receive an education for the jobs of the future? The way of the future in Daniel Yount's life was to focus on working in the mill, but not in those of his children, his grandchildren, or the mill workers. While the education necessary to work in the mill looked stable, as the industry changed, eventually all the people who worked in the mill became unemployed. While it was not apparent at the time, once they lost their source of work, it became clear that a more general education would help them find their next job. Caleb Mills's efforts to provide education to allow people to have options in their future employment, along with his efforts to build a better community and state, provided the children of the workers at Yount Mill opportunities to work in a variety of places if one mill or factory foundered.

The past four owners of Yount Mill have practiced historic preservation not as nostalgia, but as a monument to values equated with a different time and a unique way of life. Each owner has sought to find and remember the abundant life memorialized by the mill. The past four mill owners have tried to remember the Quaker values of Daniel Yount's childhood, such as simplicity, peace, integrity, community, and environment. Here simplicity might be described as meaningful work that helped farm women convert raw materials into the products they needed to clothe their families. People stayed in the stable, peaceful mill environment for generations.

The Yount family practiced integrity when they tried to alleviate the suffering of others through philanthropy; they enriched the quality of life of their neighbors and of people in the greater area. People living and working together for multiple generations defined the community, and single women or women with dependent children could find security at the mill. People could enjoy the verdant environment with low levels of pollution where they used rainwater for washing and drank from the multiple cool, flowing springs. Yount Mill stands alone on the banks of Sugar Creek at the intersection of Spring Creek in a steep-sided valley. It stands today because past owners memorialized values from other times in defiance of the popular values of the twentieth and twenty-first centuries.

The ruins of the mill played into a romanticized heritage in a deindustrialized region. The mill also stood vacant, reinforcing the emptiness of lives and the shattered dreams of industrialization. For much of the twentieth century the glass was out of the mill windows, reminding the community of the vulnerability of the building when the wind and the rain could pass through it unimpeded. The mill reminded people of the scattered community and damaged relationships of a broken world. The names of mill workers and visitors cover the walls, reminding visitors of the people who once came together to form a community and then the diaspora of the workers leaving the place they called home.

The relict and ruined landscape of the mill creates a false nostalgia for a simple time when families remained together, when work was purposeful, and when communities coalesced around agreed-upon values. People did not see the challenges of rapidly changing technologies, the stress of immigration, or the anguish of the diaspora that coincided with deindustrialization. Maybe the human mind found as much solace in what it elected to remember as in what it managed to forget. In the local memory, the relics of the mill paid homage to the beloved Daniel and his family, who ran a mill. Visitors to the site also remember the multiple connections to other families, past and present, who came to this site as immigrants looking for a better life and found it for a while. These ruins also testify that they saw change and that a prescient man from Crawfordsville realized that an educated workforce could weather the coming changes, whether at this site or someplace else.

The mill once portended economic power and prosperity, but in the end the wealth was an illusion. At the end, the mill owners staggered around bleeding money until their company fell; moreover, technology offered false promises. The much-championed hydropower in some ways supplanted steam power, but the costs of using hydrocarbons became a steady drain on the company that had once used the free weight of falling water for power. Technology did not make the community stable, and it did not preserve the family. The dreams of wealth and technology did not save the community; they just expended the community.

Today multinational corporations build manufacturing facilities in some fortunate Midwestern communities, such as the Toyota factory at Princeton, Indiana. A high school graduate finds work there right out of school, just as his grandfather found work right after World War II at Chrysler in New Castle, Indiana. These communities are the exceptions, not the rule. Mills never expected these types of jobs, but he did know that students needed experience working on farms or in their homes when they did not attend school. He felt these real-world experiences prepared students to work. A pragmatic preparation for life and work made sense at that time, as a liberal arts degree still makes sense in a changing world.

Mills worried not only about getting students enrolled, but also about getting them to materialize for school. In that context, the peculiar nature of the present superabundance of testing and assessment would be an oddity. The present wrangling over money to support public education was business as usual to Mills, but the interest in supporting a parallel system of private and charter schools would greatly disturb him since he spent so much time fighting against this in early efforts at education reform. Mills, unhappy with state institutions of higher education, would no doubt be pleased with how many private colleges exist and how many people matriculate through higher education in the Midwest. The issues and circumstances that Mills worked with remain relevant even if the details have changed.

Mills would be greatly pleased with the fine public library system available to the residents of the Midwest. He would also be pleased with the number of professional teachers trained in respectable teacher education programs. Even though Caleb Mills would be pleased with most of the changes in and opportunities provided by public education, it would be a good bet that next year Mills would be petitioning the legislature, trying to get greater accessibility, opportunities, or experiences for the youth of his state.

NOTES

Introduction

1. Some topics from this work have been previously reported. See Groover and Clark, *Yount Mill Historical Archaeology Field School Report*, 149. and Groover et al., "Landscape Reconstruction at Yount's Mill."

2. What we would call public schools.

3. Kilen, Renes, and Hermans, eds., *Landscape Biographies*. Landscapes do not have histories, but they do have stories, as reflected by the landscape biography method. The landscapes lack human agency, but natural processes impose narratives on the land. The specific decisions made by individuals and illustrated through case studies describe the environment of both structures and landscape created by humans. See Casella and Croucher, *The Alderly Sandhills Project*. Archaeologists explored a household site in Northwest England from the seventeenth to the twentieth century. They coupled traditional archaeological methods with archival research and oral history to capture family memories. The rural location felt the effects of industrialization and deindustrialization as they interacted with historic events, the domestic sphere, community and identity, and family memory.

ONE. Education in Indiana

1. Geiger, *The American College in the Nineteenth Century*.

2. "Caleb Mills House Is Steeped in History of Wabash," *Indianapolis News*, March 8, 1958.

3. Caleb Mills Papers, M 207, Letters, 1844, 1853, *Boston Recorder* vol. 29, no. 8, February 22, 1844, box 1, folder 8.

4. Carmony, *Indiana 1816–1850*, 402.

5. Ibid., 401–2.

6. Thornbrough, *Indiana in the Civil War Era*, 512.

7. Ibid.

8. Herbst, *The History of American Education*.

9. Carmony, *Indiana 1816–1850*, 394.

10. Thornbrough, *Indiana in the Civil War Era*, 770.

11. Carmony, *Indiana 1816–1850*, 372.

12. Ibid., 378.

13. Ibid., 394.

14. Thornbrough, *Indiana in the Civil War Era*, 461.

15. Caleb Mills Papers, Letters, 1844–1853, box 1, folder 8, Indiana Historical Society.

16. Ibid., Letters, 1844–1853, box 1, folder 9, Indiana Historical Society; Mills, *Caleb Mills and the Indiana School System*.

17. Carmony, *Indiana 1816–1850*, 378.

18. Ibid., 375.

19. Ibid., 379.

20. Caleb Mills Papers, I H S Address (Transcript), 1846, box 1, folder 10, Indiana Historical Society. Emphasis added.

21. Ibid. Emphasis added.

22. Ibid.

23. Ibid.

24. McDaniel, *The Contribution of the Society of Friends to Education in Indiana*, 233.

25. Ibid., 142.

26. Coffin, *The Life of Elijah Coffin*, 67.

27. Ibid., 57.

28. McDaniel, *The Contribution of the Society of Friends to Education in Indiana*, 148.

29. Carmony, *Indiana 1816–1850*, 381.

30. Ibid., 383–84.

31. Ibid., 385.

32. McDaniel, *The Contribution of the Society of Friends to Education in Indiana*, 213.

33. Caleb Mills Papers, "I H S Address: Common School Law, 1848–49; Some of its Defects," 1848–49, box 1, folder 12, Indiana Historical Society.

34. Ibid., "I H S Address: Common School Law, 1848–1849; A Remedy for the Evils before Mentioned," 1848–49, box 1, folder 12, Indiana Historical Society.

35. Ibid., "I H S Address: Financial Provision of the Law," 1848–49, box 1, folder 12, Indiana Historical Society.

36. Ibid., "I H S Address: Reasons for Voting in Favor of It," 1848–49, box 1, folder 12, Indiana Historical Society.

37. Ibid., "I H S Address: Message on Education," 1848–49, box 1, folder 12, Indiana Historical Society.

TWO. The Growth of Industry in the United States

1. Hambourge, Perrin, and Breisch, *Mills and Factories of New England,* and Prude, *The Coming of the Industrial Order.*

2. Hunter, *A History of Industrial Power in the United States,* vol. 1, 37.

3. Tucker, *Samuel Slater and the Origins of the American Textile Industry,* 35.

4. Ibid., 85, and David Nye, *Consuming Power,* 49.

5. Gordon and Malone, *The Texture of Industry,* 299–302.

6. Tucker, *Samuel Slater and the Origins of the American Textile Industry,* 122, 214.

7. Ibid., 44–45.

8. Ibid., 165, and Meyer, *The Roots of American Industrialization.*

9. Cutler, *Parents and Schools.*

10. For more on the overshot wheel, see http://www.loc.gov/pictures /resource/hhh.wv0220.photos.172730p/?co=hh. For more on the breast wheel, see http://www.loc.gov/pictures/resource/hhh.pa0837.photos.138161p/?co=hh. For more on the turbine, see http://www.loc.gov/pictures/item/wa0227.sheet.00006a /resource/.

11. Hunter, *A History of Industrial Power in the United States,* vol. 1, 64.

12. Ibid., 435. For more on this type of setup, see http://www.loc.gov/pictures /resource/hhh.ne0071.photos.346123p/?co=hh.

13. Hunter, *A History of Industrial Power in the United States,* vol. 2, 102–9.

14. Ibid., 103–4, 109.

15. Ibid., 114–15.

16. Ibid., 115.

17. Indiana Historical Bureau, "19th Century Indiana Grist Mills."

18. Indiana Historical Bureau, "Kellar Grist Mill." Adam Kellar began constructing a stone millrace on Sand Creek in 1813, and opened a grist mill in 1823. The mill was important to the local economy and was an impetus for development. The state road to the mill was established in 1834, and Brewersville was founded in 1837. Flatboats carried mill products as far as New Orleans. The mill was closed after damage from the 1937 flood.

19. Indiana Historical Bureau, "Markle Mill Site." Abraham Markle (1770–1826) had a gristmill and dam built here in 1817. The mill had an early horizontal water wheel in a splatter box located within the stone foundation of the structure. The wooden part of mill was destroyed by fire in 1938. Markle was one of founders of Terre Haute Land Company. He also ran a nearby general store, sawmill, and distillery (Indiana Historical Bureau, "Miami Indian Mills," Historical Markers, http://www.in.gov/history/markers/345.htm). The millstone is a remnant of the grist and saw mills built near here for the Miami Indians by the United States government as part of the 1818 Treaty of St. Mary's. The treaty also

established several Miami reservations in the area. It is possibly the first industrial site in what became Wabash County.

20. Indiana Historical Bureau, "Tunnel Mill." John Work (1760–1832), one of the area's most prominent businessmen, who settled on Fourteen Mile Creek in 1804, had this house built c. 1811 and built the gristmill, tunnel, and dam on the creek c. 1814–16. Over time, Work operated three gristmills, four sawmills, a powder mill, a distillery, a stone sawing mill, and a general store. Tunnel Mill, dug in near here, was six feet tall, five feet wide, and over 385 feet long and was considered a major engineering feat. Blasting through a limestone hill to build it took nearly two and a half years. Tunnel Mill served as a millrace providing a consistent water supply. The mill was three stories tall with a limestone foundation. The upper two floors were made of wood. The mill burned in 1927.

21. Indiana Historical Bureau, "Evansville Cotton Mill." Several buildings dating from 1874 remain of the Evansville Cotton Manufacturing Co., which was active from 1867 to c. 1900. It was a major employer on the lower Ohio River. Most of the workers were women. The mill had access to raw cotton via the river and to coal from local mines, and railroad transportation attracted the mill. Infant food products had been manufactured here since 1916.

22. Indiana Historical Bureau, "Lowell Mills." From 1830 to 1880 the community of Lowell Mills thrived here along the Driftwood River. There were two gristmills, a cooperage, a shoemaker's shop, a distillery, a sawmill, a woolen mill, an inn, and a general store. When the mills closed, the town was abandoned (Indiana Historical Bureau, "First Dam across the St. Joseph River–Power Race"). The original dam, providing power for which Mishawaka was noted, was completed in 1837. It was 577 feet long and 24 feet thick, and it cost $38,000. Along this race, which provided water power, and along its counterpart across the river, early Mishawaka factories were located. These produced flour, lumber, woolen goods, iron, boots, shoes, furniture, coffins, barrel staves, saddles and harnesses, and wagons valued at many hundreds of thousands of dollars each year (Thornbrough, *Indiana in the Civil War Era*, 468).

23. Crockett, *The Woolen Industry of the Midwest*, and Cole, *The American Wool Manufacture*.

24. "Montgomery County Magazine," *Journal Review*, April 1977, 10–11. Early mills were an important industry.

25. Thornbrough, *Indiana in the Civil War Era*, 413, and Trinkley and Adams, *Life Weaving Golden Thread*.

26. Thornbrough, *Indiana in the Civil War Era*, 388.

27. Ibid., 389.

28. Ibid., 432.

29. Caleb Mills Papers, "I H S Address: Fifth Annual Message," 1850, box 1, folder 13, Indiana Historical Society.

30. Ibid.

31. Ibid.

32. Ibid.

33. Ibid.

34. Indiana Constitution, art. 8, http://www.law.indiana.edu/uslawdocs /inconst/art-8.html#sec-1.

35. Caleb Mills Papers, "I H S Address: Convention for the Revision of the Constitution," box 1, folder 15, Indiana Historical Society.

36. Caleb Mills Papers, "I H S Address: Amendments of the Educational Feature of the Constitution," box 1, folder 15, Indiana Historical Society.

THREE. The Production History of Yount Mill

1. Beckwith, *History of Montgomery County*, 586.

2. William M. Reser, "Yountsville Home Coming," September 3, 1930, Alan and Barbara White Papers, mill boarding house, Yountsville, IN.

3. Ibid.

4. Ibid.

5. Molloy, *Homespun to Factory Made*.

6. M.H.K., "Indiana Woolen Mills," *Inter Ocean* (Chicago), October 23, 1888, accessed June 14, 2017, newspapers.com.

7. Reser, "Yountsville Home Coming."

8. Beckwith, *History of Montgomery County*, 586.

9. M.H.K., "Indiana Woolen Mills."

10. Reser, "Yountsville Home Coming."

11. Ibid.

12. Yount Woolen Mill, Papers, Rotary Jail Museum, Crawfordsville, IN.

13. *Atlas of Montgomery County*, 52.

14. Lake and Warner, *Map of Montgomery County Indiana*, 2; Beckwith, *History of Montgomery County*, 586.

15. Beckwith, *History of Montgomery County*, 586.

16. *Painting of Yountsville Mill*, Marian Morrison Local History Collection at the Crawfordsville District Public Library, Crawfordsville, IN.

17. *Atlas of Montgomery County*, 35.

18. Yount Woolen Mill, Papers.

19. Ibid.

20. Ibid.

21. Ibid.

22. Spring Mill, Ledger Book, 1870 Accounts, Alan and Barbara White Papers, mill boarding house, Yountsville, Indiana.

23. Spring Mill, Ledger Book, 1874 Accounts, Alan and Barbara White Papers.

24. Yount Woolen Mill, Papers.

25. Beckwith, *History of Montgomery County*, 586; *Atlas of Montgomery County*, 52, 56.

26. Yount Woolen Mill, Papers.

27. Reser, "Yountsville Home Coming."

28. Anonymous letter to D. Yount, Alan and Barbara White Papers, mill boarding house, Yountsville, Indiana.

29. Yount Woolen Mill, Papers.

30. M.H.K., "Indiana Woolen Mills."

31. Record of Teacher's Examinations and License, August 30, 1884, Yount Mill Collection, Marian Morrison Local History Collection at the Crawfordsville District Public Library, Crawfordsville, IN, available at http://history.cdpl.lib.in .us/teacher/te033.pdf.

32. Invoice, June 13, 1889, Alan and Barbara White Papers.

33. Letter, Alan and Barbara White Papers.

34. Ibid.

35. M.H.K., "Indiana Woolen Mills."

36. Ibid.

37. Ibid.

38. Ibid.

39. Ibid.

40. Ibid.

41. Ibid.

42. Reser, *John Rudolph Waymire and the First Three Generations of His Descendants*.

43. Reser, "Yountsville Home Coming."

44. Anonymous letter to Andrew Yount, Alan and Barbara White Papers.

45. Kennedy, "Old Gunkle Mill Once Played Important Part in Local History."

46. Yount Woolen Mill, Papers.

47. Ibid.

48. Ibid.

49. Ibid.

50. W. S. Blatchley, *Untitled*, photo, ca. 1900, box 3, folder 1, Mills, Rotary Jail Museum.

51. Robert Grant, letter to Andrew Yount, Alan and Barbara White Papers.

52. *Woolen Mills Co. Journal D 1899–1906*, Alan and Barbara White Papers.

53. Yount Woolen Mill, Cash Book, February 1, 1904–December 1909, Alan and Barbara White Papers.

54. Letter, Alan and Barbara White Papers.

55. Ibid.

56. Ibid.

57. Officers of the State, *Annual Reports of the State of Indiana.*

58. Anonymous letter to Andrew Yount, Alan and Barbara White Papers.

59. *Yountsville Mill Accounts Payable 1904–1909,* Alan and Barbara White Papers.

60. Yount Woolen Mill, Journal D, Jan. 3, 1898–Oct. 1906, Alan and Barbara White Papers.

61. Yount Woolen Mill, Cash Book, February 1, 1904–December 1909, Alan and Barbara White Papers.

62. William A. Reade, letter to Andrew Yount, Alan and Barbara White Papers.

63. Ibid.

64. Yount Woolen Mill, Minute Book No. 2, Rotary Jail Museum.

65. Ibid.

66. Ibid.

67. Ibid.

68. Ibid.

69. Yount Woolen Mill, Papers.

70. Yount Woolen Mill, Minute Book No. 2; Yount Woolen Mill, "Memorandum Feb 15th/10, All stock surrendered and new stock issued," Ledger, Rotary Jail Museum.

71. Yount Woolen Mill, Minute Book No. 2.

72. Ibid.

73. Ibid.

74. "Woolen Mill Wanted," *Fiber and Fabric* (Boston), September 27, 1913, http://books.google.com/books?id=Djs8AQAAMAAJ&pg=PA346.

75. Yount Woolen Mill, Minute Book No. 2.

76. Cragwall and Fitzpatrick, *Montgomery County Atlas,* 21.

77. Yount Woolen Mill, *Stock Book of the Yount Woolen Mill Company,* Rotary Jail Museum.

78. Yount Woolen Mill, Yount Woolen Mill, Minute Book No. 2.

79. Ibid.

80. Ibid.; Yount Woolen Mill, Papers.

81. Yount Woolen Mill, "Sugar Creek with Ruins of Yount's Woolen Mill Dam, photo taken November 1922," box 3, folder 1, Indiana Historical Society.

82. Yount Woolen Mill, "Abandoned and Partly Wrecked Yount Woolen Mill at Yountsville, Indiana, photo taken November 1922," box 3, folder 1, Indiana Historical Society.

FOUR. The Yount Family

1. *Atlas of Montgomery County,* 52.

2. Ibid.

3. *Crawfordsville Journal,* September 6, 1890.

4. M.H.K., "Indiana Woolen Mills," *Inter Ocean* (Chicago), October 23, 1888, accessed June 14, 2017, newspapers.com.

5. *Crawfordsville Journal,* September 6, 1890.

6. Ibid.

7. Letter to the *Crawfordsville Journal,* 1888, Alan and Barbara White Papers, boarding house, Yountsville, Indiana.

8. *Crawfordsville Journal,* September 6, 1890.

9. M.H.K., "Indiana Woolen Mills."

10. Ibid.

11. Montgomery County's Guardian's Docket, Montgomery County Clerk's Office, Crawfordsville, Indiana.

12. William M. Reser, "Yountsville Home Coming," September 3, 1930, Alan and Barbara White Papers, Yountsville, Indiana.

13. Ibid.

14. Montgomery County Will Book 3, Montgomery County Courthouse, Crawfordsville, IN, 363–365.

15. Montgomery County Circuit Court Complete Record Probate, May 1891, Montgomery County Courthouse, vol. 476, 488–502.

16. Montgomery County Clerk's Office Probate Files, Estate of Dan Yount, 1891, Personal Property, Crawfordsville, IN.

17. *Crawfordsville Journal,* September 6, 1890.

18. Wabash College Archives, DC654BJ and DC654BL, Wabash College Library, Crawfordsville, IN.

FIVE. The Lives of the Workers

1. Shackel, *Domestic Response to Nineteenth-Century Industrialization;* Halchin, *Archeological Views of the Upper Wager Block;* Greenberg, *Worker and Community;* and Green, *The Company Town,* esp. 138.

2. Gordon and Malone, *The Texture of Industry,* 359. Gordon and Malone note that over time the technology developed to have automatic fault detection, allowing workers to operate more machines at once. By the middle of the nineteenth century, the operation of increasingly complex machines in textile mills was becoming the work of skilled laborers (361).

3. Ibid., 384.

4. Mrozowski, Ziesing, and Beaudry, *Living on the Boott*, 53.

5. Nye, *Consuming Power*, 52.

6. Tucker, *Samuel Slater*, 227, and Nye, *Consuming Power*, 52; Niemi, *State and Regional Patterns in American Manufacturing.*

7. Nye, *Consuming Power*, 52.

8. Ibid.

9. Tucker, *Samuel Slater*, 252, and Nye, *America as Second Creation*, 128.

10. Nye, *America as Second Creation*, 130–31.

11. Tucker, *Samuel Slater*, 230, 250–51. The increase in urbanization and city development is noted in Hunter, Vol. 2: *Steam Power*, 103–4, 109.

12. Letter to the *Crawfordville Journal*, 1888, Alan and Barbara White Papers, Yountsville, Indiana.

13. Digby and Searby, *Children, School, and Society in Nineteenth-Century England.*

14. Copartnership of Daniel Yount and Andrew Yount, 1891, Montgomery County Clerk's Office Probate Files.

15. Ibid.

16. Ibid.

17. Wanda Howard, oral history interview, June 11, 2014.

18. Copartnership of Daniel Yount and Andrew Yount, 1891.

19. Nevitt, "Time Takes All But Memories," Alan and Barbara White Papers.

20. Ibid.

21. Ibid.

22. Ibid.

23. Ibid.

24. Ibid.

25. "Weaving Room, Lowell," NPS Lowell, https://www.youtube.com/watch?feature=player_embedded&v=B15MXVf9xS8; "Lowell National Historical Park Weaving Machines 1," NPS Lowell, https://www.youtube.com/watch?feature=player_embedded&v=FpGLVi3bVCE; "See a Room Full of Old Mill Weaving Machine," NPS Lowell, https://www.youtube.com/watch?feature=player_embedded&v=G7dxUTXX7Nk; "Mill Room, Lowell 2," NPS Lowell, https://www.youtube.com/watch?feature=player_embedded&v=rTmYV3J5JU4; "Lowell National Historical Weaving Machines 1," NPS Lowell, https://www.youtube.com/watch?feature=player_embedded&v=FpGLVi3bVCE; "Boot Textile Mill Museum at Lowell NHP," Laura Wilson-Anderson, November 8, 2008, https://www.youtube.com/watch?feature=player_embedded&v=SOBZ7bi3Z84; "Lowell National Historical Park Weaving Machines 2," NPS Lowell, https://www.youtube.com/watch?feature=player_embedded&v=_Chmn4ibx2I; "Weave

Room," NPS Lowell, https://www.youtube.com/watch?feature=player_embedded &v=KXJZR4TvJ14; and "Boott Cotton Mills Museum Weave Room," NPS Lowell, https://www.youtube.com/watch?feature=player_embedded&v=BDg Vepn4YaU.

26. Nevitt, "Time Takes All But Memories."

27. Ibid.

28. Mikel Bowman, personal correspondence with Alan and Barbara White, Alan and Barbara White Papers. "My paternal grandmother was Mary Margaret Murphy Bowman (1883–1958). I remember her verifying a story that one of my aunts told about my grandmother's older sister working at the Yountsville Mill."

29. The mill owners did not prevent the practice or attempt to discourage it by repainting the millhouse walls, and Daniel Younts himself signed the wall.

30. McDonald, *The Popular History of Graffiti*, 10, 38, 210; Milnor, *Graffiti and the Literary Landscape in Roman Pompeii*, 3; and Allen, *A Republic in Time*.

31. McDonald, *The Popular History of Graffiti*, 210.

32. Milnor, *Graffiti and the Literary Landscape*, 29.

33. Ruth Ahnert, "Writing in the Tower of London during the Reformation," 177.

34. Merrill and Hack, "Exploring Hidden Narratives," 111, and Pula, "The Writing on the Walls," 49.

35. Research on the graffiti at Yount's Mill did not extend into the attic or the basement, and it is unknown what type of graffiti, if any, is in those spaces.

36. In the areas surveyed there are a total of 1,153 graffiti markings: "Personal Identifiers" include illegible names, illegible signatures, initials, letters, and names and totaled 251. Inscriptions recorded as drawings or pictures fall under the category "Images," and there were 37 identified. All date inscriptions were categorized as dates, and there were 51 instances of these. "Words" includes all inscriptions described as lists, places, poems, quotes, ramblings, words, or writing and totaled 41. The "Numerals" category includes math graffiti, prices, tally marks, and numbers, and there were 766 identified (primarily tally marks). The category "Other" includes graffiti described as activities (i.e., tic-tac-toe), and 2 graffiti were categorized as such.

37. The interior of the mill, which is presently open space, was divided into four quadrants according to the cardinal directions. Then each quadrant was subdivided into its two walls. Graffiti were noted on each of these walls, on both the first and the second floors and in the stairwell of the mill. The graffiti locations were recorded on maps, and the graffiti contents and locations were recorded in a field notebook. The walls were also photographed to create a visual record of the graffiti.

38. To better understand the process, see the sources cited in note 25.

39. Bowman, personal correspondence with Alan and Barbara White, Yountsville, IN.

40. M.H.K., "Indiana Woolen Mills."

41. Ibid.

42. Cathy Clements, personal correspondence with Alan and Barbara White, August 14, 2010, Alan and Barbara White Papers.

43. Bodnar, *Immigration and Industrialization*; Watson, *Bread and Roses*; Taylor and McBirney, *Peopling Indiana*; and Esslinger, *Immigrants and the City*.

44. Dublin, *Women at Work*, and Cameron, *Radicals of the Worst Sort*.

SIX.   Landscape Reconstruction at Yount Mill

1. Fennell, *Perspectives from Historical Archaeology*; Branton, "Landscape Approaches in Historical Archaeology," 51–65; Yamin and Metheny, *Landscape Archaeology*; Kilen, Renes, and Hermans, *Landscape Biographies*.

2. The information in this chapter was gathered in the summer of 2014 during a Ball State University historical archaeology field school. Mark Groover supervised the field school. Six undergraduate students and a graduate field assistant conducted the archaeology at the mill. Two students who participated in the field school, former graduate student Colin MacLeod and former undergraduate student Stephen Lacey, are co-authors with me of this chapter, as noted in the chapter footnote.

3. Woods, *Rural Geography*; Hart, *The Rural Landscape*; Pacione, *Progress in Rural Geography*; Roberts, *Landscapes of Settlement*; and Kiefer, *Rush County, Indiana*.

4. The main interpretive theory presented in this book draws on strands of thought found in the Annales School of social historians, life history or site biography perspectives used by social scientists and archaeologists, and world systems theory developed by historical sociologists. An Annales perspective provides a useful temporal framework for conceptualizing the period of industrial development in the study region. A life history or site biography approach complements interpretive aspects associated with the Annales perspective. World systems theory offers a relevant economic model for examining development at regional, community, and household scales of analysis. Blumer, *Industrialization as an Agent of Social Change*; So, *Social Change and Development*; Baker and Gregory, *Explorations in Historical Geography*; and Hodder, *Interpreting Archaeology*.

The Annales School has influenced the field of history since the late 1800s. Annales studies, influenced initially by the work of Fernand Braudel, rely on time periodization and a quantitative approach. The time scales used in the Annales School consists of short-, medium-, and large-scale time intervals. Short-scale time, on the order of half a decade to a decade, refers to the time period typical of important historical events, such as major wars or the terms of presidents. Braudel, *A History of Civilizations*; Braudel, *On History*; and Braudel, *Capitalism and Material Life, 1400–1800*.

Short-scale time is often the temporal period studied in standard history. Medium-scale time encompasses a generation or several generations and can span half a century to several centuries. Large-scale time consists of intervals typical of geology, astronomy, prehistoric archaeology, and paleontology, on the order of numerous centuries and millennia or more. Large-scale periods of time are required to address topics such as astronomical, geologic, biological, and cultural evolution.

The history of Yount Mill encompasses medium-scale time, spanning over half a century. Consequently, the Yount Mill example allows consideration of the full historical trajectory of a wool mill in the region, from the beginning and middle to the end of the textile period in Indiana. This periodization approach typical of the Annales School complements perspectives in archaeology that emphasize the life history or site biography of an archaeological site, and in this case a business institution that existed for approximately seventy years. Another benefit of a medium-scale, site-biography approach is that it allows identification of the historical process associated with the subject over time. Rather than providing only a snapshot glimpse of life at the mill in 1850 or the 1850s, the roughly seventy-year interval in which the mill existed illustrates the life course of the establishment. Emphasizing the early, middle, and late periods of the mill's operation allows fine-grained reconstruction of details associated with the immediate industrial landscape, the production history of the venture, and the labor force that operated the mill. It is assumed that the specific historical details related to the mill may be unique to this example, but in general the mill probably illustrates the type of textile factories that existed in the study region.

This study also draws on theoretical stands associated with world systems theory to contextualize the economic history of the mill. World systems theory explores the development of the modern world during the past five hundred years, tracking the diffusion of capitalism across the globe since the 1500s. In world systems theory, the centers of political and economic power shift from regions and continents over time. Further, regional and global economic trends are often cyclical and punctuated by boom and bust characteristics. This economic-geographic political process is clearly illustrated at Yount Mill, where environmental factors in the 1840s encouraged mill establishment in the region. Yount Mill, in turn, prospered during the middle period of its operation, but then its prosperity was eclipsed by macro-level economic processes, such as market depression, that were beyond the control of the people who worked at and owned the mill. Later in time, after the mill had been abandoned, new industries were established in the region that created an economic upturn or boom period and significantly transformed the economy of the Midwest. By the close of the twentieth century, this second wave of economic prosperity in the region had receded with the shift of manufacturing centers to locations outside the United States. A. Burguiere, *The Annals School: An Intellectual History* (Ithaca, NY: Cornell University Press, 2009), and J. L. Bintliff, *The Annales School and Archaeology* (New York: New York University Press, 1991).

5. *Montgomery County Atlas* (Chicago: J. H. Beers and Company, 1878), http://history.cdpl.lib.in.us/images/p019-15.jpg, 34, and M.H.K., "Indiana Woolen Mills," *Inter Ocean* (Chicago), October 23, 1888, accessed June 14, 2017, newspapers.com.

6. Sanborg Maps for 1887, 1892, 1896, 1902, 1907, 1913, Montgomery County Building Department, Crawfordsville, IN.

7. M.H.K., "Indiana Woolen Mills."

8. *Montgomery County Atlas*, 1878, 34.

9. Maria Morton, interview with J. Hardick, April 19, 1990, Alan and Barbara White Papers, Yountsville, Indiana. Here she was describing her father's father.

10. M.H.K., "Indiana Woolen Mills."

11. During the course of the field school, students mapped evidence of this power distribution on all floors.

12. *Montgomery County Atlas*, 34.

13. M H K , "Indiana Woolen Mills."

14. Sanborg Maps.

15. Ibid.

16. Ibid.

17. Ibid.

18. Ibid.

19. *Montgomery County Atlas*, 34.

20. Ibid.

21. Sanborg Maps.

22. Ibid.

23. Ibid.

24. Ibid.

25. *Montgomery County Atlas*, 34.

26. Sanborg Maps.

27. Ibid.

28. Sanborg Maps.

29. M.H.K., "Indiana Woolen Mills."

30. Sanborg Maps.

SEVEN. Conclusions

1. Thornbrough, *Indiana in the Civil War Era*, 466, and Theobald, *Teaching the Commons.*

2. Theobald, *Call School.*

3. Thornbrough, *Indiana in the Civil War Era*, 466.

4. Ibid., 468.

5. Ibid., 469.

6. Caleb Mills, "I H S Address: Necessity and Expense of a Six Months School," ca. 1850, Caleb Mills Papers, box 1, folder 16, Indiana Historical Society.

7. Ibid.

8. Caleb Mills, "I H S Address: Seven Reasons for Voting in Favor of a Constitutional Convention," Caleb Mills Papers, ca. 1850, box 1, folder 16, Indiana Historical Society.

9. Thornbrough, *Indiana in the Civil War Era*, 502.

10. Ibid., 477.

11. Ibid., 476.

12. Ibid., 482.

13. Ibid., 483.

14. Ibid.

15. Ibid., 480–81.

16. Ibid., 481.

17. Ibid., 480.

18. Ibid.

19. Thornbrough, *Indiana in the Civil War Era*, 483.

20. Ibid., 478.

21. Ibid., 475.

22. "State Compulsory School Attendance Laws," Infoplease, http://www.infoplease.com/ipa/A0112617.html.

23. *Mazanec* v. *North Judson–San Pierre Sch. Corp.*, 614 F. Supp. 1152 (N.D. Ind. 1875), affirmed; 798 F. 2d 230 (7th Cir. 1986). See more at http://education.uslegal.com/compulsory-education/indiana/#sthash.tfjLxD7G.dpuf.

24. Phillips, *Indiana in Transition*, 331.

25. Cohen, *Children of the Mill.*

26. Phillips, *Indiana in Transition*, 334.

27. Ibid.

28. Vergara, *American Ruins*; Rinaldi and Yasinsac, *Hudson Valley Ruins*; and C. Bueno, *The Pursuit of Ruins.*

29. Cowie and Heathcott, *Beyond the Ruins*; E. Braae, *Beauty Redeemed*; and M. Thompson, *Ruins.*

BIBLIOGRAPHY

Collections Cited

Caleb Mills Papers. Indiana Historical Society. Indianapolis, IN.
Caleb Mills Papers. Wabash College Archive. Crawfordsville, IN.
Circuit Court Records. Montgomery County Courthouse. Crawfordsville, IN.
Clerk's Office Records. Montgomery County Courthouse. Crawfordsville, IN.
Collection of Alan and Barbara White. Private Collection. Yountsville, IN.
Indiana Room. Indiana State Library. Indianapolis, IN.
John Martz Collection. Private Collection. Crawfordsville, IN.
Sanborg Maps. Montgomery County Building Department. Crawfordsville, IN.
Yount Mill Collection. Marian Morrison Local History Collection at the
    Crawfordsville District Public Library. Crawfordsville, IN.
Yount Mill Collection. Rotary Jail Museum and Tannenbaum Cultural Center.
    Crawfordsville, IN.

Individual Works Cited

Allen, T. *A Republic in Time: Temporality and Social Imagination in Nineteenth-
    Century America.* Chapel Hill: University of North Carolina Press, 2008.
American Woolen Company. *The Manufacture of Woolen Textiles,* 1912. Library of
    Congress Prints and Photographs Division, Washington, DC. http://www
    .loc.gov/pictures/collection/coll/item/2005683436/.
Atlas of Montgomery County. Chicago: J. H. Beers & Co., 1878.
Baker, A. & D. Gregory. *Explorations in Historical Geography: Interpretative Essays.*
    Cambridge: Cambridge University Press, 1984.
Beckwith, Hiram William. *History of Montgomery County.* Chicago: H. H. Hill
    and N. Iddings, 1881.
Bintliff, J. L. *The Annales School and Archaeology.* New York: New York University
    Press, 1991.

Blumer, H. *Industrialization as an Agent of Social Change: A Critical Analysis.* New York: A. de Gruyter, 1990.

Bodnar, J. *Immigration and Industrialization: Ethnicity in an American Mill Town, 1870–1940.* Pittsburgh, PA: University of Pittsburgh Press, 1977.

Braae, E. *Beauty Redeemed: Recycling Post-Industrial Landscapes.* Risskov, Denmark: IKAROS Press; Basel: Birkhauser, 2015.

Branton, Nicole. "Landscape Approaches in Historical Archaeology: The Archaeology of Places." In *The International Handbook of Historical Archaeology,* 51–65. New York: Springer, 2009.

Braudel, F. *Capitalism and Material Life, 1400–1800.* New York: Harper and Row, 1973.

———. *A History of Civilizations.* New York: A. Lane, 1994.

———. *On History.* Chicago: University of Chicago Press, 1980.

Bueno, C. *The Pursuit of Ruins: Archaeology, History and the Making of Modern Mexico.* Albuquerque: University of New Mexico Press, 2016.

Burguiere, A. *The Annals School: An Intellectual History.* Ithaca, NY: Cornell University Press, 2009.

Burke, P. *The French Historical Revolution: The Annals School, 1929–89.* Stanford, Calif.: Stanford University Press, 1990.

Cameron, A. *Radicals of the Worst Sort: Laboring Women in Lawrence, Massachusetts, 1860–1912.* Urbana: University of Illinois Press, 1993.

Carmony, D. F. *Indiana 1816–1850: The Pioneer Era.* Vol. 2. Indianapolis: Indiana Historical Bureau and Indiana Historical Society, 1998.

Casella, E., and S. Croucher. *The Alderly Sandhills Project: An Archaeology of Community Life in (Post-) Industrial England.* Manchester, England: Manchester University Press, 2010.

Coffin, Elijah. *The Life of Elijah Coffin, with a Reminiscence by His Son, Charles F. Coffin.* Ed. Mary Coffin Johnson. Published for the family only by E. Morgan and Sons, 1863.

Cohen, R. *Children of the Mill: Schooling and Society in Gary Indiana, 1906–1960.* Bloomington: Indiana University Press, 1990.

Cole, A. H. *The American Wool Manufacture.* Cambridge: Harvard University Press, 1925.

Cowie, J., and J. Heathcott. *Beyond the Ruins: The Meanings of Deindustrialization.* Ithaca, NY: Cornell University Press, 2003.

Cragwall, J. A., and Otto F Fitzpatrick. *Montgomery County Atlas.* Chicago: Geo. A. Ogle and Company, 1917.

Crockett, N. *The Woolen Industry of the Midwest.* Lexington: University Press of Kentucky, 1970.

Cutler, W. *Parents and Schools: The 150-Year Struggle for Control in American Education.* Chicago: University of Chicago Press, 2000.

Digby, A., and P. Searby. *Children, School, and Society in Nineteenth-Century England.* New York: Macmillian, 1981.

Dublin, T. *Women at Work: The Transformation of Work and Community in Lowell, Massachusetts, 1826–1860.* New York: Columbia University Press, 1979.

Esslinger, D. *Immigrants and the City: Ethnicity and Mobility in a Nineteenth Century Midwestern Community.* Port Washington, NY: Kennikat Press, 1975.

Fennell, Christopher. *Perspectives from Historical Archaeology: Revealing Landscapes.* Bloomington, IN: Lulu Press, 2011.

Fruits, Noah. Election material, 1892–1902. Indiana State Library.

Geiger, R. *The American College in the Nineteenth Century.* Nashville, TN: Vanderbilt University Press, 2000.

Gordon, Robert, and Patrick Malone. *The Texture of Industry: An Archaeological View of Industrialization of North America.* New York: Oxford University Press, 1994.

Green, H. *The Company Town: The Industrial Edens and Satanic Mills That Shaped the American Economy.* New York: Basic Books, 2010.

Greenberg, B. *Worker and Community: Response to Industrialization in a Nineteenth-Century American City, Albany, New York, 1850–1884.* Albany: State University of New York Press, 1985.

Groover, M. D., and J. Clark. *Yount Mill Historical Archaeology Field School Report.* Prepared for Division of Historic Preservation and Archaeology, Indiana Department of Natural Resources, Indianapolis, 2018.

Groover, M. D., C. McLeod, F. Konrad, R. V. Morris, and J. Durkes. "Landscape Reconstruction at Yount's Mill." Paper presented at the Midwest Historical Archaeology Conference, Niles, Michigan, 2014.

Halchin, J., ed. *Archeological Views of the Upper Wager Block, A Domestic and Commercial Neighborhood in Harpers Ferry.* Washington, DC: US Department of the Interior, 1994.

Hambourge, S., N. Perrin, and K. Breisch. *Mills and Factories of New England.* New York: H. N. Abrams in association with the Hood Museum of Art, 1988.

Hart, J. *The Rural Landscape.* Baltimore: Johns Hopkins University Press, 1998.

Herbst, J. *The History of American Education.* Northbrook, IL: AHM Publishing, 1973.

Hodder, I. *Interpreting Archaeology: Finding Meaning in the Past.* London: Routledge, 1995.

Hunter, Louis. *A History of Industrial Power in the United States, 1780–1930.* Vol. 1: *Water Power in the Century of the Steam Engine.* Charlottesville: University Press of Virginia, 1979.

———. *A History of Industrial Power in the United States, 1780–1930.* Vol. 2: *Steam Power.* Charlottesville: University Press of Virginia, 1985.

Indiana Historical Bureau. "Evansville Cotton Mill." Historical Markers. http://www.in.gov/history/markers/328.htm.

———. "First Dam across the St. Joseph River–Power Race." Historical Markers. http://www.in.gov/history/markers/283.html.

———. "Kellar Grist Mill." Historical Markers. Accessed October 17, 2015. http://www.in.gov/history/markers/163.htm.

———. "Lowell Mills." Historical Markers. http://www.in.gov/history/markers/40.htm.

———. "Markle Mill Site." Historical Markers. http://www.in.gov/history/markers/20.htm.

———. "Miami Indian Mills," Historical Markers. http://www.in.gov/history/markers/345.htm.

———. "19th Century Indiana Grist Mills." *Indiana Junior Historian*, September 1991. Accessed October 17, 2015. http://www.in.gov/history/files/7001.pdf.

———. "Tunnel Mill." Historical Markers. http://www.in.gov/history/markers/29.htm.

Jay, Eli, ed. *Indiana Yearly Meeting Minutes: 1829–1849*. 1887. Quaker Archives, Earlham College, Richmond, IN.

Kennedy, Dumont. "Old Gunkle Mill Once Played Important Part in Local History." *Crawfordsville Journal*, December 3, 1927. Indiana Historical Society. Water Powered Mills Committee Collection box 7, folder 12 M0837.

Kiefer, W. *Rush County, Indiana: A Study in Rural Settlement Geography*. Bloomington Department of Geography, Indiana University, 1969.

Kilen, J., H. Renes, and R. Hermans, eds. *Landscape Biographies: Geographical, Historical and Archaeological Perspectives on the Production and Transmission of Landscapes*. Amsterdam: Amsterdam University Press, 2015.

Lake, O. J., and A. Warner. *Map of Montgomery County Indiana*. Philadelphia: Cowles and Titus, 1864.

M.H.K. "Indiana Woolen Mills." *Inter Ocean* (Chicago). October 23, 1888. Accessed June 14, 2017. Newspapers.com.

McDaniel, Ethel Hittle, *The Contribution of the Society of Friends to Education in Indiana*. Indianapolis: Indiana Historical Society, 1939. Indiana Historical Society Publications vol. 13, no. 2.

McDonald, Fiona. *The Popular History of Graffiti from the Ancient World to the Present*. New York: Skyhorse Publishing, 2013.

Merrill, Samuel, and Hans Hack. "Exploring Hidden Narratives: Conscript Graffiti at the Former Military Base of Kummersdorf." *Journal of Social Archaeology* 13, no. 1 (2012): 111.

Meyer, D. R. *The Roots of American Industrialization*. Baltimore: Johns Hopkins University Press, 2003.

Mills, C. *Caleb Mills and the Indiana School System*. Indianapolis: Wood Weaver Printing Company, 1905.

Milnor, Kristina. *Graffiti and the Literary Landscape in Roman Pompeii*. Oxford: Oxford University Press, 2014.

Molloy, P. *Homespun to Factory Made: Woolen Textiles in America, 1776–1876*. North Andover, MA: Merrimack Valley Textile Museum, 1977.

Mrozowski, Stephen, Grace Ziesing, and Mary Beaudry. *Living on the Boott*. Amherst: University of Massachusetts Press, 1996.

Niemi, A. *State and Regional Patterns in American Manufacturing, 1860–1900*. Westport, CT: Greenwood Press, 1974.

Nye, David. *America as Second Creation*. London: MIT Press, 2003.

———. *Consuming Power: A Social History of American Energies*. Cambridge, MA: MIT Press, 1988.

Officers of the State. *Annual Reports of the State of Indiana: For the Fiscal Year Ending October 31, 1905*. Indianapolis: Wm. B. Burford, 1906.

Pacione, M. *Progress in Rural Geography*. London: Croom Helm, 1983.

Phillips, Clifton J. *Indiana in Transition: The Emergence of an Industrial Commonwealth, 1880–1920*. Vol. 4. Indianapolis: Indiana Historical Bureau and Indiana Historical Society, 1968.

Prude, J. *The Coming of the Industrial Order: Town and Factory Life in Rural Massachusetts, 1810–1860*. Cambridge: Cambridge University Press, 1983.

Pula, James S. "The Writing on the Walls: Badger Graffiti in Civil War Virginia." *Wisconsin Magazine of History* 86, no. 3 (2003): 35–49.

Reser, William M. *John Rudolph Waymire and the First Three Generations of His Descendents*. Lafayette, IN: William Reser, 1935.

Rinaldi, T., and R. Yasinsac. *Hudson Valley Ruins: Forgotten Landmarks of an American Landscape*. Hanover, NH: University Press of New England, 2006.

Roberts, B. *Landscapes of Settlement: Prehistory to the Present*. London: Routledge, 1996.

Shackel, P. *Domestic Response to Nineteenth-Century Industrialization: An Archeology of Park Building 48, Harpers Ferry National Historical Park*. Washington, DC: US Department of the Interior, 1994.

So, A. Y. *Social Change and Development: Modernization, Dependency, and World-Systems Theories*. Newbury Park, CA: Sage Publications, 1990.

Taylor, R., and C. McBirney. *Peopling Indiana: The Ethnic Experience*. Indianapolis: Indiana Historical Society, 1996.

Theobald, P. *Call School: Rural Education in the Midwest to 1918*. Carbondale: Southern Illinois University Press, 1995.

———. *Teaching the Commons: Place, Pride, and the Renewal of Community*. Boulder: Westview Press, 1997.

Thompson, M. *Ruins: Their Preservation and Display.* London: British Museum Publications, 1981.

Thornbrough, E. L. *Indiana in the Civil War Era: 1850–1880.* Vol. 3. Indianapolis: Indiana Historical Bureau and Indiana Historical Society, 1965.

Trinkley, M., and N. Adams. *Life Weaving Golden Thread: Archaeological Investigations at the Sampson Mill Village, Greenville County, South Carolina.* Columbia, SC: Chicora Foundation, 1993.

Tucker, Barbara. *Samuel Slater and the Origins of the American Textile Industry, 1790–1860.* London: Cornell University Press, 1984.

US National Commission on Excellence in Education. *A Nation at Risk: The Imperative for Educational Reform; A Report to the Nation and the Secretary of Education.* Washington, DC: United States Department of Education, 1983.

Vergara, C. *American Ruins.* New York: Monacelli Press, 1999.

Watson, B. *Bread and Roses: Mills, Migrants, and the Struggle for the American Dream.* New York: Viking, 2005.

Woods, M. *Rural Geography: Process, Responses and Experiences in Rural Restructuring.* London: Sage Publications, 2005.

Yamin, Rebecca, and Karen Bescherer Metheny. *Landscape Archaeology: Reading and Interpreting the American Historical Landscape.* Knoxville: University of Tennessee Press, 1996.

INDEX

RONALD V. MORRIS

is a professor of history at Ball State University.

He is the author of *Bringing History to Life*.

CPSIA information can be obtained
at www.ICGtesting.com
Printed in the USA
LVHW082142130120
643535LV00009B/149/P

9 780268 106614